**Studien zur Mustererkennung**

herausgegeben von:

Prof. Dr.-Ing. Heinrich Niemann
Prof. Dr.-Ing. Elmar Nöth

Bibliografische Information der Deutschen Nationalbibliothek

Die Deutsche Nationalbibliothek verzeichnet diese Publikation in der
Deutschen Nationalbibliografie; detaillierte bibliografische Daten sind
im Internet über http://dnb.d-nb.de abrufbar.

ISBN 978-3-8325-2145-5
ISSN 1617-0695


Logos Verlag Berlin GmbH
Comeniushof
Gubener Str. 47
10243 Berlin
Tel.: +49 030 42 85 10 90
Fax: +49 030 42 85 10 92
INTERNET: http://www.logos-verlag.de

# Automatic Classification of Emotion-Related User States in Spontaneous Children's Speech

Der Technischen Fakultät der
Universität Erlangen-Nürnberg

zur Erlangung des Grades

# DOKTOR-INGENIEUR

vorgelegt von

Stefan Steidl

Erlangen — 2009

Deutscher Titel:

# Automatische Klassifikation von emotionalen Benutzerzuständen in spontaner Kindersprache

Als Dissertation genehmigt von der
Technischen Fakultät der
Universität Erlangen-Nürnberg

| | |
|---|---|
| Tag der Einreichung: | 03.09.2008 |
| Tag der Promotion: | 07.11.2008 |
| Dekan: | Prof. Dr.-Ing. habil. J. Huber |
| Berichterstatter: | Prof. em. Dr.-Ing. H. Niemann |
| | Prof. Drs. Dr. L. J. M. Rothkrantz |
| | Prof. Dr.-Ing. habil. E. Nöth |

# Acknowledgment

I am very grateful to my supervisor Prof. em. Dr.-Ing. Heinrich Niemann. Until 2005, when he became emeritus, he had been the head of the Chair of Pattern Recognition. I had the privilege to be one of his last PhD students and I appreciate it very much that I could finish my work under his guidance. Prof. Niemann reviewed my thesis very carefully and provided many hints that helped to improve the quality of my thesis.

I am deeply grateful to the head of the Speech Processing Group, Prof. Dr.-Ing. habil. Elmar Nöth, for reviewing my thesis. Many improvements are due to his suggestions. He is the one who made me enthusiastic about speech processing and who supported me over the last years. He contributes a lot to the positive atmosphere at work, which is one precondition for successful working. Because of the excellent supervision of the students within his group, I have written both my pre-diploma and my diploma thesis in the area of speech processing. I wish to thank especially Dr.-Ing. Georg Stemmer who has supervised both theses in cooperation with Prof. Nöth.

I wish to thank my second reviewer Prof. Drs. Dr. Léon J. M. Rothkrantz from Delft University of Technology for providing useful suggestions and attending my PhD defense. It has been very interesting to get a review from somebody outside the pattern recognition community. I am very grateful to all of my three reviewers for reviewing my thesis in such a short time.

Since 2005, Prof. Dr.-Ing. Joachim Hornegger has been the new head of the Chair of Pattern Recognition. I wish to thank him for welcoming me with open arms in his team, for extending my contract, and for chairing the examination committee at my PhD defense. Furthermore, I wish to thank my external reviewer Prof. Dr.-Ing. Walter Kellermann.

A thesis like this is never solely the work of the author. It is always based on the ideas and previous activities of many colleagues whose work I want to acknowledge herewith. I would like to express my deep and sincere gratitude to my supervisor Dr. phil. Anton Batliner, who is an expert in the area of speech prosody, linguistics and emotion recognition. The collaboration with him has been very successful and I enjoyed working with him very much. I am also grateful to my former colleague at work Dipl.-Inf. Christian Hacker. We have been working together very closely for many years and shared a wonderful time. Together with Dr. Batliner, we have designed the Aibo experiments and carried out the recordings and post-processings. In front of the computer science building, Christian and me designed the carpet for the parcours experiment by spraying the parcours with car lacquer onto the carpet.

My work has been embedded in two research projects funded by the European Community: PF-STAR and the Network of Excellence HUMAINE. Especially in HUMAINE, I could benefit to a large extent from the expertise of other researchers in this interdisciplinary project. I wish to thank our partners within our initiative CEICES, especially Dr.-Ing. Björn Schuller and Dr. Dino Seppi, for a very fruitful co-operation.

Over the last years, I have never had to worry about financial aspects. I have been given the opportunity to take part in many international conferences and project meetings at outstanding places within Europe and Northern America. Thanks to Prof. Nöth, Dr. Batliner, and my colleagues for many wonderful trips that we shared. I will never forget them!

My warm thanks are due to my parents. At the age of 10, I got my first personal computer, and my father taught me how to write my first small computer programs. Since then, studying computer science has not lost its fascination to me.

The last six years have been a wonderful time and I have enjoyed the merits of scientific research very much. Nevertheless, this time has also been very demanding. I owe my loving thanks to my wife Nicole for her understanding and her support over the last years and I am very proud and happy that both of us managed to finish our PhD this year.

Erlangen, November 2008
Stefan Steidl

# Abstract

The recognition of the user's emotion-related state is one important step in making human-machine communication more natural. In this work, the focus is set on mono-modal systems with speech as only input channel. Current research has to shift from emotion portrayals to those states that actually appear in application-oriented scenarios. These states are mainly weak emotion-related states and mixtures of different states. The presented FAU Aibo Emotion Corpus is a major contribution in this area. It is a corpus of spontaneous, emotionally colored speech of children at the age of 10 to 13 years interacting with the Sony robot Aibo. 11 emotion-related states are labeled on the word level. Experiments are conducted on three subsets of the corpus on the word, the turn, and the intermediate chunk level. Best results have been obtained on the chunk level where a classwise averaged recognition rate of almost 70 % for the 4-class problem *Anger*, *Emphatic*, *Neutral*, and *Motherese* has been achieved. Applying the proposed entropy based measure for the evaluation of decoders, the performance of the machine classifier on the word level is even slightly better than the one of the average human labeler. The presented set of features covers both acoustic and linguistic features. The linguistic features perform slightly worse than the acoustic features. An improvement can be achieved by combining both knowledge sources. The acoustic features are categorized into prosodic, spectral, and voice quality features. The energy and duration based prosodic features and the spectral MFCC features are the most relevant acoustic features in this scenario. Unigram models and bag-of-words features are the most relevant linguistic features.

# Kurzdarstellung

Die Erkennung des emotionalen Benutzerzustands stellt einen wichtigen Schritt dar, um die Kommunikation zwischen Mensch und Maschine natürlicher zu gestalten. Die vorliegende Arbeit konzentriert sich auf monomodale Systeme, bei denen Sprache die einzige Eingabemodalität ist. Die aktuelle Forschung auf diesem Gebiet muss ihren Schwerpunkt weg von geschauspielten Daten hinzu denjenigen emotionalen Zuständen verlagern, die in Anwendungsszenarien tatsächlich auftreten. Dies sind vor allem schwach ausgeprägte Emotionen im weiteren Sinne sowie Mischungen verschiedener Zustände. Das vorgestellte FAU Aibo Emotionskorpus stellt einen wichtigen Schritt in diese Richtung dar. Es handelt sich dabei um emotional gefärbte Spontansprache von Kindern im Alter zwischen 10 und 13 Jahren. Auf Wortebene sind 11 verschiedene Emotionszustände annotiert worden. Die Experimente wurden auf drei Teilmengen des Korpus und auf drei Analyseebenen – der Wortebene, der Turn-Ebene, und der dazwischenliegenden Chunk-Ebene – durchgeführt. Die besten Ergebnisse wurden dabei auf der Chunk-Ebene erzielt, wo für das 4-Klassen-Problem bestehend aus den vier Oberklassen *Ärger*, *Emphatisch*, *Neutral* und *Mütterlich* eine klassenweise gemittelte Erkennungsrate von fast 70 % erreicht wurde. Das vorgestellte Entropie basierte Maß zur Beurteilung von Dekodern belegt, dass der automatische Klassifikator auf Wortebene sogar etwas besser abschneidet als der durchschnittliche menschliche Bewerter. Die vorgestellten Merkmale umfassen sowohl akustische als auch linguistische Merkmale. Letztere schneiden etwas schlechter ab als die akustischen. Durch die Verknüpfung beider Wissensquellen kann eine Verbesserung der Erkennungsrate erzielt werden. Die akustischen Merkmale lassen sich in prosodische, spektrale und Stimmqualitätsmerkmale einteilen. Im Aibo-Szenario sind dabei die Energie und die Dauer basierten prosodischen Merkmale sowie die spektralen MFCC-Merkmale am wichtigsten. Die wichtigsten linguistischen Merkmale sind Unigramm-Modelle und Vektorraum-Modelle, besser bekannt als „bag-of-words"-Merkmale.

# Contents

# Chapter 1

# Introduction

## 1.1 Human-Machine Communication

Over the last 30 years, building dialog systems for spontaneous speech has been one of the main focuses of the Speech Processing and Understanding Group of the Chair of Pattern Recognition at the University of Erlangen-Nuremberg. By now, many telephone services based on automatic systems exist and provide cost-efficient services for many scenarios. The available services differ in the design of the dialog between the calling user and the system. Simple systems like the telephone answering machine service of a major German telephone company accept as input modality only input from the keypad. As a consequence, the design of the dialog is rather fixed. The disadvantages are quite obvious: as the system can only react to the entered digits and the user cannot be asked to remember the various meanings of a certain digit at a particular dialog step, the system has to inform the user about the possible actions at each step again and again. This leads to a frequent repetition of pre-recorded text modules and hence to an unnecessary delay of the whole dialog which will be annoying for experienced users.

More sophisticated systems accept speech in form of single words as an additional input modality. Often, the speech input is restricted to confirm certain dialog steps with single words like 'yes' or 'no' or to control the progress of the dialog by saying one of several given alternatives: "If you have questions regarding your bill, say *bill*". In other systems, the list of words which the system is capable to understand is not restricted to only a few given alternatives. Such a system is for example the baggage-retrieval-service of an American airline where passengers can ask the system whether their lost luggage has already been found. The system tries to understand the passenger's name and retrieves the information from a database system. If it is not able to understand the name correctly after the third try – maybe because the passenger has a foreign name –, the system hands over to a human operator.

However, state-of-the-art dialog systems allow real conversations between the human user and the machine in spontaneous speech. Although these systems are still rare, automatic dialog systems which are able to understand spontaneous speech in a limited domain are ready for commercial usage and some of them have already proven their utilizability in daily use. Such limited domains could be any kind of information system, e.g. a football league system being able to answer questions about match results, ranking, etc., a cinema information system providing the caller with information about films currently shown in the desired cinema, a timetable information system for airplanes, trains, etc., or a citizen helpdesk providing information about opening times, addresses, or phone numbers of public authorities. In 2005, Sympalog Voice Solutions[1], a spin-off company of the Chair of Pattern Recognition, built a system for a globally operating car rental company which offers:

1. a switchboard service which connects the caller to a human operator not only on the basis of a given name or department, but also on the basis of the caller's concerns which can be expressed in spontaneous speech ("I'd like to rent a car."),

2. a leasing advisor being able to answer questions concerning the leasing modalities of a car and being able to acquire and record all the necessary data of the caller, and

3. a customer service portal with full automation of standard transactions such as change of address, shipping of additional invoice copies, etc.

To be able to interpret utterances of the user in the context of previous turns[2], these systems have access to the history of the dialog. Thus, a quite natural dialog between a human and a machine is possible.

Even if this kind of new automatic dialog systems is able to understand spontaneous speech, the dialog is still not as natural as a corresponding dialog between two humans would be. One important aspect is still missing: the ability to adapt to this special person who is calling, to the individual behavior of this person, to the current mood or the emotional state of the caller. For example, if a caller is especially friendly, it would be appropriate for the system not only to be polite, as the system always should be, but to be extraordinarily friendly, even in a way which might be too exaggerated in a conversation with another user. If the system realizes that the user is hesitating, it could provide some extra help whereas this additional information is redundant and counterproductive if the user is familiar with the system. One might even think of a system which is able to detect jokes made by the caller, reacts appropriately with laughing and switches to a more casual way of conversation. Two points are necessary for this adaptation: on the one hand, the ability of the system to recognize the current state of the user, and on the other hand, the ability to change the own behavior accordingly.

Other types of human-machine communication are conversations between humans and *embodied conversational agents* (ECAs), computer animated 3D virtual characters. They provide another interface, either only a facial display (*talking heads*) or a display of the whole body. Their goal is to reduce the mental gap between users and computer systems [Take 93]. Figure 1.1 shows a muscle-based talking head with different facial expressions [Albr 05]. Particularly in conversations with such a realistic looking agent, the need to model facial expressions becomes obvious. Showing emotions comprises the synthesis of emotional speech, facial expressions (including lip movements), gestures, and body movements as well as strategies at which point

---

[1]`http://www.sympalog.de`, last visited 01/12/2009
[2]In a dialog, a turn consists of all utterances of one speaker from the moment this speaker starts speaking to the moment he/she hands over to the dialog partner.

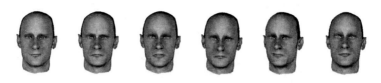

Figure 1.1: Expression of emotions in a muscle-based talking head: joy, anger, fear, sadness, disgust, surprise (from left to right) [Albr 05]

of time which emotions are appropriate. Obviously, the latter depends on the behavior of the human conversational partner. Hence, the emotional states of the partner have to be recognized automatically. It can be recognized from speech input (acoustic information from audio data as well as linguistic information from the textual information). Other input modalities that can be analyzed are facial expressions, gestures, body movements, and physiological signals.

## 1.2 State-of-the-Art

This work addresses the classification of emotional and emotion-related states from speech only. In the following, an overview is given of the current state-of-the-art in this special area of research.

For more than 50 years, psychologists have been investigating the influence of emotions on speech. The basis of these investigations were examples of prototypical emotions. Over the last ten years, computer scientists got more and more involved in the problem of recognizing emotions automatically and have started to classify emotions with pattern recognition techniques. Automatic analysis allows to process a large amount of data in adequate time, but collecting a huge amount of training data necessary to train statistical classifiers turned out to be a problem itself. Many of the corpora available today consist of emotional data portrayed by actors.

The popularity of acted emotional speech is rooted in the intrinsic advantages of this approach of data collecting:

1. Emotion portrayals yield intense, prototypical expressions of emotion. Hence, the search for acoustic correlates and the subsequent automatic classification is considerably easier.

2. The studio recordings are of high audio quality avoiding problems in signal processing with reverberated or noisy speech.

3. A balanced distribution of all emotions can be guaranteed improving the performance of many machine classification techniques without the need to upsample (repetition of samples of less frequent emotions) or downsample (reduction of the data of frequent emotions) the data. Thus, the *sparse data problem* one has to face in real application scenarios can be avoided.

4. Data can be collected in a relatively short time and at low cost compared to other elicitation techniques (s. Chapter 2.4).

5. Post-processing of the data is rather simple in comparison to recordings of spontaneous speech since no labeling of emotions is needed as the intended emotion is known in advance. Additionally, the verbal content produced by the actors is standardized by that restricting the transliteration of the actually spoken utterances to the correction of a few misspeakings.

Such material typically is read, non-interactive speech, and the text itself is typically non-emotional, making the analysis of acoustic characteristics easier, but rendering any linguistic analysis impossible.

Corpora of acted emotional speech exist for many languages. An overview up to 2003 is given in [Verv 03]. Another attempt to catalog all existing emotion databases has been made within the European Network of Excellence HUMAINE[3]. The web site lists three different categories of corpora: multi-modal databases (audio-visual, audio-visual and gestures, audio and physiological measured data), speech only databases, and databases for facial expressions. The individual databases differ in a number of properties: the type of emotion elicitation (acted, induced, or real life data), the emotional content (number, type and intensity of the emotions or emotion-related states that are represented in the data), the number of subjects, the type of speech (spontaneous speech, scripted sentences, single words, or nonsense speech), and the availability (available for research or protected by copyright, legal issues, etc.).

Exemplarily, three widely used corpora of emotion portrayals are mentioned here: the English *Emotional Prosody Speech and Transcripts* corpus of the Linguistic Data Consortium (LDC)[4], the *Danish Emotional Speech Corpus* [Engb 96], and the German *Berlin Emotional Speech Database* [Burk 05]. The corpus of the LDC contains semantically neutral utterances (dates and numbers) portrayed by eight actors in fourteen distinct emotions which are selected according to Banse and Scherer's study of vocal emotional expression in German [Bans 96]. The Danish Emotional Speech Corpus contains scripted, not emotionally colored material (single words, sentences, and text passages) in the four emotions *anger, sadness, joy,* and *surprise* portrayed by four subjects. The Berlin Emotional Speech Database contains scripted, semantically neutral sentences portrayed by ten subjects in the six emotions *hot anger, disgust, fear/panic, happiness, sadness/sorrow,* and *boredom*. Additionally, all three corpora contain material in a neutral state.

State-of-the-art recognition performances reported for acted speech are very high, even if many different emotions are to be distinguished. In [Schu 06], for example, a classification accuracy of 74.5 % is reported on the Danish Emotional Speech Corpus for the five class problem, and even 87.5 % for the seven class problem on the Berlin Emotional Speech Database. These results are remarkable since they do not only lie clearly above chance level, but also slightly above the human ability to recognize these emotions. The average human accuracy is 67.3 % on the Danish corpus, and 84.3 % on the German corpus. The human accuracy is evaluated in human perception tests where subjects who are listening to an isolated utterance of an unfamiliar person have to decide for one of the given emotion categories. This situation corresponds to the information given to the machine classifier. The human ability to perceive emotions

---

[3]http://emotion-research.net/databases, last visited 01/12/2009
[4]http://www.ldc.upenn.edu/Catalog/, last visited 01/12/2009

is considerably higher if the labeler is familiar with the subject and knows the context of the present situation. Then, humans can perceive even subtle emotional changes.

Besides the general interest in automatic classification of emotional speech, there is also growing interest in the applicability of emotion recognition in special applications. Speech processing moves more and more from the task of understanding *what is spoken* to the task of *how something is produced*. As pointed out in the first section, information *how* something is spoken can be useful in any kind of human-machine communication. Studies of emotions in realistic scenarios are rare. A large-scale study where test users call dialog systems built by various sites to make air travel arrangements is reported in [Ang 02]. Smaller studies are reported in [Lee 05] and [Batl 03b]. But automatic emotion recognition can also be useful in human-human communication. In [Gupt 07], emotion recognition in call-center dialogs between a calling person and a human operator is employed to identify dialogs of extreme emotional characteristics like happy or angry moods with the purpose to help call-center supervisors to monitor the calls and to identify agents who are not able to satisfy the customer. Another application mentioned in [Clav 06] is public surveillance where critical situations, e. g. situations where people are threatened, are to be detected.

The emotion categories listed in Table 3.2, 3.4 and 3.5 demonstrate that the emotional states that can be observed in real applications differ from the emotions typically portrayed in acted corpora. Naturally occurring emotional states are rather emotion-related than pure emotions (s. Chapter 2.1 for terminology), occur only infrequently, and the emotional intensity is quite low.

Unfortunately, collecting data of naturally occurring emotions itself is a rather problematic task. Some studies use human-human dialogs to obtain naturally occurring emotions. In [Vidr 05], dialogs between a human agent and a client in a stock exchange customer service center are used. The speech data used in [Devi 06, Vidr 07] are recordings of real conversations between an agent and a client in a real-life medical call center. Other studies try to elicit emotions (s. Chapter 2.4).

In real applications, the actually occurring emotional states heavily depend on the chosen scenario. A lot of studies focus on the detection of a single emotional state like anger [Arim 07, Kawa 07, Yaco 03], fear [Clav 06], or annoyance and frustration [Ang 02, Kapo 07]. Related studies aim at classifying laughter [Knox 07, Lask 07], sleepiness [Kraj 07], suicidal speech [Ying 07], or deception [Enos 07]. The large area of research on pathological voices is also closely related to this field.

So far, a large number of different features has been proposed to recognize emotional states. The features can be categorized in prosodic, spectral, and voice quality features. Besides these acoustic features, linguistic features provide another source of information in real application scenarios. In the following, the most common features of each group as well as recent studies where these features are used are listed in order to provide an overview over currently used features. Neither the list of features, nor the cited studies claim to be complete. A detailed description of the features used in this thesis is given in Chapter 6.

**Prosodic Features** The most commonly used features in speech emotion recognition are prosodic features. Prosody characterizes suprasegmental speech phenomena,

i. e. properties attributed to speech segments that are larger than phonemes like syllables, words, phrases, or whole turns of a speaker [Noth 99]. Perceived characteristics
are, for example, pitch, loudness, speaking rate, duration, pause, and rhythm. The
most important prosodic functions are the marking of boundaries ("Kohl said: 'Strauß
will never be chancellor'" vs. "'Kohl', said Strauß, 'will never be chancellor'"), phrasal
accents ("I will go" vs. "I will go"), sentence mood ("On Monday." vs. "On Monday?"),
and emotional state of the speaker ("Yes, sure." (*positive*) vs. "Yes, sure." (*ironic*)).

In general, the perceived characteristics do not have unique acoustic equivalents in
the speech signal, but there are acoustic features which highly correlate with them like
the *fundamental frequency* $F_0$, which highly correlates with perceived pitch, and the
*short time signal energy* correlating with perceived loudness. The prosodic features
can be categorized into $F_0$ features, *energy* features, and *duration* features.

$F_0$ features characterize the change of the $F_0$ values over time within one word,
phrase, or turn. If features for the whole segment are desired, functionals are applied
to the $F_0$ base contour. Common functionals are the mean, the median, the maximum,
the minimum, the standard deviation, and the range. Less frequently, the first and
the third quartile, the centroid, and the third and the fourth standardized moment
are used. The third standardized moment, the skewness, is a measure of the asymme-
try, the fourth standardized moment, the kurtosis, a measure of the "peakedness" of a
probability density. Even though the positions of the extrema describe the $F_0$ contour,
they are temporal measures and are therefore related to the group of duration features. Often, these functionals are also applied to the first derivative of the $F_0$ contour
($\Delta$ features) and sometimes also to the second derivative ($\Delta\Delta$ features). Numerous
studies calculate their features using this procedure, but differ in the number of calculated features and the way the base features are normalized. Exemplarily, these studies are listed: [Ang 02, Gupt 07, Hu 07a, Kraj 07, Schu 04, Schu 07a, Yild 04, Vogt 05].

Energy features describe the change of the signal energy over time. The approach
is basically the same as for $F_0$ features: functionals are applied to the contour of the
short time signal energy values. In general, studies using $F_0$ features also employ energy features. Hence, the same exemplary studies as mentioned above for $F_0$ features
can be cited.

Duration based features model the effect of the speaking style on the duration of
the spoken utterance. It can be measured on various units like phonemes (especially
vowels), single words, or the whole utterance. Other units are regions of voiced and
unvoiced sounds with the advantage that no alignment of the spoken word chain to
the sound signal is required. The speaking style also affects the duration of pauses
between words. Again, functionals like mean, median, standard deviation, etc. are
applied. A popular duration feature is the speaking rate defined as the ratio of the
observed duration and the expected duration of the segment. Often, it is approximated by alternatives which are easier to calculate like the number of vowels [Ang 02]
or phonemes [Yild 04] per second, or the temporal distance between energy extrema
[Vogt 05]. Features related to pauses are the ratio of speech to pause time, the duration of the longest pause or the number of long pauses inside an utterance [Ang 02].
As mentioned above, the position of the energy and $F_0$ extrema belong to the group
of duration features, too.

**Spectral Features** Conventionally, prosodic features only comprise $F_0$, energy, and duration. Spectral features describe the characteristics of a speech signal in the frequency domain besides $F_0$ like harmonics and formants. Harmonics are multiples of the fundamental frequency and are specified by their frequency and their amplitude. They are used for speech emotion recognition in [Kraj 07]. Formants are amplifications of certain frequencies in the spectrum resulting from resonance in the vocal tract. They are characterized by their frequency, their amplitude, and their bandwidth. Voiced phones have four or more formants. In general, the two lowest ones are sufficient to disambiguate vowels. The applicability of formant features for emotion recognition is demonstrated in [Hu 07a, Kraj 07, Vlas 07]. Other spectral features calculate the spectral energy in various frequency bands [Kraj 07, Ying 07]. The *energy slope* is the ratio of the spectral energy above a certain frequency (e. g. 1 kHz) to the spectral energy below this threshold [Huan 06].

Further spectral features are the standard features used in speech recognition: the *mel frequency cepstral coefficients* (MFCC). Although they have been designed to extract *what* is spoken, they have been used successfully in emotion recognition to recognize *how* something is spoken [Lee 04, Buss 07, Hu 07b, Seth 07]. These features are calculated for quasi-stationary extracts of the speech signal. Additionally, the first and the second derivative of the MFCC values are used [Knox 07, Kraj 07, Vlas 07]. The features can either be averaged over the whole segment (*long-term average spectrum*, LTAS) as in [Kraj 07] or classified directly on the frame level. The a posteriori scores on the turn level can be used in combination with other turn level features to improve the classification [Vlas 07]. The MFCC can be replaced by other well-known speech recognition features like *linear predictive cepstral coefficients* (LPCC) or *mel filter bank* (MFB) features. The latter are investigated in [Buss 07].

**Voice Quality** Voice qualities are speaking styles like modal (neutral) voice, breathy, whispery, creaky, harsh, or falsetto voice. They have been characterized by Laver in terms of the three physiological parameters *adductive tension* (action of the interarytenoid muscles adducting the arytenoids), *medial compression* (adductive force on the vocal processes adducting the ligamental glottis), and *longitudinal tension* (tension of the vocal folds themselves) [Lave 80]. According to Fant's *source-filter model* [Fant 85], speech production may be modelled as the convolution of the source signal and the vocal tract filter response. Voice quality is characterized by the form of the source signal.

Scherer states that "although fundamental frequency parameters (related to pitch) are undoubtedly important in the vocal expression of emotion, the key to the vocal differentiation of discrete emotions seems to be *voice quality*" [Sche 86]. Especially in the differentiation of subtle variations in emotional states, voice quality seems to play an important role [Gobl 03]. Experiments in speech synthesis demonstrate that differences in voice quality alone can evoke different emotional colorings in an otherwise neutral utterance. In reverse, voice quality features should be able to provide cues for emotion recognition. Nevertheless, state-of-the-art voice quality features have fallen short of the high expectations put upon them so far.

The major problem in voice quality research is the estimation of the glottal source. *Inverse filtering* (IF) of the speech signal is a non-invasive technique to separate the source signal by canceling the effects of the vocal tract. Numerous automatic inverse filtering algorithms have been proposed (for an overview, please see [Gobl 03]). The voice quality measures can be determined directly from the IF signal like the glottal-to-noise excitation ratio [Mich 97] used in [Fern 05], the *aperiodic frequency range* [Ohts 01] used in [Mori 07], or the parabolic spectral parameter [Alku 97] used in [Fern 05]. Unfortunately, these measures are very sensitive to noise. Instead, parametric models like the *four-parameter model of the glottal flow derivative* of Fant and Liljencrants (*LF-model*) [Fant 85] are fitted to the signal [Fern 05]. This source model is integrated in the IF algorithm proposed in [Froh 01] resulting in an improved estimation of the vocal tract resonance filter. Nevertheless, fully automatic methods tend to perform least well when there is no true closed phase to the glottal cycle and where automatic estimation of formant peaks is least reliable, as it is the case for many non-modal voice qualities.

An alternative to inverse filtering are source-related measures obtained from the spectrum of the speech signal. The two most popular voice quality features are *jitter* and *shimmer* which measure the cycle-to-cycle variation of the period length (reciprocal of the fundamental frequency) and the peak (or average) amplitude, respectively. They are used for emotion recognition in [Fern 05, Hu 07a, Kraj 07, Mich 97, Vlas 07]. Another voice quality feature is the *harmonics-to-noise ratio* (HNR) [Boer 93], a measure of the degree of periodicity of a sound, used, for example, in [Hu 07a, Kraj 07, Vlas 07]. Other measures result from a comparison of the first harmonic with the first formant or the second harmonic, or the balance of higher versus lower frequencies (see section on spectral features). However, these measures always reflect source as well as filter characteristics resulting in an overlap of spectral and voice quality features.

**Linguistic Features**   Many emotion corpora contain emotion portrayals of non-emotional text in order to make the analysis of acoustic features easier. Hence, linguistic features are often disregarded. Nevertheless, they can provide additional cues in real application data.

One approach is the estimation of the probability $P(\Omega_\kappa | w_1 w_2 \ldots w_U)$ of an emotion category $\Omega_\kappa$ given the word sequence $w_1 w_2 \ldots w_U$ of an utterance. Like in language models for speech recognition [Noth 01], $n$-grams $P(\Omega_\kappa | w_{U-n+1} \ldots w_U)$ to reduce the context and smoothing techniques to handle unobserved $n$-grams are used. Due to low observation frequencies of $n$-grams with $n \geq 3$ in the training data, only unigrams [Devi 03] and bigrams [Polz 00] are promising. Trigrams are used in [Ang 02] but only with minor success. In [Lee 02], unigrams are only considered for *salient* words. Emotional salience is defined as the amount of information that a specific word contains about the emotion category. In [Schu 05], the *information gain ratio* (IGR) is applied to select the seven best emotion discriminating words. Eleven alternatives to $\prod_w P(\Omega_\kappa | w)$ are considered.

Another way to use lexical information are *bag-of-words* representations of an utterance known from automatic document categorization. Each component of a feature vector corresponds to one entry of the lexicon and contains the (absolute or relative) frequency of the respective word in the given utterance. Alternatively, the absolute term frequency can be weighted with the *inverse document frequency* [Salt 88] and/or the logarithm can be taken. Thereby, information about the order of the words within one utterance is lost. Different techniques to reduce the size of the feature vector exist. *Stopping* defines a list of words which are excluded from the vector. *Stemming* clusters words of the same stem in one category. With *principal component analysis* (PCA) or feature selection techniques like *sequential forward floating search* (SFFS), the dimension can be further reduced. Experimental results are reported in [Schu 05, Schu 07a]. In [Gupt 07], words are clustered by building emotion-dependent dictionaries of words and phrases that are frequently used in the respective emotion. Words can also be clustered using *part-of-speech* (POS) features. In [Bulu 07], the analysis of utterances in four emotions using 13 POS tag types shows that emotions can be differentiated at the POS level.

The third method mentioned here is a spotting approach for emotional keywords or phrases which is based on *Belief Networks*. In [Schu 04], a network of five levels performing a clustering from words to super-words, phrases, super-phrases, and finally to emotions is suggested. On the word level, evidence in form of word confidence scores of the ASR hypothesis is fed into the net.

In the last sections, different types of features have been described that are relevant to distinguish a set of emotional and emotion-related states from each other. But the choice of the right features is only one aspect in the automatic classification of emotional or emotion-related states. Another aspect is the choice of an appropriate machine classifier.

**Machine Classifiers** From the area of *machine learning*, a large number of machine classifiers is known and many of them have been applied in emotion recognition. One simple linear classifier is *linear discriminant analysis* (LDA) which is, e. g., used in [Kraj 07, Batl 06b]. Very popular, but more complex classifiers are *artificial neural networks* (ANN), used in [Knox 07, Kraj 07], and *support vector machines* (SVM), applied in [Schu 04, Lee 04]. Other classification techniques are *classification and regression trees* (CART) [Ang 02] or *random forrests*. Classifiers which are especially suited to classify features on the frame level are *Gaussian mixture models* (GMM). In order to get classification results on a higher level such as the word or the turn level, GMM classification can be combined with other classifiers like SVM [Hu 07b, Vlas 07]. To model the variation of the features in time, *hidden Markov models* (HMM) are applied as in [Nogu 01, Schu 03, Lee 04].

Although the LDA classifier is simple, resulting in fast training and test cycles, it seems to be rather robust towards overlapping class areas and, surprisingly, its recognition performance if often comparable to much more complex classifiers. In [Batl 06b], LDA is compared to SVM and random forrests. The accuracies in terms of the average recall (definition in Chapter 4.2.1) are 57.9 % for SVM, 58.7 % for random forrests, and 56.3 % for LDA. In a study by Krajewski and Kröger on sleepiness detection, LDA even outperforms ANN [Kraj 07]. The different results show that there is no one best classifier. Which classifier yields the best results depends on the data actually used and in the end also on the expertise of the user to get the best out of the classifier by adequate pre-processing of the data and the right choice of parameters. For the purpose of comparing different features or feature types, the absolute accuracy is of minor importance. The classifiers used within this work are described in Chapter 4.1.

## 1.3   Contribution to the Research on Emotion

The overview of current research in the area of emotion recognition from speech demonstrates that numerous classification techniques as well as a large number of features can be used to automatically recognize emotional states. By now, the performance of automatic recognition systems is high – even if many emotions are to be distinguished – and is comparable to the human ability to distinguish emotional states, at least if the utterances are labeled without context and the subject is unknown to the labeler. However, most of the studies are based on speech data from emotion portrayals. The excellent classification results obtained so far allow to raise the level of difficulty by focusing on noisy or reverberated speech data [Schu 07c] or by turning towards the recognition of naturally occurring emotional states as they can be observed in real application scenarios. We consider the latter to be the most important stage in the research on automatic emotion recognition, similar to the change in speech recognition from read speech to spontaneous speech.

Unfortunately, adequate speech corpora of naturally occurring emotions are rare or are not available for research. Our new *FAU Aibo Emotion Corpus* contains naturally occurring emotional speech of children playing with Sony's robot Aibo. Besides *neutral*, the emotional/emotion-related states *joyful, surprised, motherese, bored, emphatic, helpless, touchy, reprimanding, angry,* and *other* are annotated. Problems of the elicitation of emotional speech in the chosen Wizard-of-Oz experiment are the sparse-data problem and the low emotional intensity. Although the chosen scenario is very specific, the study gives further evidence that emotional states that can be observed in real scenarios are not the full-blown emotions that have been studied mainly so far. Based on the one hand on the decisions of the reference labelers and on the other hand on acoustic features, the dimensions *valence* and *interaction* could derived from the data. *Valence* is one of the dimensions postulated by psychologists. However, the second dimension on this type of data cannot be interpreted as one of the well-known dimensions *arousal* and *control*.

A new measure to evaluate decoders (single human labelers or machine classifiers) is proposed which weights a classification error, i. e. any deviation from the majority vote of the group of reference labelers, w. r. t. the decisions of the single reference labelers for the specific segment under consideration. Applied to the FAU Aibo Emotion Corpus, our classification system proves to be comparable to the average human labeler of our group of labelers w. r. t. both the number and the type of errors – even on this difficult type of data.

This new corpus provides the common data basis of the project CEICES, a unique initiative, launched by our research group, where the participating international partners contribute their feature sets in order to compare different feature types across the borders of individual research institutes.

In this thesis, features covering prosodic, spectral, voice quality as well as linguistic features are presented. The different types of features are evaluated separately and promising types are combined by early and late fusion resulting in a very competitive, but compact set of features. Since emotional states can change rather quickly, even within one turn, the emotional state is labeled on the word level. By calculating features on the word level, our approach differs from those of most other research groups. In order to find out which unit of analysis is the most appropriate one for emotion recognition, classification experiments on the word, the chunk, and the turn level are carried out. The best results are obtained on the chunk level, which is a compromise between the length of the unit and the homogeneity of the emotional state within this unit. Duration based and $F_0$ based features rely on a correct word segmentation and $F_0$ extraction, respectively. Features based on an automatic word segmentation and on automatically calculated $F_0$ values are compared to those features that are based on a manually corrected version. Different types of errors are quantified. It can be shown that the impact of segmentation and $F_0$ extraction errors on emotion recognition is not significant.

This work has been part of the European Network of Excellence HUMAINE, an international and interdisciplinary research project on human-machine interaction and emotion. Scherer has suggested to base theory and research in the vocal communication of emotion on a modified version of Brunswik's functional lens model of perception. Parts of this work – the evaluation of decoders (both human labelers and machine classifiers) and the evaluation of acoustic and linguistic features – fit nicely into this framework.

## 1.4 Structure of this Work

The following chapter *Human Emotions and Emotion-related User States* defines the term *emotion* together with other terms in this context, in particular the broader term *emotion-related state* which defines the states that are subject of the presented work. Different emotion theories from the psychology of emotion are addressed. These theories constitute what emotions are and how many emotions exist. Emotion theories have an impact on how emotions can be described and thereby on the labeling process of emotional data. Furthermore, the chapter addresses how emotions affect the human vocal communication and different types of studies on vocal communication of emotion are presented. The chapter closes describing possibilities to elicit emotions. These elicitation techniques influence the building of new emotion corpora.

Chapter 3, *Labeling of User States*, deals with two alternatives of labeling, namely category and dimensional labeling, and the problems that arise if application-oriented emotional data is labeled. In addition, possibilities of labeling emotions that change over time are addressed and an extension of category labels to soft decisions is introduced. Finally, measures of inter-labeler agreement for nominal data are presented.

Chapter 4, *Classification and Visualization Techniques*, presents the fundamental principles of statistical machine classification and the principles of the machine classifiers which are actually used in the experiments of this work, namely Gaussian mixture models, linear discriminant analysis, and artificial neural networks. Besides established ways of evaluating classifiers, e. g. calculating the recognition rate, recall, precision, or F-measure, a new measure based on the entropy is introduced which compares the decision of the decoder to the decisions of the reference labelers and weights errors according to this comparison.

Chapter 5, *FAU Aibo Emotion Corpus* , describes the emotion speech corpus used in this thesis from the design and the recording settings, to the segmentation of the audio stream and the transcription of the speech, to various annotation steps. The alignment of the data segments to the pre-defined behavior of the robot dog, the manual corrections of the segmentation on the word level and the $F_0$ values, and the annotated emotion, prosodic, and syntactic labels are described. Various data sets used in the experiments are defined and an analysis of both the German and the English version of the corpus is performed. The emotion-related user states are arranged and visualized in a low-dimensional space using nonmetric dimensional scaling on the basis of confusions between labelers. The chapter ends with a description of the CEICES initiative launched by our research group. With the FAU Aibo Emotion Corpus, CEICES offers a commonly available emotional speech database and facilitates research on emotional speech by bringing together competence and feature sets of the participating partners.

Chapter 6, *Features for Emotion Recognition from Speech*, introduces the different features used in the experiments. The experimental results are presented in Chapter 7, *Experimental Results on Emotion Recognition*. Different types of features are evaluated w. r. t. their applicability in an automatic classification system for emotion-related user states. The feature types are features of the existing *Erlangen Prosody Module*, which are based on energy, $F_0$, duration, and pauses, frequency features like DFT, MFCC, and TRAPS features known from speech recognition, voice quality features like shimmer, jitter, and harmonics-to-noise ratio, linguistic features based on the spoken word chain, and features based on the behavior of the pet robot which is known in the case of the FAU Aibo Emotion Corpus. The feature types are evaluated on the word, the turn, and the chunk level to compare different segmentations.

The thesis closes with the two remaining chapters 8 and 9. Chapter 8 gives an outlook on future research in the area of automatic emotion recognition from speech whereas Chapter 9 summarizes the presented aspects of emotion recognition together with the main experimental results.

# Chapter 2

# Human Emotions and Emotion-related User States

The question about the nature of emotions is very old, dating back to at least the Hellenistic philosophers. Nevertheless, it is still a topic of ongoing debate and research in modern psychology. Thereby, many modern psychological models of emotion are highly influenced by historical perspectives. Discrete emotion models, assuming that only a small number of basic emotions exist, for example, are based on the Darwinian perspective and have influenced many researchers also from other areas like computer science to focus mainly on data containing only the "Big Six" emotions. In the following section, before presenting modern emotion theories and their historical roots, various terms associated with the phenomenon *emotion* are defined and delimited from each other. Then, vocal expressions of emotions, as they have been found in emotion psychology experiments, are summarized. The last section presents different possibilities to elicit emotions.

## 2.1   Terminology

The definition of the term *emotion* is the basis for any kind of research in this area. Only a common definition allows to compare results of different research groups and to avoid misunderstandings. The way emotions are defined also determines the kind of phenomena being examined in emotion research. For the purposes of this work, a working definition by Scherer [Sche 00] is used, which defines *emotions* as

> "episodes of coordinated changes in several components (including at least neurophysiological activation, motor expression, and subjective feeling but possibly also action tendencies and cognitive processes) in response to external or internal events of major significance to the organism".

The triggering external events can be, for example, the "behavior of others, a change in a current situation, or an encounter with novel stimuli" [Sche 00]. Internal events are, for example, thoughts, memories, and sensations. Besides all definitional debates, this definition mentions different elements of emotions for which according to [Sche 00] increasing consensus can be found in the literature:

1. Emotions are of episodic nature and are highly distinctive [Cowi 03]. The underlying assumption is that a noticeable change in the functioning of the organism is caused by some triggering external (e. g. the behavior of others) or internal (e. g. thoughts, memories, sensations) event. Emotion episodes last for a certain duration and normally do not stop abruptly, but fade out with decreasing intensity making the detection of the offset harder than the onset.

2. Emotions consists of several components, including the *reaction triad* of emotion (cf. [Sche 00]), namely physiological arousal, motor expression, and subjective feeling. Necessary components may also be action tendencies and cognitive processes being involved in the evaluation of the eliciting events and the regulation of the ongoing emotional processes.

3. The emotion triggering internal or external stimuli or events are of major significance to the organism. Thus, emotions have been called *relevance detectors* [Frij 86]. The required evaluation of events with respect to their meaning for the organism determines the functional response (adaptation to or mastery of the situation) of the organism as well as the nature of the organismic and mental changes that will occur during the emotional episode.

4. Emotional episodes are of unitary character. They require interdependent and synchronized changes in the component processes.

Various terms highlighting the episodic and distinctive character of emotions exist, each of them carrying specific theoretical implications: 'primary emotions' [Plut 84], 'basic emotions' [Stei 92], 'modal emotions' [Sche 94], or 'acute emotions' [Laza 94]. In order not to prejudge theoretical issues, Cowie et al. [Cowi 01] use Scherer's term 'full-blown emotion' [Sche 99] as a neutral way to refer to episodes that would be widely regarded as prime examples of emotion.

With the given definition, Scherer tells apart emotions from other affective phenomena like moods, interpersonal stances, attitudes, or personality traits as listed together with brief definitions in Table 2.1. Table 2.2 contrasts emotions from these other four affective states on a number of design features which typically include the intensity and the duration of the state, the degree of synchronization of different organismic systems during the state, the extent to which the change in state is triggered by or focused on an event or situation, the influence of the antecedent evaluation or appraisal of the situation, the rapidity of change, and the influence on the behavior.

In this work, different states of children (see Table 5.10) are investigated which are not emotions according to the given definition above. Cowie prefers the term *emotion-related states* [Cowi 03], whereas Scherer calls them *affective states* [Sche 00], using the term *affect* as cover term for all states related to emotion in a broad sense. Theses states explicitly include states focusing on the cognitive (states like alert, hopeful, sincere), or on the cognitive and behavioral component (states like funny, sarcastic). In contrast, Frijda defines *affect* as the "irreducible aspect that gives feelings their emotional, *non-cognitive* character" [Frij 93]. Within this work, the term *emotion-related* is preferred. In the special context of human-machine interaction, the state of the human conversational partner in the interaction with the machine is called *emotion-related user state.*

| affective state | brief definition | examples |
|---|---|---|
| emotion | relatively brief episode of synchronized response of all or most organismic subsystems in response to the evaluation of an external or internal event as being of major significance | angry, sad, joyful, fearful, ashamed, proud, elated, desperate |
| mood | diffuse affect state, most pronounced as change in subjective feeling, of low intensity but relatively long duration, often without apparent cause | cheerful, gloomy, irritable, listless, depressed, buoyant |
| interpersonal stances | affective stance taken toward another person in a specific interaction, coloring the interpersonal exchange in that situation | distant, cold, warm, supportive, contemptuous |
| attitudes | relatively enduring, affectively colored beliefs, preferences, and predispositions towards objects or persons | liking, loving, hating, valuing, desiring |
| personal traits | emotionally laden, stable personality dispositions and behavior tendencies, typical for a person | nervous, anxious, reckless, morose, hostile, envious, jealous |

Table 2.1: Brief definition of five affective states with examples after [Sche 00]

## 2.2 Emotion Theories

Emotion theories in the psychology of emotion predict the number of different emotions that can be expected, how these emotions are differentiated, and why and in which situations emotions are elicited. Thus, the impact of emotion theories on other areas of research like affective computing in computer science is extraordinarily high. They influence the content of emotion databases and by that the basis of recognition experiments. They control the way data of unknown emotional state is labeled. In synthesis of emotions, they define the point in time when an embodied conversational agent reacts emotionally, the selection of the most suited emotion, its intensity, and the way how emotions are synthesized.

In modern psychology of emotion, many concurrent emotion theories exist, each of them capturing and explaining at least some aspects of the complex phenomenon *emotion*. A short overview over modern emotion theories emotion theories as well as their historical development can be found, e.g., in [Corn 00], a more detailed one in [Sche 00] which the following brief overview is based on. Basic emotion models and multidimensional models are most relevant for this thesis. The classification experiments are based on discrete emotional states. However, the states are rather emotion-related than emotions proper. Dimensions of emotions are derived in a data-driven approach and compared to those ones postulated by multidimensional models.

| type of affective state | intensity | duration | synchronization | event focus | appraisal elicitation | rapidity of change | behavioral impact |
|---|---|---|---|---|---|---|---|
| emotion | ++ - +++ | + | +++ | +++ | +++ | +++ | +++ |
| mood | + - ++ | ++ | + | + | + | ++ | + |
| interpersonal stances | + - ++ | + - ++ | + | ++ | + | +++ | ++ |
| attitudes | o - ++ | ++ - +++ | o | o | + | o - + | + |
| personality traits | o - + | +++ | o | o | o | o | + |

o: low, +: medium, ++: high, +++: very high, -: indicates a range

Table 2.2: Design feature delimitation of different affective states after [Sche 03a]

## 2.2.1   Historical Roots

The following conceptions and debates show the continuity of some argumentation strands that are used currently in debates about emotions. They are essential for the understanding of current theories and research objects in the psychology of emotion.

### Plato

More than two millennia ago, the ancient Greek philosopher Plato (427-347 BC) suggested that the soul has a tripartite structure, composed of three separate and opposing areas: cognition, emotion, and motivation. This postulate of three separate systems has been a near-constant controversial issue in the psychology of emotion. In recent years, this debate has been reinvigorated under the name of "cognition-emotion debate". 50 years after Plato formulated the doctrine of the tripartite soul, Aristotle argued for the impossibility of such a separation and for the assumption of an interaction of the different levels of psychological functioning. Many modern psychologists try to overcome thinking in separate systems and emphasize the interlacement of the cognitive, motivational, and emotional processes.

### Descartes

Descartes (1596-1650), a French philosopher, mathematician, scientist, and writer, revolutionized the psychology of emotion by proposing to handle mental and physiological processes at the same time. Since that time, the relationship between mental and bodily phenomena is discussed undiminishedly in the so called "mind-body debate". Examples of current debates are the nature of physiological patterning for specific emotional states or the potential retroaction of expressive innervation of the muscles on mental states.

### Darwin

In his book "The Expression of the Emotions in Man and Animals" [Darw 72] from 1872, Charles Darwin (1809-1882), an English naturalist, described the facial expressions and bodily movements that come along with several emotions in humans and animals together with a simple theory of the evolution of such expressions and movements.

According to Darwin, emotions are survival-related patterns that have evolved to solve certain problems that a species has faced over its evolutionary history. They have to be understood in terms of their function, namely their survival value. Consequently, emotions have to be, more or less, the same in all humans and, in particular, independent of the culture. In addition, because of the common evolutionary past of humans and other animals, similarities in the emotions should be observable for closely-related species.

In the tradition of Darwin, many researchers have tried to demonstrate the universality of emotions, especially of certain human facial expressions (Ekman, Izard, Fridlund, Tompkins). Over the last 30 years, they have collected an impressive amount of evidence for the universality of a small number of facial expressions of emotions. This number is varying depending on different research groups. Ekman uses six universal facial expressions, namely happiness, sadness, fear, disgust, anger, and surprise, sometimes also seven, including contempt. This smaller set is often called the "Big Six" [Corn 96]. According to Izard, there are ten universal facial expressions, Plutchik identifies eight ones. In general, this number varies between six and 14.

Anthropologists as well as social psychologists have strongly attacked Darwin's theory, regarding emotions as sociocultural products determined by learned social rules. This controversy is known as "biology versus culture" debate.

Nevertheless, Darwin's theory is probably the one with the most imposing and enduring impact on the modern psychology of emotion. It has led to the strong focus on emotion expression in face, body, and voice, and has encouraged many current intercultural studies and developmental approaches.

### James

In his 1884 article "What is an emotion?" [Jame 84], William James (1842-1910), an American psychologist and philosopher, postulated that emotions do not elicit physiological changes, but that emotion *is* the feeling of the bodily changes as they occur. These changes are caused by the perception of an exciting fact. Consequently, emotions cannot occur without any bodily changes and the body always responds first before the experience of the bodily changes constitutes what is called emotion. James said, "we feel sorry because we cry, angry because we strike, afraid because we tremble" [Jame 84, p. 190]. The experience of different emotions implies the existence of unique patterns of bodily responses.

Whereas Darwin concentrated on how emotions are *expressed*, James tried to explain the nature of emotional *experience*. James agreed with Darwin that emotions are adaptations to the environment helping the organism to survive. Darwin as well as James considered emotions as more or less distinctive, automatic, and preprogrammed responses to environmental events. They are predispositions to act in a certain way. In comparison, contemporary emotion theorists in the tradition of Darwin and James consider emotions as *action tendencies* [Frij 86].

Today, most theorists agree that feeling as the reflection of what is happening in other components or modalities is at least one of the components of emotion. After more than a century of research, three conclusions related to James's theory seem to be warranted according to Cornelius [Corn 00]:

1. James assumed that someone with no body "would be excluded from the life of the affections" [Jame 84]. Studies of people with spinal cord injuries [Hohm 66, Chwa 88] confirm that feedback of the body plays at least an important role in experiencing emotions, mainly those emotions associated with anger. In particular, the degree of impairment seems to correlate negatively with the intensity of the experienced emotion. Nevertheless, other emotions like love and compassion seem to be experienced with a higher intensity after injury.

2. According to studies by Levenson et al. [Leve 92a, Leve 90], emotions can be differentiated at the level of the autonomic nervous system. This supports the theory of unique bodily response patterns. Reliable differences in the patterns of heart rate and finger temperature change associated with fear, anger, disgust, and happiness could be found.

3. Different studies ([Leve 90, Lair 84, Stra 88, Step 93]) have shown that facial expressions and bodily postures may drive emotional experience. Several theorists (e.g., Levenson et al. [Leve 90]) have proposed the existence of *affect programs* that activate a number of expressive, motor, and experiential systems. Is any one of these programs activated, it may also activate others. With respect to speech, prosody would be expected to be one of the systems being activated by affect programs and, vice versa, should be able to activate them.

The cited examples of current research demonstrate the great influence the historical theories mentioned above have had on the psychology of emotion and still have. The next section outlines modern psychological models of emotion.

## 2.2.2  Current Psychological Models of Emotion

Emotion theories define the number of existing emotions that can be distinguished as well as the principles that lead to this differentiation. With respect to both aspects, current emotion theories differ greatly.

### Dimensional Models

Dimensional models distinguish emotions according to different characteristics such as the degree of excitation, pleasantness, or relaxation. These models can be discriminated on the basis of the number and the kind of dimensions employed.

**Unidimensional Models**   Although proponents of unidimensional models acknowledge a variety of fine distinctions between emotional states, they claim that the basic distinction between different emotions can be made on the basis of only one single dimension. Depending on the theorist, this dimension is either *activation/arousal* – the subjective state feeling activated or deactivated – or *valence* – the subjective feeling of pleasantness or unpleasantness.

For the activation/arousal dimension, the major difference between emotions is the degree of arousal from very little to very much. Duffy went even to the lengths of abolishing the term *emotion* in favor of the adoption of terms denoting general excitation [Duff 41]. The level of activation can be thought of the strength of the person's disposition to take some action linking the activation dimension to James' understanding of emotions as dispositions to act in certain ways and Frijda's action tendencies.

If the dimension is valence, the most important distinguishing mark between emotions is the degree of pleasantness, ranging from unpleasant, bad, or disagreeable on the one pole to pleasant, good, or agreeable on the opposite one. In this way, positive and negative emotions can be discriminated, reflecting the two fundamental behavioral orientations *approach* and *avoidance* [Schn 59].

**Multidimensional Models**   In multidimensional models, emotional states can be represented as coordinates in a low-dimensional space. In 1874, Wundt suggested the three independent dimensions pleasantness–unpleasantness, rest–activation, and relaxation–attention [Wund 10]. In the mid twentieth century, multidimensional models were taken up again by several researchers. In 1954, Schlosberg pointed out the relevance of the two dimensions *valence* and *arousal* [Schl 54]. He demonstrated that this two-dimensional space is applicative to represent a considerable amount of information about emotion. Plutchik [Plut 62, Plut 80] and Russel [Russ 80, Russ 83] also contributed to the popularity of this two-dimensional model. Cowie et al. call this space activation-evaluation space [Cowi 01]. Full-blown emotions form a roughly circular pattern in this space.

The activation-evaluation model provides a way of describing emotional states that is more tractable than using words and, hence, especially attractive to computationally oriented research. Nonetheless, emotion-related words can be translated into positions within the two-dimensional space and, vice versa, positions can be translated back into verbal descriptions. Two-dimensional spaces can be illustrated graphically and similarities and differences of emotions can be expressed and visualized as Euclidean distances between points in this space.

However, the reduction of the multidimensional space to only two dimensions goes with a loss of information. The close neighborhood of anger and fear in the activation-evaluation space, for example, makes an effective separation of both emotions impossible. The problem can be solved by adding *perceived control* or *inclination to engage* as a third dimension. In both cases, anger is positive whereas fear is negative. Unfortunately, adding one more dimension yields only a few more emotional states that can be separated and once one starts to add further dimensions, the question arises where to stop [Cowi 03].

**Discrete Emotion Models**

In contrast to dimensional emotion models, discrete models claim that only a few discrete emotions exist.

**Circuit Models**   Circuit models are used in the neuropsychology of emotion. The basic assumption is that evolutionarily developed neural circuits determine the number of fundamental emotions as well as their differentiation. Panksepp [Pank 82, Pank 89] argues for the existence of four fundamental circuits which produce well-organized, clear behavioral sequences for rage, fear, expectancy, and panic. Additionally to these primary order emotive states, the theory suggests the existence of emotive states of secondary order, that are produced by blending activities across the primary systems, in order to be able to explain not only the emotional behavior of lower mammals but also of primates, especially humans.

**Basic Emotion Models**    Theories suggesting the existence of basic or fundamental emotions such as anger, fear, disgust, sadness, and joy belong to the most popular conceptualizations of the nature of emotion. They are strongly supported by the existence of corresponding verbal labels used frequently in everyday life. Similar to circuit models, theorists in this tradition proceed on the assumption that a number of major adaptive emotional strategies has developed over the course of evolution that consist of a limited number of fundamental emotions. These emotions can be distinguished according to their specific elicitation conditions and their physiological, expressive, and behavioral reaction patterns. In general, the number of basic emotions varies between six and 14.

Many of these models are derived from Darwin's work [Darw 72] where he demonstrated the functionality, evolutionary history, and universality across species, ontogenetic stages, and cultures for a number of major emotion terms in the English language. Tomkins [Tomk 62, Tomk 84] extended Darwin's theorizing: he regarded basic or fundamental emotions as phylogenetically stable neuromotor programs. The reactions range from peripheral physiological responses to muscular innervation, particularly in the face. They are automatically triggered by specific eliciting conditions which differ in the gradient of neural firing. The face is of important relevance as it is considered to be the primary differentiating effector system.

Izard and Ekman extended Tomkins' theory and contributed substantially to the popularity of his concept. They attempted to obtain empirical evidence, particularly with respect to the following three aspects: firstly, the early ontogenetic onset of discrete emotion patterns [Izar 80, Izar 94, Izar 95], secondly, the discrete patterning of prototypical facial expressions for a number of basic emotions, and thirdly, the universality of these patterns [Ekma 72, Ekma 73, Ekma 80, Ekma 94, Ekma 92, Izar 72, Izar 90, Izar 94, Leve 92b].

The large variety of emotional states cannot be explained with the limited number of basic emotions. Mechanisms to mix or blend basic emotions had to be postulated. Plutchik, also supporting Darwin's evolutionary theory, assumes eight basic emotions, made up of four pairs of opposites: joy and sadness, acceptance and disgust, fear and anger, and surprise and anticipation [Plut 80]. Opposite emotions inhibit or neutralize each other and, hence, are arranged as opposite sectors in his *emotion wheel* (Figure 2.1 right). In contrast, *primary dyads*, mixtures of two adjacent emotions, can be experienced at the same time as blended emotions. The complex emotion of contempt, for example, is produced by mixing the basic emotions anger and disgust. *Secondary* and *tertiary dyads* are mixtures of two primary emotions that are once and twice respectively removed on the circle. Nevertheless, emotion names could not be found for each of these mixtures, suggesting that mixtures of emotions that are more widely separated on the emotion circle are harder to imagine or less likely to be experienced than those that are closer. Also mixtures of three basic emotions, so-called *triads*, might be possible.

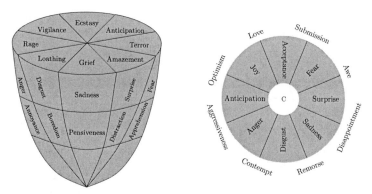

Figure 2.1: Left: Plutchik's Emotion Solid; the vertical dimension represents intensity. Right: cross section of the Emotion Solid with eight basic emotions (also known as Plutchik's Emotion Wheel) and the primary dyads resulting from mixing two adjacent primary emotions; after [Plut 80, p. 157 ff.]

According to Plutchik, emotions vary also in their intensity. For each basic emotion, he defines an intense version and a less intense one (Figure 2.1 left). Nevertheless, the less intense emotions are, the more difficult it is to distinguish them.

Also Ekman and Izard have elaborated their theories to account for the large variety of emotional states as well as for environmental and cultural effects on the emotional development [Ekma 94, Izar 94]. In this context, Ekman introduced the concept of *emotion families.*

## Meaning Oriented Models

**Lexical Models** Theorists in this tradition assume that the wisdom of the language can be used to discover the underlying structure of psychological phenomena. The basis of lexical models is the structure of semantic fields of emotion terms. Although psychophysiological processes are largely unconscious and it is unclear whether the semantic structures of the emotion lexicon can be mapped onto them, this approach is appealing as it activates common cultural interpretation patterns.

Ortony et al. performed a structural analysis of the emotion lexicon to demonstrate the underlying semantic implicational structure [Orto 88]. Shaver et al. built trees of emotion terms with differential degrees of generality in the classification of emotional states by cluster analysis methods [Shav 87].

**Social Constructivist Models** According to the social constructivist theories, socioculturally determined behavior and value patterns make up the meaning of emotion in general. Although psychobiological components of emotion are not denied, they are considered secondary to the meaning that emotion attains in the sociocultural context. This holds both for the interpretation of the eliciting event or situation and the role of the emotion reaction in the person's sense-making and social interaction. As in lexical models, emotion lexicons are of major importance as emotion labels available in a language are considered to reflect the emotional meaning structure in the respective culture.

### Componential Models

Componential models assume that emotions are elicited by a cognitive (but not necessarily conscious or controlled) evaluation or appraisal of antecedent situations or events. The result of this evaluation determines the patterning of the reactions in the different response domains (physiology, motor expression, action tendencies, and feeling).

In the context of explaining the elicitation of emotions, the term *appraisal* was first used by Arnold [Arno 60]. She distinguished three different appraisal dimensions: beneficial vs. harmful, presence vs. absence of some object, and relative difficulty to approach or avoid the latter. Lazarus argued for a two-stage process where, in the first stage, the significance of the event for one's well-being and, in the second stage, the ability to cope with the consequences of the event is evaluated [Laza 66].

Among others, appraisal theories differ in the conceptualization of emotion differentiation. Four major strands can be distinguished depending on whether events are appraised with respect to certain postulated criteria, attributions, themes, or meanings [Sche 99]. According to the classic approach to appraisal, based on the early work of Arnold and Lazarus, individuals use a fixed set of criteria to evaluate the significance of the events that happen to them. These criteria comprise intrinsic characteristics of the objects or events such as novelty or agreeableness, the significance of the event for one's needs and goals, the individual's ability to cope with the consequences of the event, and the compatibility of the event with social or personal standards, norms, or values. Table 2.3 lists the major criteria as postulated by Frijda [Frij 86], Roseman [Rose 84, Rose 91, Rose 96], Scherer [Sche 84b, Sche 84a, Sche 86, Sche 88], and Smith/Ellsworth [Smit 85].

Appraisal theories also differ in the number of predicted major emotions. Typically, the ensuing emotion is determined by specific profiles of appraisal outcomes. In Scherer's component process model, there are as many different emotional states as differential patterns of appraisal results exist.

Ortony et al. developed a computationally tractable model of emotion especially to be used in artificial intelligence systems [Orto 88]. Emotions are valanced reactions to certain cognitions and interpretations determined by the appraisal of consequences of *events* for oneself or for others, own *actions* or actions of other agents, and aspects of *objects*. The structure of emotion types in the theory of Ortony et al. is presented in Figure 2.2.

## 2.3  Vocal Expression of Emotion

Emotional expression plays an important role in human speech communication and has a powerful impact on the listener. This fact has been recognized throughout history. Already Greek and Roman manuals on rhetoric (e. g., by Aristotle, Cicero, Quintilian) pointed out the strategic use of emotionally expressive speech [Kenn 72]. In [Sche 03a], Scherer gives a short overview of the history of research in the field

| Scherer | Frijda | Roseman | Smith/Ellsworth |
|---|---|---|---|
| novelty | change | | attentional activity |
| • suddenness | | | |
| • familiarity | familiarity | | |
| • predictability | | | |
| intrinsic pleasantness | valence | | pleasantness |
| goal significance | | appetitive/aversive | |
| • concern relevance | focality | motives | importance |
| • outcome probability | certainty | certainty | certainty |
| • expectation | presence | | |
| • conduciveness | open/closed | motive consistency | perceived obstacle/ |
| • urgency | urgency | | anticipated effort |
| coping potential | | | |
| • cause: agent | intent/self-other | agency | human agency |
| • cause: motive | | | |
| • control | modifiability | control potential | situational control |
| • power | controllability | | |
| • adjustment | | | |
| compatibility standards | | | |
| • external | value relevance | | legitimacy |
| • internal | | | |

Table 2.3: Comparison of different appraisal criteria after [Sche 99]

of vocal expression of emotion. The main milestones are briefly mentioned here: In the 19th century, the emergence of modern evolutionary biology (cf. Chapter 2.2.1) boosted the interest in the expression of emotion in face and voice. First empirical investigations of the effect of emotion on the voice were conducted at the beginning of the 20th century. With the help of newly developed methods of electroacoustic analysis, psychiatrists tried to diagnose emotional disturbances. Inventions like the telephone and the radio and their rapid and wide distribution promoted the scientific interest in the communication of speaker attributes and vocal cues in speech. In the 1960s, systematic research programs started involving many different research areas: Psychiatrists renewed their interest in diagnosing affective states via vocal expressions, non-verbal communication researchers investigated the way emotions are carried by different bodily channels, emotion psychologists explored the expression of emotion in different modalities, and linguists and phoneticians studied the relevance of pragmatic information in speech. Progress in acoustic signal processing allowed engineers and phoneticians to use more sophisticated technologies in the analysis of speech and, at the same time, to process a larger amount of data. Recently, due to advances in automatic speech processing and understanding, speech scientists and engineers directed their attention to the recognition of affective user states and to the synthesis of emotions with the goal to increase the naturalness of a human-machine dialog and, hence, to increase the acceptability of such systems for human users.

Scherer suggested [Sche 78, Sche 03a] to base theory and research in the vocal communication of emotion on a modified version of Brunswik's functional lens model of perception [Brun 56] – a metaphor highlighting the probabilistic relationships be-

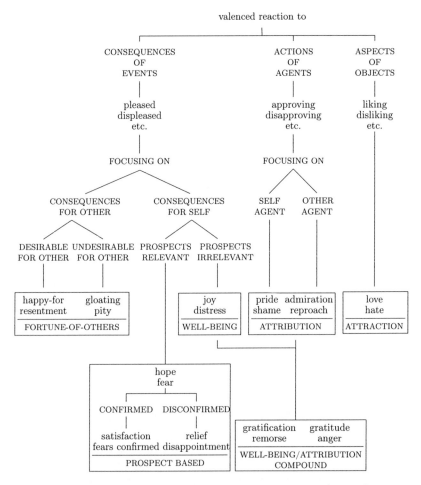

Figure 2.2: OCC model: structure of emotion types after [Orto 88]

tween an ecological criterion and the sensory cues that an organism uses to judge this criterion. The cues are focused by cognitive processes like rays of light. The model adapted to the vocal communication of emotion is depicted in Figure 2.3. The emotional state of the speaker is expressed – or encoded – by certain voice and speech characteristics which can be measured objectively in the speech signal. Physiological changes with effect on the respiration, phonation, and articulation produce specific patterns of acoustic parameters for each emotion. For an observer, these acoustic changes can be cues to the speaker's emotional state and are called *distal cues* (distal in the sense of distant from the observer). As part of the speech signal, they are

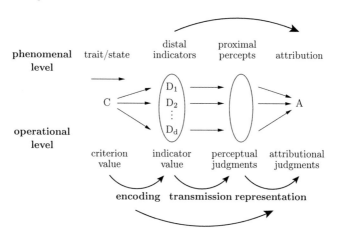

Figure 2.3: Scherer's modified version of Brunswik's functional lens model of perception after [Sche 78, Sche 03a]

transmitted to the listener who perceives them via the auditory perceptual system. Emotional states might not always produce reliable externalizations in form of specific distal cues in the voice. In Brunswik's terminology, *ecological validity* is the degree of correlation between such characteristics and the underlying speaker state.

The perceived cues of the speaker's emotional state are called *proximal cues* (in the sense of close to the observer). Whereas Brunswik saw the proximal stimulus as close but still outside the organism, Scherer places them inside the organism. In auditory perception, the fundamental frequency of a speech signal, for example, represents the distal cues. Each phase of the input, transduction, and coding process – beginning with the impact on the pattern of vibration along the basilar membrane and, in turn, on the pattern of excitation along the inner hair cells, to the subsequent excitation of the auditory neurons, and finally, to the representation in the auditory cortex – might be considered as proximal representation. Since it is difficult to measure the raw input directly, Scherer argues to extend this term to the neural representation of the stimulus information as coded by the respective neural structures. Thus, the proximal cue for fundamental frequency would be perceived pitch. At least the conscious part of this representation can be assessed via self-report. Various influences of the transmission channel (e.g., reverberation, noise) and the structural characteristics of the perceptual organ and the transduction and coding process (e.g., selective enhancement of certain frequency bands) may modify or distort the distal cues in such a way that they no longer carry the essential information. Thus, distal characteristics are not necessarily equivalent to the proximal cues produced in the observer.

Finally, if the distal cues are valid and the proximal cues reliably map them, it is still possible that the inference mechanism of the respective listener leads to the wrong conclusion about the speaker's emotional state.

By means of Scherer's functional lens model, major research issues in the area of vocal communication of emotion can be identified (indicated by curved arrows in Figure 2.3):

**Encoding Studies**  Emotions can only be communicated reliably via vocal expression alone if unique patterns of acoustic parameters, or distal cues in the context of a Brunswikian lens model, exist for different types of emotion. In the psychology of emotion, many empirical encoding studies have been conducted over the last six decades, attempting to determine which acoustic changes correspond to which emotional speaker states. These studies differ in the kind of speech data being investigated. According to the type of emotion elicitation (see Chapter 2.4), they can be categorized into three groups: natural vocal expression, induced emotional expression, and simulated emotional expression.

So far, only a limited number of acoustic cues has been studied by psychologists. They can be classified into four categories [John 00]:

1. time-related measures like rate and duration of vocal sounds and pauses, phrase duration and word rate,

2. intensity-related measures like the logarithmic transform of the signal energy,

3. measures related to the fundamental frequency like $F_0$ floor, $F_0$ range, $F_0$ variance, $F_0$ skewness, jitter, spectral slope of the glottal spectrum, and the ratios of the energy of the harmonics and the fundamental frequency, and

4. combined time-frequency-energy measures like formant amplitudes and bandwidths, long-term resonance characteristics of the vocal tract obtained by a long-term average spectrum (LTAS) calculated separately for voiced and unvoiced sections of speech, and various parameters characterizing the sound produced at the glottis prior to the effects of the vocal tract resonance (glottal waveform analysis).

Johnstone and Scherer ([John 00], see also [Sche 86, Bans 96, Sche 03a]) have reviewed the converging evidence from various studies with respect to the acoustic patterns characterizing the vocal expression of the major modal emotions anger/rage, fear/panic, sadness, joy/elation, boredom, and stress (although stress is not a single, well-defined emotion). Table 2.4 shows the results.

Much of the consistency is due to differential levels of arousal for the target emotions. In the past, it has often been assumed that voice can only mark physiological arousal but, in contrast to facial expressions, cannot communicate qualitative differences between emotions. In contrast, decoding studies (see below) have demonstrated that human judges can infer different emotions from vocal expressions with nearly the same accuracy as from facial expressions and thus, clearly disprove this assumption. According to Scherer [Sche 03a], the difficulty in demonstrating qualitative differentiation of emotions apart from arousal is based on two facts: (1) Only a limited number of acoustic cues, mainly $F_0$, energy, and speech rate, have been studied so far whereas only a few studies have analyzed frequency spectrum or formant parameters. It is possible that qualitative differences have a stronger impact on source and articulation

|                              | anger/ rage | fear/ panic | sadness | joy/ elation | boredom | stress |
|------------------------------|:-----------:|:-----------:|:-------:|:------------:|:-------:|:------:|
| Intensity                    | ↗           | ↗           | ↘       | ↗            |         | ↗      |
| $F_0$ floor/mean             | ↗           | ↗           | ↘       | ↗            |         | ↗      |
| $F_0$ variability            | ↗           |             | ↘       | ↗            | ↘       |        |
| $F_0$ range                  | ↗           | ↗(↘)[1]     | ↘       | ↗            |         | ↘      |
| Sentence contour             | ↘           |             | ↘       |              |         |        |
| High frequency energy        | ↗           | ↗           | ↘       | (↗)[2]       |         |        |
| Speech and articulation rate | ↗           | ↗           | ↘       | (↗)[2]       | ↘       |        |

[1] Banse and Scherer found a decrease in $F_0$ range [Bans 96].
[2] inconclusive evidence

Table 2.4: Influence of basic emotions on acoustic parameters after [Sche 03a]

characteristics whereas $F_0$, energy, and speech rate may be most indicative of arousal. (2) Arousal differences within emotion families have been neglected. Discrepancies in different studies may result from different forms of anger (hot anger, explosive rage versus cold, subdued or controlled anger) as most studies do not specify which kind of anger has actually been produced or portrayed.

**Decoding Studies**   This kind of studies examines to what extent human lay judges are able to infer emotions from speech samples. In general, actors have been asked to portray a limited number of emotions by producing speech utterances with standardized or nonsense content. Thus, the speech samples do not contain any linguistic information and the judgment of the listeners is based on acoustic parameters only. The judges are provided with a list of emotion labels and are requested to decide for one of the given alternatives. Consequently, decoding studies tend to be discrimination studies rather than recognition studies.

In [Sche 89], Scherer reviews approximately 30 studies which have been conducted up to the early 1980s and where only normal voice portrayals have been used (excluding pathological voice samples and filtered speech). In these studies, the average accuracy with which human listeners can infer emotions is about 60 % for up to ten emotions. This is about five to six times higher than chance level. Similar accuracies have been reported in more recent studies: [Bezo 84] reports a mean accuracy of 65 % for eight different emotions (disgust, surprise, shame, interest, joy, fear, sadness, and anger). In a study by Scherer et al. with a variety of different types of listeners and age groups, a mean accuracy of 56 % for five emotions (disgust, joy, fear, sadness, and anger) has been obtained [Sche 91].

Results from a cross-cultural study [Sche 01b] with listener-judges from nine countries in Europe, Asia, and the United States also indicate that to some degree universal inference rules from vocal characteristics to specific emotions even exist across different cultures since confusion patterns across different cultures were similar.

In comparison to the decoding studies for vocal expressions mentioned above, facial expression studies generally report higher average recognition accuracies (around 75 %). The difference of about 15 percentage points is mostly due to expressions of joy and disgust which can be recognized with almost 100 % accuracy from facial expressions since facial actions are highly specific for both emotions (smiling for joy

| acoustic parameters | ARO/ STR | HAP/ ELA | ANG/ RAG | SAD | FEA/ PAN | BOR |
|---|---|---|---|---|---|---|
| **speech rate and fluency** | | | | | | |
| number of syllables per second | > | ≥ | <> | < | > | < |
| syllable duration | < | ≤ | <> | > | < | > |
| duration of accented vowels | ≥ | ≥ | > | ≥ | < | ≥ |
| number and duration of pauses | < | < | < | > | <> | > |
| rel. duration of voiced segments | | | > | | <> | |
| rel. duration of unvoiced segments | | | < | | <> | |
| **voice source–$F_0$ and prosody** | | | | | | |
| $F_0$ mean[3] | > | > | > | < | > | ≤ |
| $F_0$: 5th percentile[3] | > | > | = | ≤ | > | ≤ |
| $F_0$ deviation[3] | > | > | > | < | > | < |
| $F_0$ range[3] | > | > | > | < | <> | ≤ |
| Frequency of accented syllables | > | ≥ | > | < | | |
| Gradient of $F_0$ rising and falling[3,6] | > | > | > | < | <> | ≤ |
| $F_0$ final fall: range and gradient[3,4,7] | > | > | > | < | <> | ≤ |
| **voice source–vocal effort and type of phonation** | | | | | | |
| intensity (dB) mean[5] | > | ≥ | > | ≤ | | ≤ |
| intensity (dB) deviation[5] | > | > | > | < | | < |
| gradient of intensity rising and falling[2] | > | ≥ | > | < | | ≤ |
| rel. spectral energy in higher bands[1] | > | > | > | < | <> | ≤ |
| spectral slope[1] | < | < | < | > | <> | > |
| laryngealization | | = | = | > | > | = |
| jitter[3] | | ≥ | ≥ | | > | = |
| shimmer[3] | | ≥ | ≥ | | > | = |
| HNR[1,3] | | > | > | < | < | ≤ |
| **articulation–speed and precision** | | | | | | |
| formants–precision of location | ?[1] | = | > | < | ≤ | ≤ |
| formants bandwidth | < | | < | > | | ≥ |

Notes:
1. depends on phoneme combinations, articulation precision or tension of the vocal tract
2. depends on prosodic features like accent realization, rhythm, etc.
3. depends on speaker-specific factors like age, gender, health, etc.
4. depends on sentence mode
5. depends on microphone distance and amplification
6. for accented segments
7. for final portion of sentences

In specific phonemes, < "smaller," "lower," "less," "flatter," or "narrower"; = equal to "neutral"; > "bigger," "higher," "faster," "more," "steeper," or "broader"; ≤ smaller or equal, ≥ bigger or equal; <> both smaller and bigger have been reported

ARO: arousal, STR: stress, HAP: happiness, ELA: elation, ANG: anger, RAG: rage, SAD: sadness, FEA: fear, PAN: panic, BOR: boredom

[1] explanation of '?' missing in [Sche 03b]

Table 2.5: Effect of emotion on acoustic parameters: a synthetic review of the empirical findings after [Sche 03b]

and nose wrinkling for disgust). Whereas sadness and anger are generally recognized best vocally followed by fear, the accuracies for vocal expression of joy vary rather strongly for different studies which is probably due to the fact that different members of the same emotion family are portrayed. Exuberant joy and quiet happiness, for example, show important vocal differences, but generally, the studies do not specify which kind of joy has actually been used [Sche 03a]. In contrast, disgust is recognized very poorly from voice throughout all studies with accuracies barely above chance level suggesting that voice is more suited to the expressive and communicative needs of certain emotions than of others. Obviously, voice is ideally suited to warn (fear) or threaten (anger) others in a fairly indirect way over large distances whereas facial expressions might be most adequate to prevent conspecifics being at the same place from eating rotten food (disgust) [John 00].

The lower accuracies for vocal expressions lie, according to Scherer, also in the dynamic nature of vocal stimuli resulting in less stable patterns compared to facial expressions where the major emotions seem to be identified by basic muscle configurations.

**Inference Studies** Whereas decoding studies focus on the ability of listeners to recognize the emotional state of the speaker, inference studies investigate the underlying voice–emotion inference mechanism. By varying the acoustic cues in sample utterances, they determine the relative effect of particular parameters on the emotion judgment. Three different methods exists to systematically manipulate the parameters: (1) cue measurement and regression, (2) cue masking, and (3) cue manipulation via synthesis.

(1) *Cue measurement and regression* measures the acoustic characteristics of vocal emotion portrayals and correlates them with the listener's judgment of the underlying emotion or attitude of the speaker. Highly correlated parameters are likely to have determined the judge's inference.

(2) *Cue masking* masks, distorts, or removes certain verbal/vocal cues from vocal emotion expressions and determines the influence of the modified material on the emotion inference. Different techniques like (low-pass) filtering, randomized splicing, playing backwards, pitch inversion, and tone-silence coding have been used.

(3) *Cue manipulation via synthesis* uses synthesis and copy synthesis methods where vocal parameters can be systematically manipulated to determine the effect of these changes on the judgment of the listener. The improvements of text-to-speech systems will allow a large number of systematic variations of acoustic parameters and result in natural sounding emotional speech.

For a more detailed review see [John 00, Sche 03b, Sche 03a].

**Transmission Studies** The Brunswikian lens model, trying to model systematically all aspects of the communication process, also allows to model the transmission of the distal signal of the sender to the receiver where it is represented on a subjective, proximal level. Thereby, the transmission process can systematically change the nature of the distal cues and thus be responsible for inference errors due to nonrepresentative proximal cues. Two major aspects are (1) the transmission of sound through space and (2) the transform functions in perception as determined by the nature of human hearing mechanisms [Sche 03b].

Factors influencing the transmission of sound through space are, for example, the distance between sender and receiver and the presence of other sounds or background noise. In order to communicate over large distances, the articulation has to be rather precise and the mode of production changes. A higher vocal effort is needed to produce more intense speech changing not only the intensity but also affecting a large number of characteristics related to voice production at the larynx. On the other hand, facial expressions and gestures, especially head movements, are expected to have less effect on the intensity and spectral distribution of the acoustic signal with increasing distance since they cannot be communicated over long distances (see [Lave 91]). Thus, transmission also constraints the way voice can be used to signal emotions.

The perceptual representation of sounds does not correspond in a one-to-one fashion to objectively measured properties of the sound. A few selected examples from [Sche 03b] are given here: The perceived loudness of voiced speech signals, for example, correlates more strongly with the amplitude of a few or even a single harmonic than with its overall intensity [Gram 88, Titz 92]. $F_0$ movements are only perceived as melodic movements if they cross the glissando threshold which depends on the frequency and on the slope of the $F_0$ change (see [dAll 95]). Oscillating $F_0$ values around a fixed or slowly varying value are perceived as voice quality effects (tremor, jitter) rather than melodic movements. The correlation between physical signal length and perceived duration of fluent speech segments is generally very weak. Higher $F_0$ or an $F_0$ rise at the end of an utterance, for example, is perceived as a faster speaking rate [Kohl 95].

**Representation Studies**   These studies focus on the mental algorithms that are used by listeners to infer emotion on the basis of proximal cues. The Brunswikian lens model requires these proximal cues to be directly measured. So far, the only possibility is to rely on the listener's verbal description of his/her subjective impressions of the speaker's voice and speech which is constrained by the semantic categories for which there are words in a specific language. Unfortunately, in most languages, including English, only relatively few words exist describing vocal qualities. Furthermore, only a subset of those is frequently used in normal speech or literature but this is required in order to study naïve, untrained listeners. Due to these difficulties, the number of representation studies is quite low.

Many aspects of this work fit nicely into the framework of the presented Brunswikian lens model and the studies that emerge from it. The task of finding good features to be able to train an automatic classifier for emotion-related user states (see Chapter 6 and 7) is comparable to encoding studies where the goal is to identify acoustic parameters (distal cues) which characterize different emotions. The question how good human listeners are in recognizing emotions from vocal expressions, addressed in decoding studies, is important for the interpretation of the inter-labeler agreement for the manually labeled data being used in this work (see Chapter 3.5 and 5.3.7). Although the influence of reverberation as part of the transmission channel on the recognition accuracy of a machine classifier is not part of this work, we have conducted experiments with different levels of reverberation on our data [Schu 07c].

Most studies have used emotion portrayals produced by actors. The next sections lists different ways of emotion elicitation and contrasts the advantages and drawbacks of each method.

## 2.4  Elicitation of Emotions

Three different groups of methods to elicit vocal expression of emotion are presented: simulated vocal expression, induced vocal expression, and natural vocal expression.

**Simulated Vocal Expression**   The preferred way in most previous studies in all areas from the psychology of emotion to speech synthesis and speech recognition has been the use of emotional speech produced by professional or lay actors, based on emotion labels and/or typical scenarios.  In [Sche 03a] relevant studies in the psychology with simulated vocal expressions are listed.

The main advantage of emotion portrayals is the production of intense, prototypical expressions of emotion. Other advantages have already been mentioned in Chapter 1.2. The intended emotion is known as the actor/actress is told what emotion to portray, and subsequent perception tests demonstrate that listener-judges can reliably recognize the intended emotion from the speech. If necessary, samples with a low recognition accuracy are excluded from the study.

Unfortunately, this approach also entails some disadvantages: The emotions under examination are generally limited to only a few basic emotions. As actors are influenced by conventionalized stereotypes of vocal expression, relatively obvious cues might be overemphasized whereas more subtle ones, which possibly appear in natural expression of emotion, may be missed [Sche 86]. Emotion portrayals might reflect sociocultural norms more than the psychophysiological effects on the voice whereas supporters of simulated vocal expressions argue that all publicly observable expressions are subject to social constraints and hence, are "portrayals" to some extent [Sche 03a]. Often, the expression of personal feelings or emotions is suppressed due to sociocultural norms whereas in other situations, it is preferable to express emotions although they are not felt [Camp 00]. Campbell stresses the importance to distinguish between intended expression of emotion as in case of emotion portrayals and unintended revelation of the speaker's state. The fact that emotion portrayals are recognized correctly does not exclude the possibility that at the same time, listener-judges are aware that the speaker is consciously intending to express the particular emotion instead of actually being emotional. People respond negatively to displays of emotions that are perceived as simulated [Cowi 03].

**Induced Vocal Expression**   Induction techniques try to effectively change the subject's emotional state. In [Gerr 94], nearly 250 mood induction studies focusing on the induction of elation and depression are reviewed and the effectiveness of the mood induction procedure (MIP) is analyzed. The different MIPs are categorized into the following five groups:

1. *MIPs based on the free mental generation of emotional states:* The applied
stimuli are not presented by the experimenter, but are activated by the subjects
themselves. Examples are the Hypnosis MIP (subjects in a deep trance are
instructed to remember and imagine a certain situation of their own choice in
which they felt happy or sad) and the Imagination MIP (subjects are instructed
to imagine or re-experience situations).

2. *MIPs based on the guided mental generation of emotional states:* Emotion-
inducing material is presented with the instruction to get into the suggested
emotional state. Examples are the Veltin MIP (subjects are instructed to use
self-referent statements describing positive or negative self-evaluations and bodily sensations as auto-suggestions, i. e. to try to feel the emotion described by
the statement), Film/Story$^+$ MIP[1] (imagination of the situation presented in a
film or story and 'getting involved' in the suggested feelings), and the Music$^+$
MIP (listening to mood-suggestive pieces of classical or modern music).

3. *MIPs based on the presentation of emotion-inducing material:* Unlike the methods of the previous category, emotional stimuli are presented without instructing
the subjects to get into the emotional state suggested. Thereby, it is avoided
that subjects actively try to get into the prescribed state. MIPs of this group
are the Film/Story MIP, the Music MIP, and the Gift MIP (unexpected gifts
are expected to evoke elation).

4. *MIPs based on the presentation of need-related emotional situations:* Emotions
often arise from the satisfaction or frustration of needs. Thus, Success/Failure
MIPs (false-positive or false-negative feedback in tests alleged to assess the
subject's cognitive abilities) activate the need of achievement, Social Interaction MIPs (exposing subjects to certain social interactions arranged by the
experimenter) the need of affiliation.

5. *MIPs aiming at the generation of emotionally relevant physiological states:* As
many theorists claim that emotions in general presuppose an unspecific physiological arousal, Drug MIPs induce physiological arousal by administering psychoactive drugs like antidepressants [Helf 94] or adrenaline. In the Facial Expression MIP, subjects are asked to frown or smile. In accord with the facial
feedback hypothesis [Leve 80], the contraction and relaxation of different muscles can induce negative and positive emotional states.

Apart from elation and depression, these techniques have also been applied to
other emotions. According to [Cowi 03], films/videos and still photographs, such as
the *Philadelphia Morgue* set for fear and disgust, are widely used for a variety of
emotions. Sadness and depressive-like affect can be reliably induced using sad music.
To increase the effectiveness, different types of MIPs can be combined.

However, most of these techniques have neither been developed particularly for
elicitation of speech, nor is it obvious how easily they can be adapted for that purpose [Cowi 03]. A few induction techniques specifically designed to elicit speech are,
for example, a difficult spelling task to elicit negative emotion [Bach 99], a mental

---

[1]The '+' stands for the explicit instruction to get into the suggested emotional state

arithmetic task to elicit speech under stress conditions [Fern 03], and a Wizard-of-Oz-scenario, developed at our institute, where a malfunctioning system is simulated to evoke anger [Batl 03a].

Although induction techniques are applicable to evoke emotions, the following drawbacks exist: Generally, the elicited emotions are relatively weak. This seems to be true especially for systems specifically designed to elicit emotional speech. Furthermore, the exact emotional state produced in the individuals is unknown due to individual differences in the event appraisal. A study with three different laboratory mood/emotion induction procedures shows that the resulting emotional states tend to be mixtures of multiple affective states rather than single, discrete emotions [Poli 81]. Moreover, physiological evidence exists that emotional states induced by imaging techniques differ substantially from those states induced by external events [Stem 01]. In induction techniques, the content of the spoken utterances cannot be controlled. In order to be able to analyze the more spontaneous data statistically, the size of the corpus has to be increased drastically. Besides the technical problems, it is morally arguable if emotions may be induced deliberately only for the purpose of collecting scientific data [Camp 00].

**Natural Vocal Expression**  The ideal research paradigm seems to be the use of recordings of naturally occurring voice changes in emotionally charged situations like dangerous flight situations for pilots, affectively loaded therapy sessions, talk and game shows on TV, or journalists reporting emotion-eliciting events [Sche 03a]. In the radio news broadcast of the crash of the Hindenburg, for example, excitement and panic are clearly audible in the speech of the witnesses.

An existing database of naturally occurring emotional speech is, for example, the *Geneva Airport Lost Luggage* study, where 112 passengers have been interviewed after having reported their luggage lost to the baggage retrieval service of the airline [Sche 97]. The arising emotions are anger, resignation, worry, and good humor. Another example is the *Belfast Naturalistic Database* consisting of video clips (10-60 seconds long) taken from television chat shows, current affairs programs, and interviews conducted by the research team [Doug 03, Doug 00].

By nature, the ecological validity of naturally occurring emotions is high. Unfortunately, copyright and other legal issues often prohibit the publication of the material and preclude the use for scientific research. Furthermore, the recordings often suffer from bad audio quality, are generally very brief, and cover only a small number of speakers. In addition, the determination of the precise nature of the underlying emotion is a serious problem [Sche 03a]. In many situations, even self-assessments of the participants cannot be considered since the subjects have not been recorded primarily for the purpose of emotion elicitation. Another difficulty is known as the *Observer's Paradox* attributed to Labov: Investigators observing or interviewing people to find out about their habits of speech will, by their own presence and participation, tend to influence the forms of speech that are used. Consequently, recordings ought to be observer-free and hence, cannot be designed in the traditional scientific sense [Camp 03]. Moreover, the emerging lack of control will result in unbalanced data. And even more problematically, the unobtrusive recording of people is ethically highly questionable if not illegal.

Apart from the aspired naturalness of the data, Douglas-Cowie et al. mention further issues that should be considered in developing a new generation of databases of emotional speech. The main issues are the scope of the data, the context of the content, and the descriptors to describe the emotional content [Doug 03].

Amongst others, the 'scope' covers the number and the gender of the speakers, the language and type of dialect spoken, and the social/functional setting. All these aspects are likely to influence the signs by which a given emotion may be expressed. For the purpose of recognizing emotion, databases are necessary that encompass as many of these signs as possible. Another aspect of scope is the range of emotions under consideration. Speech in daily life tends to express moderate emotional states and emotion-related states rather than full-blown basic emotions [Cowi 03]. The scope of the database may have to be very large – standard lists for (non-basic) emotions contain more than a hundred words – but at the same time, data collection must be kept manageable. Studies prove that listeners determine the emotional significance of vocal features differently if listening to utterances in the context of a dialog compared to isolated utterances [Caul 00]. Thus, databases for emotional speech need to incorporate the context of the expression of emotion. Douglas-Cowie et al. distinguish four different types of context: semantic context, structural context, intermodal context, and temporal context. The following Chapter 3, *Labeling of User States*, is dedicated to descriptors needed to describe the emotional content.

The one and only emotion database satisfying all needs of researchers from the different areas of emotion research does not exist (and will not exist in the near and middle term). The requirements of the participating research disciplines are too different. Because of the need for a database of naturally occurring emotions suitable for machine classification, we have recorded our own emotional speech database, the FAU Aibo Emotion Corpus, in a Wizard-of-Oz experiment with children playing with the Sony robot Aibo. The corpus is described in detail in Chapter 5.

**Summary**   *Emotions* are relatively brief episodes of synchronized response of several organismic subsystems in response to the evaluation of external or internal events being of major significance to the organism. The observable states of the users in a human-machine interaction, e. g. *helpless*, are rather *emotion-related* than emotions proper and are called *emotion-related user states* henceforth. Emotion theories define what emotions are, how many emotions exist and how they can be differentiated. Modern emotion theories are highly influenced by historical theories of Darwin, James, and others. Related work in the area of computer science has been strongly influenced by *basic emotion models* suggesting the existence of only a few fundamental emotions. Consequently, research has been mainly focusing on the investigation of a small number of full-blown emotions portrayed by actors. *Dimensional models* describe emotions in terms of only a few dimensions. The most widely used dimensions are *valence* and *arousal*. Speech is one important modality in which emotions are expressed. Psychologists have identified various speech parameters (e. g. prosodic parameters such as speech rate, fluency, $F_0$, and intensity parameters, voice quality parameters) changing with the emotional state of the speaker. Scherer's modified version of the Brunswikian lens model of perception defines various research issues in the area of vocal expression of emotion. Many aspects of this work like the evaluation of both human and machine decoders (decoding studies) and the choice of adequate features (encoding studies) fit nicely into this framework. The chapter ends with the presentation of three types to elicit emotions: simulated, induced, and natural vocal expressions. From an application-oriented point of view, natural vocal expressions of those states that actually occur in a human-machine communication are preferable. However, certain disadvantages (unknown precise nature of the underlying emotion, sparse data problem, Observer's Paradox, etc.) exist. Eventually, the need for a new speech database of naturally occurring emotion-related states, which is appropriate for machine learning, is pointed out.

# Chapter 3

# Labeling of User States

The primary objective of this thesis is the automatic classification of emotion-related user states in speech. Chapter 4.1 will explain the main principles of statistical machine classification. It will be shown that machine classification requires a labeled sample set $\omega$ of representative patterns for each of the classes that are to be distinguished. The information which class a pattern belongs to (called the *label*) is necessary in the training phase of the classifier to learn the class areas. Furthermore, the class affiliation is required to evaluate the performance of the classifier on a test set (see Chapter 4.2).

For many typical classification problems in pattern recognition, the class affiliation is given and is assumed to be correct. If acted data is used, this also holds for emotion recognition from speech since the emotion is known which the actress/actor is asked to portray. It is assumed that the actresses/actors are able to portray the emotional state convincingly. Additionally, this can be assured by human perception tests and the subsequent elimination of samples which are recognized poorly by humans.

In all other ways of eliciting emotions (see Chapter 2.4), the emotion is not known and has to be described by humans, either by the person who experienced the emotion (self report), or by a reasonably representative group of human labelers who describe the emotion they perceive while listening to or looking at the emotional data. Thereby, the observer's impression of the subject's state is described, not necessarily the emotional state itself that led the speaker to produce that kind of speech. According to [Cowi 01], this type of research is called *effect-oriented* in contrast to *cause-oriented* research. In general, lay judges are employed for this purpose in order to reflect the perception of an average human being.

Unfortunately, no generally accepted methodology for describing emotions exists [Cowi 03]. Instead, labeling of emotion itself is part of the research on emotion and is strongly influenced by the underlying emotion theory. The emotional or emotion-related state of the speaker – or the user in a human-machine conversation – can be described using category labels or dimensional labels. In general, dimensional labels have a continuous range of values, which can be predicted automatically by regression techniques. Using category labels, a small set of discrete categories is defined and each pattern is assigned one of these category labels. The patterns can be classified automatically using classification techniques. The term *labeling* is used if human judges annotate the emotional or emotion-related state. In the context of pattern recognition, the discrete categories/category labels are denoted as *classes*. The process of classifying the emotional/emotion-related state automatically is called *classification*. Henceforth, the terms *category labels*, *categories*, and *classes* are used as synonyms.

## 3.1   Category Labels

Category labels drawn from everyday language are the most familiar way of describing emotions. Indeed, this approach is so familiar that it is easily assumed that it is self-evidently the correct way [Cowi 03]. Nevertheless, research on these categories reveals a lot of difficulties.

The size of an emotion lexicon is remarkable. For English, the *Semantic Atlas of Emotional Concepts* lists as many as 558 words "with emotional connotation" [Aver 75]. In studies which focus only on terms describing emotion proper, the amount of emotion words is significantly lower and varies from about 100 (107 in [Whis 89], 135 in [Stor 87], 142 in [Plut 80]) to more than 200 (196 in [Fehr 84], 213 in [Shav 87]). Ortony et al. lists about 250 emotion terms in a broad sense of emotion and about half as many in a narrower sense [Orto 88]. Studies for other languages yield comparable sizes of the emotion lexicon: 235 emotion terms for German in [Sche 84a] and 153 words for Italian in [Zamm 98].

Cowie and Cornelius state that "languages do not generally multiply terms unless they are needed" [Cowi 03]. In order to attain a sufficiently high precision of the descriptive system, i. e. that descriptors of genuinely different states are different as well, at least 60 categories are needed to describe emotions that occur with a reasonable frequency in everyday life according to Cowie and Cornelius. Although this is a low estimate and not every shade of emotion that humans can distinguish is covered, it directly raises the problem of tractability. Statistically reliable conclusions can only be reached with a far smaller number of categories or an enormous amount of data but corpora of such size are not available. If automatic classification systems (see Chapter 4.1) are to be trained, even more data is needed. As it is shown in the examples below, the problem is aggravated by the unbalanced distribution of the emotional states in data of naturally occurring emotions.

The overview in Table 3.1 [Cowi 03] opposes the lists of key emotions of Lazarus, Ekman, Buck, Lewis/Haviland, Banse/Scherer and Cowie et al. The number of key emotions varies between 12 and 21 which is a tractable number of emotions.

Application-oriented corpora of emotional speech show that only a part of the emotions that could be expected on the basis of the key word lists in Table 3.1 actually occur in a specific scenario. On the contrary, other user states that are not mentioned in these lists like *helpless*, *tired*, or *emphatic* can be observed. Some emotional states occur but not frequently enough to train a classification system (known as the *sparse data problem*) what necessitates the mapping of rare emotional states onto broader cover classes.

In the following, our experience with category labeling of emotional data from two application-oriented corpora, the one of the SmartKom project [Wahl 06] and the SympaFly corpus [Batl 04b], are described. Both corpora contain emotional speech data of users in a human-machine conversation with an automatic dialog system. Part

| Lazarus [Laza 99] | Ekman [Ekma 99] | Buck [Buck 99a] | Lewis/Haviland [Lewi 93] | Banse/Scherer [Bans 96] | Cowie et al. [Cowi 99] |
|---|---|---|---|---|---|
| anger | anger | anger | anger/hostility | rage/hot anger irritation/ cold anger | angry |
| fright | fear | fear | fear | fear/terror | afraid |
| sadness | sadness/ distress | sadness | sadness | sadness/ dejection grief/ desperation | sad |
| anxiety | | anxiety | anxiety | worry/anxiety | worried |
| happiness | sensory pleasure | happiness | happiness | happiness | happy |
| | | | | elation (joy) | |
| | amusement | | humor | | amused |
| | satisfaction | | | | pleased |
| | contentment | | | | content |
| | | interested | | | interested |
| | | curious | | | |
| | | surprised | | | |
| | excitement | | | | excited |
| | | bored | | boredom/in- difference | bored |
| | | | | | relaxed |
| | | burnt out | | | |
| disgust | disgust | disgust | disgust | disgust | |
| | contempt | scorn | | contempt/scorn | |
| pride | pride | pride | pride | | |
| | | arrogance | | | |
| jealousy | | jealousy | | | |
| envy | | envy | | | |
| shame | shame | shame | shame | shame/guilt | |
| guilt | guilt | guilt | guilt | | |
| | embarrass- ment | | embarrassment | | |
| | | | | | disappointed |
| relief | relief | | | | |
| hope | | | | | |
| | | | | | confident |
| gratitude | | | | | |
| love | | | love | | loving |
| | | | | | affectionate |
| compassion | | pity | | | |
| | | moral rap- ture | | | |
| | | moral indig- nation | | | |
| esthetic | | | | | |

Table 3.1: Recent list of key emotions after [Cowi 03]

of the German SmartKom system is a 'next generation' multi-modal communication telephone booth, called SmartKom-Public. The user can communicate with a virtual agent who is, together with other information, being displayed on a graphical inter-

| emotion-related | number of words | |
| user state | absolute | relative |
|---|---|---|
| joyful (weak) | 580 | 3.4 % |
| joyful (strong) | 93 | 0.5 % |
| surprised | 31 | 0.2 % |
| neutral | 15,390 | 88.9 % |
| helpless | 654 | 3.8 % |
| angry (weak) | 418 | 2.4 % |
| angry (strong) | 138 | 0.8 % |

Table 3.2: SmartKom: emotional user states and their frequencies in the SmartKom corpus [Batl 03c]

| joyful (weak) | joyful (strong) | surprised | neutral | helpless | angry (weak) | angry (strong) |
|---|---|---|---|---|---|---|
| joyful | | surprised | neutral | helpless | angry | |
| joyful | | | neutral | helpless | angry | |
| joyful | | | neutral | problem | | |
| no problem | | | | helpless | angry | |
| no problem | | | | problem | | |
| not angry | | | | | angry | |

Table 3.3: SmartKom: different mappings of emotional user states onto cover classes [Batl 03c]

face. In a human-machine dialog, the user can get information associated with hotels, restaurants, cinemas, etc. Examples are information about existing cinemas close-by, films currently being shown, or ticket reservation. In this context, non-prompted, spontaneous speech data and video recordings of the subject's face and body have been collected in a large-scaled Wizard-of-Oz scenario where subjects were using the (pretended) SmartKom system. The emotion-related user states *joy/gratification*, *anger/irritation, helplessness, surprised*, and *neutral* are labeled holistically, i. e. the labeler can look at the person's facial expression, the body gestures, and listen to the speech recordings. Additionally, it is marked whether the emotional state is perceived as weak or strong. Table 3.2 is a compilation of the user states and the frequencies of their occurrence in terms of the number of words contained in the turns labeled with the respective user state [Batl 03c]. The frequency of the user state *neutral* (15,390 words, 88.9 %) outweighs the other user states (1,914 words, 11.1 %) by far illustrating the sparse data problem in application scenarios. Furthermore, the emotional user states *angry* and *joyful* are perceived in most cases only as weak emotions.

For statistical classification, emotion-related user states have to be subsumed under broader cover classes. Table 3.3 shows the different mappings onto cover classes being investigated in classification experiments in [Batl 03c]. If data is not to be discarded (as it cannot be done in a real application), rare user states have to be mapped onto a special reject class or onto cover classes which may then contain dissimilar user states. From a theoretical point of view, this will not always make sense. Unfortunately, it is often inevitable from a practical point of view. In the SmartKom scenario, the state *surprised* stands for *positive surprise*. Hence, *joyful* and *surprised* are mapped onto the same cover class in the given example. As the

| user state | cover class | number of words | |
| --- | --- | --- | --- |
| | | absolute | relative |
| joy | | 58 | 0.3 % |
| neutral | neutral | 15,390 | 72.9 % |
| ironic | | 395 | 1.9 % |
| emphatic | emphatic | 3,708 | 17.6 % |
| surprised | | 31 | 0.1 % |
| helpless | helpless | 654 | 3.1 % |
| panic | | 43 | 0.2 % |
| touchy | marked | 806 | 3.8 % |
| angry | | 40 | 0.2 % |

Table 3.4: SympaFly: emotional user states and their frequencies [Batl 04b]

| user state | number of labels | |
| --- | --- | --- |
| | absolute | relative |
| neutral | 41,545 | 83.8 % |
| annoyed | 3,777 | 7.6 % |
| frustrated | 358 | 0.7 % |
| tired | 328 | 0.7 % |
| amused | 326 | 0.7 % |
| other | 115 | 0.2 % |
| not-applicable | 3,104 | 6.2 % |

Table 3.5: DARPA Communicator project: emotional user states and the frequencies of the annotated raw labels [Ang 02]

names of the cover classes may be misleading, it is highly important to make clear that a cover class subsumes different states and to denominate these states in order to avoid inconsistent results across different studies.

Another application is the automatic dialog system *SympaFly*, a telephone system for the reservation and booking of flights. Speech data has been collected in three evaluation stages in the development phase of the system. The naturally occurring emotion-related states of the callers testing the system are labeled with the categories *joy, ironic, emphatic, surprised, helpless, panic, touchy, angry* and *neutral* [Batl 04b]. The frequencies of the user states in terms of words which are contained in the turns labeled with the respective user state are given in Table 3.4. Again, *neutral* is the most frequent state (72.9 %) whereas some states, namely *angry, panic, surprised,* and *joy* are quite rare and have to be mapped onto cover classes. The user state *emphatic* needs some explanation: This state is labeled if the user speaks pronounced, accentuated, or hyper-articulated but without showing any emotion. It is labeled since any marked deviation from a neutral speaking style can – but need not – be a possible indication of some (starting) trouble in communication [Batl 03a].

In a very similar scenario developed in the DARPA Communicator project, test users were also calling an automatic dialog system to make air travel arrangements [Walk 01]. Besides *neutral*, the emotional user states *annoyed, frustrated, tired, amused,*

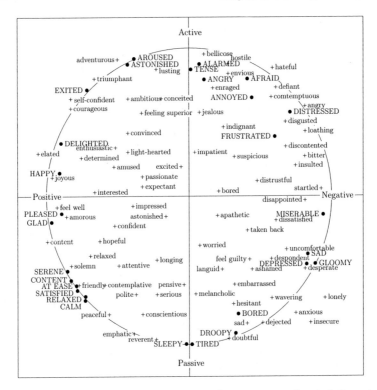

Figure 3.1: A two-dimensional representation of emotion terms (vertical dimension: active/passive; horizontal dimension: positive/negative) after [Sche 01a]

*other*, and *not-applicable* are labeled. 49,553 emotion classifications were made on 21,889 utterances (on average, each utterance has been labeled by 2.26 labelers). The distribution of these 'raw' labels are given in Table 3.5. In this study, most labels are *neutral* (83.8 %), too.

## 3.2   Dimensional Labeling

An alternative to category labeling is the use of dimensional labels. The 'dimensional model' emotion theory, described in Chapter 2.2.2, states that emotions can be distinguished by means of certain characteristics. Unidimensional models assume that only one such dimension is sufficient to distinguish emotions whereas multidimensional models argue that more – generally two or three – dimensions are necessary to capture the main differences. Based on these dimensional models, emotions can be labeled by specifying a value for each dimension.

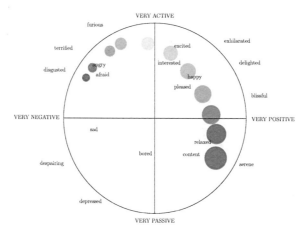

Figure 3.2: FeelTrace: dimensional labeling in the activation-evaluation space after [Cowi 00]

As supporters of both category and dimensional labeling claim that their technique is suited to describe emotions, a mapping of categories onto dimensions and vice versa should be possible. In most studies concerning this aspect, a two-dimensional space spanned by the dimensions 'evaluation' (positive/negative or pleasant/unpleasant) and 'activation' (high/low or active/passive) is used. "Researchers have been [...] able to locate particular emotion labels (or facial expressions) in clearly identified regions of the two-dimensional space, independently of the language or culture in which these studies have been conducted" [Sche 01a]. Figure 3.1 shows an arrangement by Scherer of 80 emotion terms (in lower case) [Sche 84a, Sche 01a]. The plot is the result of a multidimensional scaling (s. Chapter 4.3.2) based on the similarity matrix obtained by human lay judges assessing the similarity of the given emotion terms. The exact position of the terms depends on the number and the choice of emotion terms. In the circumplex model postulated by Russel [Russ 80], the positions of 28 major emotions form a circumplex illustrated in Figure 3.1 by the circle and the emotion terms in capital letters. Nevertheless, if more emotion terms are arranged, the whole two-dimensional space is filled and the positions of some terms change.

A tool for labeling the perceived emotional state on the basis of the common two dimensions 'activation' and 'evaluation' is *FeelTrace*, developed by Cowie et al. at Queen's University Belfast [Cowi 00]. It is suited to label both audio and video data. States at the limit of emotional intensity define a circle with alert neutrality at the center of this circle. By that, they are equidistant from an emotionally neutral point. The labeler moves a pointer in form of a colored disc within this circle to the appropriate point in the two-dimensional space. Mouse movements are made visible by displaying the disc at recent mouse positions on the screen and having the discs shrink gradually over time. Figure 3.2 shows the instrument and a mouse movement starting at *afraid*, moving to *interested*, *happy*, *relaxed*, and finally to the emotional state *content*.

To ensure that labelers are fully aware of the meaning of the selected cursor position at any given instant, two main devices are used: the color coding of the pointer and the placement of verbal landmarks at strategic points in the space. The color coding of the pointer used in FeelTrace is derived from Plutchik. It is reasonably intuitive so that it can be readily associated with the relevant emotional state. Pure red signifies the most negative evaluation possible and neutrality with respect to activation. On the opposite side pure green signifies the most positive evaluation possible and neutrality with respect to activation. In the perpendicular direction pure yellow signifies the most active state and neutrality with respect to evaluation and pure blue the least active state possible and also neutrality with respect to evaluation. The color at intermediate states is set by a straightforward additive rule. *Neutrality* at the the center of the circular space is white.

As a supplement of the color coding, nine key emotion words are placed at the periphery of the circle. They identify the strong, archetypical emotions associated with broad sectors of the circle and are provided by representations by Plutchik [Plut 94] and Russel [Russ 97]. The emotion words within the circle represent less extreme emotional states. The words and their positions within the circular space are taken from the *Basic English Emotion Vocabulary* study [Cowi 99]. Ten of the twelve items most often included in a subject's basic emotion vocabulary are displayed.

The resolving power of FeelTrace is comparable to an emotion vocabulary of 20 non-overlapping words, but allows intermediate ratings.

The *Geneva Emotion Wheel* [Banz 05, Sche 05] is another labeling tool. It combines dimensional and category labeling. In contrast to FeelTrace, the underlying dimensions are perceived control (high/low control) and valence (negative/positive, unpleasant/pleasant). Several prototypes exists which differ slightly in the number of emotion families and their order in the emotion wheel. The following description refers to a version of 16 emotion families. They are arranged as sectors in a circle according to their postulated position in the two-dimensional space as illustrated in Figure 3.3. Each emotion family consists of four members of varying intensity which are depicted as colored circles within the respective sector and all of them have the same color hue. Both the size and the color saturation of the member circles increase with the intensity of the attributed emotion adjective. The members are arranged that way that the intensity of the emotion increases with the distance from the center. The names of the emotion families as well as the adjectives attributed to the respective members are given in Table 3.6. If the tool is used in its electronic version, the names of the emotion adjectives appear when the mouse cursor moves over the colored circles. They are not given in the paper-and-pencil version of the tool.

Various experiments to validate the instrument [Banz 05] have shown that the structure of the emotion wheel seems to match to a large extent the spatial organization of the 16 emotion families in terms of similarity ratings (emotion families rated similar are adjacent in the emotion wheel) and in terms of direct ratings of the underlying dimensions 'valence' and 'control'. Furthermore, most participants of the study classified a large majority of the attributed adjectives into the predicted categories. However, the average intensity rank order of the adjectives within one emotion family obtained in the study did not match the predicted order in most cases. Because of this mismatch, the labeling of intermediate intensities with different labels has been

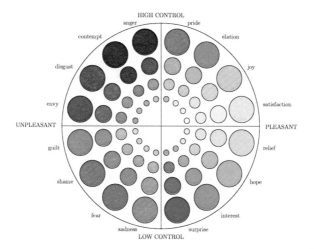

Figure 3.3: Geneva Emotion Wheel after [Banz 05]

| emotion family | adjectives with emotional intensity varying from | | | |
|---|---|---|---|---|
| | low | ⟵⟶ | | high |
| **pride** | gratified | self-satisfied | proud | flushed with pride |
| **elation** | in high spirits | elated | exhilarated | exalted |
| **joy** | cheerful | happy | joyful | overjoyed |
| **satisfaction** | pleased | satisfied | content | delighted |
| **relief** | feeling unburdened | relieved | feeling at ease | feeling comfortable |
| **hope** | expectant | hopeful | optimistic | confident |
| **interest** | attentive | interested | fascinated | enthralled |
| **surprise** | puzzled | astonished | surprised | stupefied |
| **sadness** | in low spirits | sad | dejected | despaired |
| **fear** | nervous | apprehensive | fearful | panicked |
| **shame** | embarrassed | feeling disgrace | shameful | feeling disreputable |
| **guilt** | feeling at fault | feeling blameworthy | deserving reproach | feeling guilty |
| **envy** | feeling distrust | grudging | envious | jealous |
| **disgust** | feeling dislike | feeling distaste | feeling disgust | revolted |
| **contempt** | disdainful | scornful | contemptuous | feeling repulsion |
| **anger** | aggravated | irritated | angry | full of rage |

Table 3.6: Geneva Emotion Wheel: adjectives attributed to the four colored circles of each emotion family with intensity varying from low (small circles) to high (big circles) after [Tran 04]

abandoned. Only the rating of the intensity for each emotion family in four discrete steps remains.

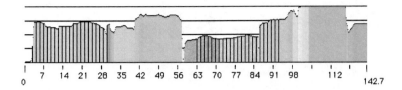

Figure 3.4: FeelTrace: emotional intensity (axis of ordinates) and coordinates in the activation/valence space (color coding) over time [Cowi 00]

## 3.3   Time Dependent Labels

In the previous two sections the labelers are given pieces of (speech) data of variable length to which they have to assign the appropriate emotional state using category or dimensional labels. It is assumed that the subject's emotion or emotional state is nearly constant for the whole data segment under consideration. This assumption makes sense for acted data where the actor/actress produces pre-defined utterances in a given emotion. The segment boundaries directly result from these specifications. However, in most cases where recordings of induced or naturally occurring emotions are used, these boundaries are not known. The observed emotional state of the subject is rarely constant but shifts over time. These changes can either be sharp or gradual. Frequently, the latter prevail and the determination of the segment boundaries is not clear-cut in these cases. Therefore, looking for segments of constant emotion is rather difficult. Furthermore, the tasks of defining the segments and labeling the emotional content fuse what complicates the labeling process if the data is labeled by more than one labeler as all labelers should work on the same segments. One solution to this problem is to choose segments which are small enough so that constant emotion can be assumed. Thereby, consecutive segments of the same emotion can occur. Often, speech data is segmented into single utterances, but the emotional state that can be observed (not necessarily the underlying emotional state) can even change within one utterance. Regarding the FAU Aibo Emotion Corpus described in Chapter 5, the data is even broken down to the word level for the purpose of labeling.

Another way is to give the labeler the opportunity to change the emotion label while listening to the speech data or watching the video data. The labeling process happens in real-time. The segmentation of the data is superfluous. FeelTrace, described in the last section, records the position of the mouse pointer in the two-dimensional space over time. The recorded information contains both the observed emotional state and the perceived emotional intensity. A point in the two-dimensional space spanned by the dimensions 'activation' and 'evaluation' is given in polar co-ordinates by its angle and its radius. The emotional state corresponds to the angle and the intensity to the radius. The results over time of one labeler are shown in Figure 3.4. The intensity (the radius) is shown on the ordinate whereas the emotional state (the angle) is depicted by the color coding as indicated in Figure 3.2.

Labeling at the same time both the emotional state and the emotional intensity in a two-dimensional space in real-time is a rather complex task which can also be

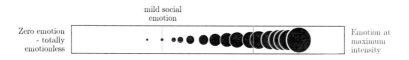

Figure 3.5: ETraceScale: real time labeling of emotional intensity over time (labeling increasing emotional intensity by moving the mouse from left to right)

Figure 3.6: ETraceCat: variant of ETraceScale where the intensity range is divided into three categories

broken down into several smaller tasks like labeling the emotional intensity only or labeling both the degree of activation and the degree of valence separately. Figure 3.5 shows *ETraceScale*, a tool developed by Cowie et al. at Queen's University Belfast. By moving the mouse, the degree of emotional intensity can be specified. Additionally to the position of the mouse, the intensity value is coded with colors ranging from blue (zero intensity) to red (maximum intensity). Mouse movements like the one from left to right in Figure 3.5 are depicted by circles of diminishing size. Additionally, certain positions in the intensity range can be marked like the 'mild social emotion' position at one third of the maximum intensity in Figure 3.5 to give the labeler a feeling for different intensities. Figure 3.6 shows *ETraceCat*, an alternative version of ETraceScale, where the intensity range is divided into the three categories 'completely emotionless', 'partial emotion', and 'emotion in the full sense'. By changing the meaning of low and high values, the program can easily be adjusted to be used for other purposes.

# 3.4 Soft Decisions for Category Labels

Often, the observable emotional state is ambiguous. Our tool *eLabel* gives the labeler the possibility to decide for more than one category in the case that he/she cannot decide for a single class. The tool has been developed with the purpose of labeling the FAU Aibo Emotion Corpus on the word level. Figure 3.7 shows the situation where the labeler is asked to decide between the four cover classes **Motherese, Emphatic, Anger**, and **Neutral**. These cover classes are to be distinguished in the classification experiments described in Chapter 7. Details on the categories and the mapping onto cover classes are given in Chapter 5.3.7. The labeler is not sure whether the subject's voice sounds still **Neutral** or if the observed emotion-related state belongs already to the state **Motherese**. By setting the bar for **Motherese** to 60 % and the one for **Neutral** to 40 %, the labeler expresses that he/she would decide for **Motherese** if asked for a hard decision but that he/she is quite uncertain about this decision. It

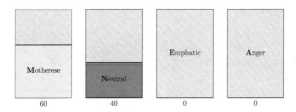

Figure 3.7: eLabel: soft decisions for category labels

could also be **Neutral** albeit the labeler considers **Neutral** to be less probable than **Motherese**.

The percentages for all category labels always sum up to 100 %. If the labeler changes one bar, eLabel changes the other three bars automatically keeping the ratios among the other three states constant. The percentages can be regarded as confidence information of the labeler. In the case of the FAU Aibo Emotion Corpus, these soft labels are not intended to be used to label the components of emotion blends where the percentage of each emotion specifies the proportion of the respective emotion contained in the total blend. They are also not applicable to label the intensity of the respective emotional state. 60 % **Motherese** does not mean that the labeler perceived a slight form of **Motherese** (and that he/she is maybe sure about this decision). Quite the contrary, it means that the labeler is not sure about his/her decision for **Motherese** and no statement about the emotional intensity is made at all. Nevertheless, if the labeler cannot decide for one single emotional state, the emotion under consideration is likely to be weak. In case of labeling emotional intensities, the percentages would not need to sum up to 100 %.

## 3.5   Measures of Inter-Labeler Agreement

Since emotions are perceived differently by individuals, the data is labeled by a reasonably representative group of labelers and the final label generally results from the majority vote of all participating labelers. The inter-labeler agreement (often also called inter-rater agreement) gives information about the agreement between the labelers and by that also about the appropriateness of the labels used and the difficulty of the labeling task. The latter affects the evaluation of the performance of an automatic classification system. In the following, only measures of inter-labeler agreement for nominal data are presented since the experiments of this thesis are based on category labels only. A description of agreement measures for ordinal or cardinal data can be found, for example, in [Hade 07]. For nominal data, a data set of $N$ samples is labeled by a group of $L$ labelers, $L \geq 2$. For each sample, each labeler decides for one of $K$ categories/classes. Let $\eta_\kappa^{(l)}$ be the number of cases where labeler $l$ decides for category $\kappa$ and $\eta_{\kappa_1,\kappa_2}^{(l_1,l_2)}$ be the number of cases where the two labelers $l_1$ and $l_2$ decide for category $\kappa_1$ and $\kappa_2$, respectively. Furthermore, let $p_\kappa^{(l)}$ be the probability that labeler $l$ chooses class $\kappa$ and $p_{\kappa_1,\kappa_2}^{(l_1,l_2)}$ the probability that the two labelers $l_1$ and $l_2$ choose class $\kappa_1$ and $\kappa_2$, respectively.

## 3.5.1 Cohen's Kappa

Cohen's kappa was originally designed to evaluate the agreement of only two labelers for nominal labels [Cohe 60]. The observed agreement of the labelers $p_o$ is compared to the "by chance"-agreement $p_c$ that is expected if statistical independence of the decisions of both labelers is assumed.

$$\text{Cohen's } \kappa := \frac{p_o - p_c}{1 - p_c} \tag{3.1}$$

The difference $p_o - p_c$ represents the proportion of cases in which "beyond-chance agreement" occurs. It is normalized by the probability of disagreement $1 - p_c$ which is expected by chance. The probability $p_o$ is estimated by the proportion of cases where both labelers agree on a common category:

$$\hat{p}_o = \sum_{\kappa=1}^{K} \hat{p}_{\kappa,\kappa}^{(1,2)} = \sum_{\kappa=1}^{K} \frac{\eta_{\kappa,\kappa}^{(1,2)}}{N} \ . \tag{3.2}$$

Assuming statistical independence, the probability $p_c(\kappa)$ that two labelers agree by chance on class $\kappa$ is the product of the a priori probabilities $p_\kappa^{(1)}$ and $p_\kappa^{(2)}$ of the two labelers. Then, the probability $p_c$ is the sum over all classes $\kappa$ of the probability $p_c(\kappa)$. The corresponding estimates are given by the following equation:

$$\hat{p}_c = \sum_{\kappa=1}^{K} \hat{p}_c(\kappa) = \sum_{\kappa=1}^{K} \hat{p}_\kappa^{(1)} \cdot \hat{p}_\kappa^{(2)} = \sum_{\kappa=1}^{K} \frac{\eta_\kappa^{(1)}}{N} \cdot \frac{\eta_\kappa^{(2)}}{N} \ . \tag{3.3}$$

If the agreement equals chance agreement, Cohen's $\kappa$ is equal to zero. Positive values indicate better than chance agreement. The maximum of one is reached if (and only if) both labelers agree perfectly. As a rough guideline, kappa values between 0.4 and 0.75 can be considered to express a moderate agreement whereas values above 0.75 express a good agreement. In the context of emotion recognition, the emotion label reflects the emotional state the rater perceives and is inherently highly subjective. Hence, a lower threshold for 'good agreement' seems to be appropriate.

## 3.5.2 Weighted Kappa

In many cases, confusions differ in the degree of severity. Obviously, a confusion of slight anger with the neutral state is less severe than a confusion of full-blown anger with joy. The *weighted kappa* is an extension of Cohen's kappa and allows for the specification of a weight function $w(\kappa_1, \kappa_2)$ which assigns weights to a confusion of category $\kappa_1$ with category $\kappa_2$ [Cohe 68, Flei 69]. The weights are restricted to the following conditions: (1) a perfect agreement has the maximal weight $w(\kappa, \kappa) = 1$, (2) disagreements are given positive weights less than the maximal weight: $0 \leq w(\kappa_1, \kappa_2) < 1$ for $\kappa_1 \neq \kappa_2$, and (3) two labelers are considered symmetrically: $w(\kappa_1, \kappa_2) = w(\kappa_2, \kappa_1)$. The probability estimates $\hat{p}_o$ and $\hat{p}_c$ are substituted by their weighted equivalents:

$$\hat{p}_{o,\text{weighted}}(w) = \sum_{\kappa_1=1}^{K} \sum_{\kappa_2=1}^{K} \hat{p}_{\kappa_1 \kappa_2}^{(1,2)} \cdot w(\kappa_1, \kappa_2) \quad \text{and} \tag{3.4}$$

$$\hat{p}_{c,\text{weighted}}(w) = \sum_{\kappa_1=1}^{K} \sum_{\kappa_2=1}^{K} \hat{p}_{\kappa_1}^{(1)} \hat{p}_{\kappa_2}^{(2)} \cdot w(\kappa_1, \kappa_2) \ . \tag{3.5}$$

Referring to Equation 3.1, the weighted kappa for two labelers is defined as

$$\text{Weighted } \kappa(w) := \frac{\hat{p}_{\text{o,weighted}}(w) - \hat{p}_{\text{c,weighted}}(w)}{1 - \hat{p}_{\text{c,weighted}}(w)} . \tag{3.6}$$

It is identical to Cohen's kappa if the weights for disagreement are equal to zero: $w(\kappa_1, \kappa_2) = 0$ for $\kappa_1 \neq \kappa_2$. If the numerals $1, 2, \ldots, K$ are assigned to the $K$ categories and the differences between the category numbers can be interpreted meaningfully as confusion weights, the following weight function $w_1$, as proposed in [Cohe 68] and [Cicc 72], can be applied:

$$w_1(x, y) = 1 - \left| \frac{x - y}{K - 1} \right| . \tag{3.7}$$

Another weight function is, for example,

$$w_2(x, y) = 1 - \left( \frac{x - y}{K - 1} \right)^2 . \tag{3.8}$$

### 3.5.3   Extension to Several Labelers

In 1982, Davies and Fleiss proposed an extension of Cohen's kappa to evaluate the agreement of several labelers [Davi 82]. In contrast to Fleiss' former work from 1971 [Flei 71], it is assumed that all $N$ samples are labeled by the same $L$ labelers and that the information which labeler decided for which class is known for each sample. Let $\eta_\kappa(n)$ be the number of labelers who labeled sample $n$ as belonging to category $\kappa$. In order to determine $\hat{p}_\text{o}$ for the whole data set, the value $\hat{p}_\text{o}(n)$ is determined for each sample $n$ first. $\hat{p}_\text{o}(n)$ is the proportion of pairs of decisions of two labelers for sample $n$ where both labelers agree. If $\eta_\kappa(n)$ labelers agree on class $\kappa$ for sample $n$, the number of pairs where two labelers agree on this class is $\binom{\eta_\kappa(n)}{2}$. The sum of this term over all $K$ classes yields the number of pairs where two labelers agree on a common class. The proportion $\hat{p}_\text{o}(n)$ results from dividing this sum by the maximum number of possible pairs which is $\binom{L}{2}$ for $L$ labelers.

$$\hat{p}_\text{o}(n) = \frac{\sum_{\kappa=1}^{K} \binom{\eta_\kappa(n)}{2}}{\binom{L}{2}} = \frac{\sum_{\kappa=1}^{K} \eta_\kappa(n)\big(\eta_\kappa(n) - 1\big)}{L(L-1)} \tag{3.9}$$

Finally, $\hat{p}_\text{o}$ is the average of $\hat{p}_\text{o}(n)$ over all $N$ samples:

$$\hat{p}_\text{o} = \frac{1}{N} \cdot \sum_{n=1}^{N} \hat{p}_\text{o}(n) \tag{3.10}$$

$$= \frac{1}{N\,L\,(L-1)} \cdot \sum_{n=1}^{N} \sum_{\kappa=1}^{K} \eta_\kappa(n)\big(\eta_\kappa(n) - 1\big) \tag{3.11}$$

$$= \frac{1}{L\,(L-1)} \cdot \sum_{l_1=1}^{L} \sum_{\substack{l_2=1 \\ l_2 \neq l_1}}^{L} \sum_{\kappa=1}^{K} \hat{p}_{\kappa,\kappa}^{(l_1, l_2)} . \tag{3.12}$$

The estimate of the probability that any two labelers agree by chance is the estimated probability $\hat{p}_c^{(l_1,l_2)}$ that two labelers $l_1$ and $l_2$ agree by chance averaged over all possible combinations of pairs of labelers.

$$\hat{p}_c = \frac{1}{L(L-1)} \cdot \sum_{l_1=1}^{L} \sum_{\substack{l_2=1 \\ l_2 \neq l_1}}^{L} \hat{p}_c^{(l_1,l_2)} \qquad (3.13)$$

The estimated probabilities $\hat{p}_c^{(l_1,l_2)}$ are the sum over all $K$ categories of the probability $\hat{p}_{\kappa,\kappa}^{(l_1,l_2)}$ that labelers $l_1$ and $l_2$ agree both by chance on class $\kappa$. Again, statistical independence between the decisions of the two labelers is assumed. Hence, $\hat{p}_{\kappa,\kappa}^{(l_1,l_2)}$ can be expressed as the product of the a priori probability estimates $\hat{p}_\kappa^{(l_1)}$ and $\hat{p}_\kappa^{(l_2)}$ that the respective labeler decides for class $\kappa$.

$$\hat{p}_c^{(l_1,l_2)} = \sum_{\kappa=1}^{K} \hat{p}_{\kappa,\kappa}^{(l_1,l_2)} = \sum_{\kappa=1}^{K} \hat{p}_\kappa^{(l_1)} \cdot \hat{p}_\kappa^{(l_2)} \qquad (3.14)$$

Equation 3.12 and 3.14 can easily be extended to a weighted version of kappa for several labelers like the way it is done in Equation 3.4 and 3.5.

A further extension of the weighted multi-labeler kappa is Krippendorff's alpha which can handle missing data [Krip 04, Krip 07]. Like Fleiss' approach from 1971 [Flei 71], it abandons the speaker dependent a priori probabilities $\hat{p}_\kappa^{(l)}$. Instead, speaker independent a priori probabilities $p_\kappa$ are used which are estimated over the ratings of all labelers. Krippendorff proposes different weight functions for nominal, ordinal, interval, and ratio data. The one for interval data is comparable to Equation 3.8 and yields reliability values of the same size. As the problem of missing data does not occur in the experiments of this thesis, no further description of Krippendorff's alpha is given.

**Summary** In contrast to emotion portrayals, the subject's emotional state is not given if naturally occurring emotions or emotion-related states are considered. Instead, human labelers are asked to describe their impression of the subject's state while listening to the recorded data. Emotion category labels are most widely used for this purpose. There is a trade-off between the precision of the descriptive system and its tractability. If application scenarios are in the focus, the categories have to be adapted to the states which actually occur in the specific scenario. For statistical analysis, rare states have to be mapped onto cover classes. Another approach is dimensional labeling motivated by dimensional emotion theories. Mainly, the two dimensions 'evaluation' and 'activation' (as in FeelTrace) or alternatively 'evaluation' and 'control' (as in the Geneva Emotion Wheel) are used. Emotion terms can be assigned positions in these dimensional spaces allowing to map categories onto dimensions and vice versa. However, the exact positions depend on the number and the choice of the emotion terms. The emotional content is assumed to be (nearly) constant within the whole segment to be labeled. If the segments of constant emotional content are not known prior to emotion labeling, the data is segmented into small units like sentences or even single words. Alternatively, in FeelTrace and its variants, the labeler can describe the emotional content in real-time by changing the position in the dimensional space while listening to the data without the need to segment the data. As the emotional state is often ambiguous, soft decisions for category labels are introduced where the labeler can specify confidence scores for the categories being considered. Since emotions are perceived differently by individuals, more than one observer is asked to label the emotional content. To evaluate the agreement of the labelers, Cohen's kappa for two labelers and its extension to several labelers is presented. The weighted version of kappa allows to punish confusions of similar categories less than those of dissimilar ones.

# Chapter 4

# Classification and Visualization Techniques

In order to classify emotion-related user states automatically, statistical classification techniques are applied. After describing the fundamentals of statistical classification, the classifiers that are used in the experiments of this thesis (s. Chapter 7) – Gaussian mixture models, linear discriminant analysis, and artificial neural networks – are introduced. Furthermore, existing methods to evaluate machine classifiers are presented. A new method based on the entropy is proposed, which is better suited to compare the performance of a machine classifier to the one of a human labeler. It implicitly weights classification errors accordingly to the decisions of the reference labelers. At the end of this chapter, two visualization techniques for high-dimensional data – the Sammon transformation and the nonmetric multidimensional scaling – are described.

## 4.1 Statistical Classification

### 4.1.1 Fundamentals

Figure 4.1 shows the structure of a classification system following [Niem 90, Niem 03]. In the first step, patterns $\boldsymbol{f}^i$ are recorded. Concerning speech, a pattern is a one-dimensional function $f(t)$ specifying the amplitude of the speech signal for a point at time $t$. These patterns are digitized and preprocessed in order to reduce the effort of the subsequent processing steps and/or to increase the later classification performance. From each pattern $\boldsymbol{f}^i$, a feature vector $\boldsymbol{c}^i$ is extracted which contains the important information in order to classify the pattern. The set of feature vectors is denoted with $\mathcal{C} = \{\boldsymbol{c}^1, \ldots, \boldsymbol{c}^N\}$. Finally, each feature vector $\boldsymbol{c}^i$ is mapped onto a class $\Omega_\kappa$ in the classification module:

$$\boldsymbol{c} \longrightarrow \Omega_\kappa, \quad \kappa \in \{0, \ldots, K\} \quad \text{or} \quad \kappa \in \{1, \ldots, K\} \ . \tag{4.1}$$

If desired the possibility to reject a pattern by mapping it onto the reject class $\Omega_0$ can be allowed. In order to classify feature vectors, the class areas have to be known. They are learned during a training stage using a sample set $\omega$ which consists of representative patterns of each clas

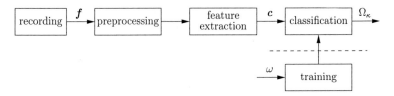

Figure 4.1: Structure of a classification system following [Niem 90, Niem 03]

**Optimal Classifier**   The statistical classifier assumes that the a priori probabilities $p_\kappa$ as well as the conditional densities $p(c|\Omega_\kappa)$ of each class are known. In addition, the costs $r_{\kappa\lambda}$ that result from classifying a pattern of class $\Omega_\kappa$ as belonging to class $\Omega_\lambda$ have to be specified. The costs are subject to the following reasonable restrictions:

$$0 \le r_{\kappa\kappa} < r_{\kappa 0} < r_{\kappa\lambda}, \quad \kappa \ne \lambda \ . \tag{4.2}$$

The probability that the classifier decides for class $\Omega_\kappa$ if the feature vector $c$ is observed, is given by the decision rule $\delta(\Omega_\kappa|c)$. Initially, it is assumed that the decision rule is a random variable with $\sum_{\kappa=0}^{K} \delta(\Omega_\kappa|c) = 1$. The expectation value of the costs $V(\delta)$ is composed of the costs $V(\delta|\Omega_\kappa)$ that emerge from the feature vectors of class $\Omega_\kappa$:

$$V(\delta) = \sum_{\kappa=1}^{K} p_\kappa V(\delta|\Omega_\kappa) \tag{4.3}$$

$$= \sum_{\kappa=1}^{K} p_\kappa \left[ \sum_{\lambda=0}^{K} r_{\kappa\lambda} \int_{R_c} p(c|\Omega_\kappa)\delta(\Omega_\kappa|c)\,\mathrm{d}c \right] \tag{4.4}$$

$$= \int_{R_c} \sum_{\lambda=0}^{K} \underbrace{\left[ \sum_{\kappa=1}^{K} r_{\kappa\lambda} p_\kappa p(c|\Omega_\kappa) \right]}_{=:u_\lambda(c)} \delta(\Omega_\kappa|c)\,\mathrm{d}c \ . \tag{4.5}$$

The optimal classifier applies that decision rule which minimizes the expected costs:

$$\delta^* = \operatorname*{argmin}_{\delta} V(\delta) \ . \tag{4.6}$$

To minimize the term $V(\delta)$ in Equation 4.5, the term $u_\lambda(c)\delta(\Omega_\kappa|c)$ has to be minimal for each vector $c$. Thus, the classifier decides for that class $\Omega_\lambda$ whose test variable $u_\lambda(c)$ has the smallest value which results in the following nonrandomized decision rule:

$$\delta^*(\Omega_\kappa|c) = \begin{cases} 1 & \text{if } u_\kappa(c) = \min_\lambda u_\lambda(c) \\ 0 & \text{else} \end{cases} \ . \tag{4.7}$$

For a two-class problem and an only one-dimensional feature $x$, the right plot of Figure 4.2 shows the two test variables $u_1(x)$ and $u_2(x)$. The probability density functions $p(c|\Omega_\kappa)$ are modeled by the two univariate Gaussians shown in the left figure. In the demonstrated case, the decision rule corresponds to a threshold decision. The threshold $\theta$ is the intersection of $u_1(x)$ and $u_2(x)$. All values $x < \theta$ are classified as belonging to class $\Omega_1$, all others as belonging to class $\Omega_2$.

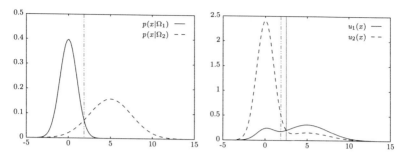

Figure 4.2: The optimal classifier: the right figure shows the test variables $u_\lambda(x)$ for a 2-class problem with $p(x|\Omega_\lambda)$ modeled by the univariate Gaussians shown in the left figure (priors $p_1 = p_2 = 0.5$, costs $r_{11} = 0.5$, $r_{12} = 2.0$, $r_{21} = 6.0$, $r_{22} = 1.0$)

**Bayes Classifier**  For many cases, a $(0,1)$-cost function $(\forall \kappa, \lambda \in \{1, \dots, K\} : r_{\rm c} = r_{\kappa\kappa} = 0, r_{\rm e} = r_{\kappa\lambda} = 1, \lambda \neq \kappa)$ is assumed and a decision is forced, i. e. the classifier cannot reject a feature vector. Under these constraints the optimal classifier is called Bayes classifier. The Bayes classifier minimizes the error probability $p_{\rm e}$ and assigns $c$ to the class with the highest a posteriori probability $p(\Omega_\lambda|c)$.

$$\delta^*(\Omega_\kappa|c) = \begin{cases} 1 & \text{if } p_\kappa p(c|\Omega_\kappa) = \max_\lambda p_\lambda p(c|\Omega_\lambda) \\ 0 & \text{else} \end{cases} \qquad (4.8)$$

Figure 4.2 shows the effect of the cost function ($r_{11} = 0.5$, $r_{12} = 2.0$, $r_{21} = 6.0$, $r_{22} = 1.0$, vertical continuous line) on the threshold compared to a $(0,1)$-cost function (vertical dashed line).

## 4.1.2  Gaussian Mixture Models

The optimal classifier assumes that the probability density functions $p(c|\Omega_\kappa)$ are given which unfortunately is not the case in real applications. In Gaussian mixture models (GMMs) these probability density functions are modeled by a mixture of $M$ multivariate Gaussians:

$$p(c|\theta) = \sum_{m=1}^{M} \alpha_m \cdot \mathcal{N}(c|\mu_m, \Sigma_m) \quad \text{with} \quad \sum_{m=1}^{M} \alpha_m = 1 \ . \qquad (4.9)$$

The parameter set $\theta$ represents the mixture weights $\alpha_m$ as well as the mean vectors $\mu_m$ and the covariance matrices $\Sigma_m$ of the $M$ Gaussians. The maximum likelihood principle states that those parameters $\theta$ are chosen which maximize the probability density of the observed data $\mathcal{C}$.

$$\hat{\theta} = \operatorname*{argmax}_{\theta} p(\mathcal{C}|\theta) = \operatorname*{argmax}_{\theta} \prod_{i=1}^{N} p(c^i|\theta) \qquad (4.10)$$

$$= \operatorname*{argmax}_{\theta} \sum_{i=1}^{N} \log p(c^i|\theta) \qquad (4.11)$$

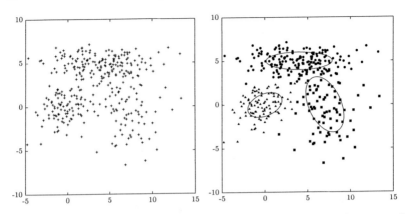

Figure 4.3: Randomly generated vectors $c \in \mathbb{R}^2$ of a mixture model which consists of three Gaussians (left). The Information by which mixture component a vector was generated is shown in the right plot, but is not available for the learning process

Often, it is easier to optimize the logarithm of the probability density $p(\mathcal{C}|\boldsymbol{\theta})$ as the product in Equation 4.10 turns into a sum (Equation 4.11). Since the logarithm is a monotonic function, this does not influence the estimates $\hat{\boldsymbol{\theta}}$. Unfortunately, differentiation of the log-likelihood function and setting it equal to zero in order to find its maximum does not yield a closed solution for Gaussian mixture models with $M > 1$. Numerical optimization techniques like the co-ordinate ascent or the Newton-Raphson technique and its alternatives are available, but all of them suffer from either the sensitivity to initial conditions or high computational costs. The EM algorithm offers better convergence properties and its computation for GMMs is simple.

**EM Algorithm**   The expectation-maximization algorithm relies on the existence of intermediate variables, called *latent data*, in the estimation problem. In 1977, Dempster et al. successfully handled the general case without assuming a specific likelihood function [Demp 77]. Concerning GMMs, the unobserved data $\boldsymbol{z} = \{z_1, \ldots, z_N\}$, $z_i \in \{1, \ldots, M\}$ contains the information which component density "generated" a data item $\boldsymbol{c}^i$ (illustrated in Figure 4.3). Introductions to the general EM algorithm and to its application to the parameter estimation of GMMs can be found in [Taga 98] and [Bilm 98], respectively.

For the probability density function of the complete data, the definition of conditional probabilities results in the following equation

$$p(\boldsymbol{z}, \mathcal{C}|\boldsymbol{\theta}) = p(\boldsymbol{z}|\mathcal{C}, \boldsymbol{\theta}) \cdot p(\mathcal{C}|\boldsymbol{\theta}) \,, \tag{4.12}$$

which can be transformed by rearranging and taking the logarithm into

$$\log p(\mathcal{C}|\boldsymbol{\theta}) = \log p(\boldsymbol{z}, \mathcal{C}|\boldsymbol{\theta}) - \log p(\boldsymbol{z}|\mathcal{C}, \boldsymbol{\theta}) \,. \tag{4.13}$$

Equation 4.13 is an identity which holds for any value $\boldsymbol{z}$ plugged into the right hand side, thus also for values of $\boldsymbol{z}$ which are generated accordingly to the distribution

$p(z|\mathcal{C}, \boldsymbol{\theta}^{(k)})$. The expected value of the left hand side is independent of $z$ and results in

$$\sum_z \log(p(\mathcal{C}|\boldsymbol{\theta}))\, p(z|\mathcal{C}, \boldsymbol{\theta}^{(k)}) = \log p(\mathcal{C}|\boldsymbol{\theta}) \sum_z p(z|\mathcal{C}, \boldsymbol{\theta}^{(k)}) = \log p(\mathcal{C}|\boldsymbol{\theta}) \; . \qquad (4.14)$$

The right hand side is

$$\underbrace{\sum_z \log(p(z,\mathcal{C}|\boldsymbol{\theta}))\, p(z|\mathcal{C}, \boldsymbol{\theta}^{(k)})}_{=:Q(\boldsymbol{\theta},\boldsymbol{\theta}^k)} - \underbrace{\sum_z \log(p(z|\mathcal{C}, \boldsymbol{\theta}))\, p(z|\mathcal{C}, \boldsymbol{\theta}^{(k)})}_{=:H(\boldsymbol{\theta},\boldsymbol{\theta}^k)} \; . \qquad (4.15)$$

Putting left and right hand side back together results in

$$\log p(\mathcal{C}|\boldsymbol{\theta}) = Q(\boldsymbol{\theta}, \boldsymbol{\theta}^k) - H(\boldsymbol{\theta}, \boldsymbol{\theta}^k) \; . \qquad (4.16)$$

In an iteration process, parameters $\boldsymbol{\theta}^{(k+1)}$ have to be found so that

$$\log p(\mathcal{C}|\boldsymbol{\theta}^{(k+1)}) \geq \log p(\mathcal{C}|\boldsymbol{\theta}^{(k)}) \; . \qquad (4.17)$$

Using Jensen's inequality, it can be shown that

$$H(\boldsymbol{\theta}^{(k+1)}, \boldsymbol{\theta}^{(k)}) \leq H(\boldsymbol{\theta}^{(k)}, \boldsymbol{\theta}^{(k)}) \qquad (4.18)$$

holds for any value of $\boldsymbol{\theta}^{(k+1)}$. The mathematical proof can be found in [Taga 98]. This reduces the problem of maximizing the log-likelihood function to finding parameters $\boldsymbol{\theta}$ that maximize $Q(\boldsymbol{\theta}, \boldsymbol{\theta}^{(k)})$:

$$\boldsymbol{\theta}^{(k+1)} = \underset{\boldsymbol{\theta}}{\operatorname{argmax}}\, Q(\boldsymbol{\theta}, \boldsymbol{\theta}^{(k)}) \; . \qquad (4.19)$$

Equation 4.19 is the EM algorithm. Starting with an initial point $\boldsymbol{\theta}^{(0)}$, this equation is applied iteratively to obtain a sequence $\boldsymbol{\theta}^{(k)}$. Usually, maximizing of $Q(\boldsymbol{\theta}, \boldsymbol{\theta}^{(k)})$ is much easier than the original maximization problem in Equation 4.11. In the case of Gaussian mixture models, the log-likelihood function of the complete data $\log p(z, \mathcal{C}|\boldsymbol{\theta})$ and the likelihood function of the latent data $p(z|\mathcal{C}, \boldsymbol{\theta}^{(k)})$ are

$$\log p(z, \mathcal{C}|\boldsymbol{\theta}) = \sum_{i=1}^{N} \log(\alpha_{z_i} \cdot \mathcal{N}(c^i|\mu_{z_i}, \Sigma_{z_i})) \quad \text{and} \qquad (4.20)$$

$$p(z|\mathcal{C}, \boldsymbol{\theta}^{(k)}) = \prod_{i=1}^{N} p(z_i|c^i, \boldsymbol{\theta}^{(k)}) \; . \qquad (4.21)$$

Both functions are plugged into Equation 4.19 which then can be simplified and solved by differentiation of $Q(\boldsymbol{\theta}, \boldsymbol{\theta}^{(k)})$ with respect to the parameters $\boldsymbol{\theta}$ and setting the results equal to zero. The resulting formulae are

$$\alpha_m^{(k+1)} = \frac{1}{N} \sum_{i=1}^{N} p(m|c^i, \boldsymbol{\theta}^{(k)}) \; , \qquad (4.22)$$

$$\mu_m^{(k+1)} = \frac{\sum_{i=1}^{N} c^i\, p(m|c^i, \boldsymbol{\theta}^{(k)})}{\sum_{i=1}^{N} p(m|c^i, \boldsymbol{\theta}^{(k)})} \; , \quad \text{and} \qquad (4.23)$$

$$\Sigma_m^{(k+1)} = \frac{\sum_{i=1}^{N} p(m|c^i, \boldsymbol{\theta}^{(k)})(c^i - \mu_m^{(k)})(c^i - \mu_m^{(k)})^t}{\sum_{i=1}^{N} p(m|c^i, \boldsymbol{\theta}^{(k)})} \; . \qquad (4.24)$$

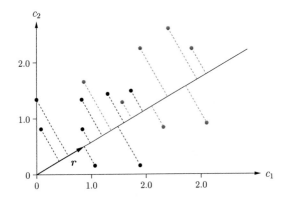

Figure 4.4: Projection of samples $c^i$ of two classes (black and gray) onto a straight line in direction $r$

The mathematical derivation of the formula can be found in [Bilm 98].

For each class in a $K$-class problem, $p(c|\Omega_\kappa)$ is modeled by a separate GMM. The classifier decides for the class with the highest posterior probability $p(\Omega_\kappa|c)$.

### 4.1.3   Linear Discriminant Analysis

In classical discriminant analysis the features $c^i \in \mathrm{R}^d$ are projected onto a straight line with direction $r$ as illustrated in Figure 4.4. The goal is to identify the orientation $r$ in order that the projected samples are well separated. The projection $\tilde{c} \in \mathrm{R}$ of a sample $c$ is given by the linear combination of the components of $c$:

$$\tilde{c} = r^t c, \qquad \|r\| = 1 \ . \tag{4.25}$$

For a two-class classification problem, the set of samples can be divided into the two subsets $\mathcal{C}_1$ and $\mathcal{C}_2$ containing $N_1$ samples labeled $\Omega_1$ and $N_2$ samples labeled $\Omega_2$, respectively. For each subset, the mean vector $\boldsymbol{\mu}_i$ and the scatter matrix $\boldsymbol{S}_i$ can be computed as follows:

$$\boldsymbol{\mu}_i \ = \ \frac{1}{N_i} \sum_{c \in \mathcal{C}_i} c \quad \text{and} \tag{4.26}$$

$$\boldsymbol{S}_i \ = \ \sum_{c \in \mathcal{C}_i} (c - \boldsymbol{\mu}_i)(c - \boldsymbol{\mu}_i)^t \ . \tag{4.27}$$

$\boldsymbol{S}_\mathrm{W} = \boldsymbol{S}_1 + \boldsymbol{S}_2$ is called the *within-class scatter* matrix. The *between-class scatter* matrix $\boldsymbol{S}_\mathrm{B}$ is defined as

$$\boldsymbol{S}_\mathrm{B} = (\boldsymbol{\mu}_1 - \boldsymbol{\mu}_2)(\boldsymbol{\mu}_1 - \boldsymbol{\mu}_2)^t \ . \tag{4.28}$$

Similarly, the mean and the scatter for the subsets $\tilde{\mathcal{C}}_1$ and $\tilde{\mathcal{C}}_2$ of the projected samples is given by:

$$\tilde{\mu}_i = \frac{1}{N_i} \sum_{\tilde{c} \in \tilde{\mathcal{C}}_i} \tilde{c} = \frac{1}{N_i} \sum_{c \in \mathcal{C}_i} r^t c = r^t \mu_i \quad \text{and} \tag{4.29}$$

$$\tilde{s}_i^2 = \sum_{\tilde{c} \in \tilde{\mathcal{C}}_i} (\tilde{c} - \tilde{\mu}_i)^2 = \sum_{c \in \mathcal{C}_i} (r^t c - r^t \mu_i)^2 = r^t S_i r . \tag{4.30}$$

The *Fisher linear discriminant* employs that direction $r$ for which the linear function $r^t c$ yields the maximum ratio of between-class scatter to within-class scatter:

$$J(r) = \frac{|\tilde{\mu}_1 - \tilde{\mu}_2|^2}{\tilde{s}_1^2 + \tilde{s}_2^2} . \tag{4.31}$$

$J(\cdot)$ is obtained as an explicit function of $r$ by substituting $\tilde{\mu}_i$ and $\tilde{s}_i$ found in Equation 4.29 and 4.30, respectively, into Equation 4.31.

$$J(r) = \frac{r^t S_B r}{r^t S_W r} \tag{4.32}$$

This expression is known as the *generalized Rayleigh quotient*. A vector $r$ which maximizes the criterion function $J(\cdot)$ is at the same time a solution of the following generalized eigenvalue problem:

$$S_B r = \lambda S_W r . \tag{4.33}$$

As $S_B r$ is always in the direction of $\mu_1 - \mu_2$, it is not necessary to solve for the eigenvalues and eigenvectors of $S_W^{-1} S_B$. The direction that maximizes $J$ is

$$r = S_W^{-1}(\mu_1 - \mu_2) . \tag{4.34}$$

Finally, the data is classified by applying a threshold to the projected data. For each class, the projected samples can, e.g., be fit with a univariate Gaussian. The threshold is given by the intersection of the posteriors in these one-dimensional distributions.

In the case of $K$ classes, Fisher's linear discriminant is generalized by using $K - 1$ discriminant functions. Thus, the samples are projected from a $d$-dimensional space to a $K-1$-dimensional subspace. Further information on multiple discriminant analysis can be found in [Duda 00].

The LDA classifier is equivalent to a multivariate Gaussian classifier if the covariance matrices are presumed to be identical for all classes resulting in a linear decision boundary [Frie 89]. The implementation used for the experiments in this thesis is based on such a Gaussian classifier.

## 4.1.4 Artificial Neural Networks

Artificial neural networks try to simulate the functionality of the brain of vertebrate animals. The human brain consists of approximately $10^{11}$ neurons. They are the core component of the brain and process and transmit information. Information is

encoded in the frequency of action potentials, "spikes" of electrical discharge, which
are transmitted over nerve tracts from one neuron to others. Synapses are the junc-
tions between the nerve tracts and the neuron. They are located on the surface of the
cell body and on the dendritic tree (cellular extensions in form of many branches).
On average, each neuron of an adult human brain has about 7,000 synaptic connec-
tions to other neurons. In chemical synapses, action potentials release excitatory or
inhibitory post-synaptic potentials in the neuron. These electrical potentials sum up
and trigger a new action potential at the axon of the neuron if a certain threshold is
exceeded. The threshold is not reached if the number of activated inputs is too small,
the frequency of the incoming action potentials is too low, or due to asynchronism of
the incoming action potentials.

In the following, multilayer perceptrons, a very popular kind of artificial neural
networks, are introduced.

**Multilayer Perceptrons**   A multilayer perceptron consists of $L + 1$ layers of neurons, $L \geq 1$. $M^{(l)}$ denotes the number of neurons or nodes in layer $l$. The first
layer ($l = 0$) is called *input layer*, the last layer ($l = L$) *output layer*, and all other
layers ($0 < l < L$) inbetween *hidden layers*. Each node of layer $l - 1$ transmits its
information to all nodes of the following layer $l$, $l \in \{1, \ldots, L\}$, resulting in the unidi-
rectional graph shown in Figure 4.5. Weights are assigned to all edges in this graph.
The weight $w_{ij}^{(l)}$ denotes the weight assigned to the edge from node $i$ of layer $l - 1$
to node $j$ of layer $l$. The net activation of a unit is the weighted sum of its inputs
minus a neuron specific threshold $w_{0j}^{(l)}$.

$$\text{net}_j^{(l)} = \sum_{i=1}^{M^{(l-1)}} y_i^{(l-1)} w_{ij}^{(l)} - w_{0j}^{(l)} \qquad (4.35)$$

Equation 4.35 can be expressed as the scalar product $(\boldsymbol{y}^{(l-1)})^t \boldsymbol{w}_j^{(l)}$ of the inputs
and the weights if the input vector as well as the weight vector are augmented by
appending -1 and $w_{0j}^{(l)}$, respectively. Thus, the bias $w_{0j}^{(l)}$ can be treated mathematically
like any other weight. The emitted output of a unit is obtained by applying an
activation function $f$ which is generally a non-linear function, e. g. the sign function.

$$y_j^{(l)} = f(\text{net}_j^{(l)}) \qquad (4.36)$$

The training algorithm described in the following section requires the activation function to be differentiable. Hence, the sigmoid or the hyperbolic tangent function shown
in Figure 4.6 are frequently used activation functions.

The input layer distributes the values of a feature vector $\boldsymbol{c}$ to the neurons of
the first hidden layer. Thus, the number of nodes in the input layer is equal to the
dimension of the feature vector. Applying Equation 4.35 and 4.36, the input is fed
forward from the input layer through the hidden layers to the output layer. In general,
the number of nodes in the output layer $M^{(L)}$ is equal to the number of classes $K$. If
so, the multilayer perceptron decides for the class with the highest output value $y_j^{(L)}$.

Theoretical constructions show that already multilayer perceptrons with only one
hidden layer can implement every desired function, given a sufficient number of hidden

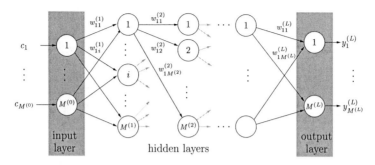

Figure 4.5: Topology of a multi-layer perceptron (MLP)

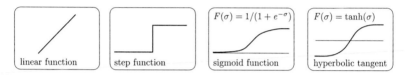

Figure 4.6: Different activation functions for artificial neural networks [Kies 97]

nodes, proper nonlinearities, and weights. Unfortunately, these considerations are of greater theoretical interest than of practical use since they are not a constructive proof and neither give the number of hidden units required nor the proper weights. Furthermore, the desired function is also not known as it is related to the training patterns in a very complicated way.

**Backpropagation Algorithm** The Backpropagation algorithm is a supervised training for multilayer networks. Using a gradient descent the weights are adjusted in order to reduce the training error $\varepsilon$:

$$\Delta w_j^{(l)} = -\eta \frac{\partial \varepsilon}{\partial w_{ij}^{(l)}} \ . \tag{4.37}$$

A typical error function is the mean squared error $\varepsilon_{\mathrm{MSE}}$ defined as the sum of the squared differences between the desired target output $t_j$ and the actual output $y_j^{(L)}$ of the units in the output layer $L$.

$$\varepsilon_{\mathrm{MSE}}(\boldsymbol{w}) = \frac{1}{2} \sum_{k=1}^{M^{(L)}} (t_k - y_k^{(L)})^2 \tag{4.38}$$

The error depends on all weights $w_{ij}^{(l)}$ in the network which are subsumed in the vector $\boldsymbol{w}$. In general, $t_j$ equals 1 if the feature vector belongs to class $\Omega_j$ and -1 if it belongs to another class. For the output layer, the desired outputs $t_k$ are known. In order to differentiate with respect to the weights $w_{jk}^{(L)}$ between the last hidden layer and the output layer, the chain rule of differentiation is applied:

$$\frac{\partial \varepsilon_{\mathrm{MSE}}}{\partial w_{jk}^{(L)}} = \frac{\partial \varepsilon_{\mathrm{MSE}}}{\partial \mathrm{net}_k^{(L)}} \cdot \frac{\partial \mathrm{net}_k^{(L)}}{\partial w_{jk}^{(L)}} = -\delta_k^{(L)} \cdot y_j^{(L-1)} \, . \tag{4.39}$$

The term $\delta_k^{(L)}$ is called *sensitivity* and describes how the overall error changes with the net activation of unit $k$ of the output layer. Applying the chain rule again results in:

$$\delta_k^{(L)} = -\frac{\partial \varepsilon_{\mathrm{MSE}}}{\partial \mathrm{net}_k^{(L)}} = -\frac{\partial \varepsilon_{\mathrm{MSE}}}{\partial y_k^{(L)}} \cdot \frac{\partial y_k^{(L)}}{\mathrm{net}_k^{(L)}} = (t_k - y_k^{(L)}) f'(\mathrm{net}_k^{(L)}) \, . \tag{4.40}$$

Unfortunately, the desired output values for the hidden layers are not known. Again, the chain rule is applied several times in order to differentiate w.r.t. the weights $w_{ij}^{(L-1)}$ of the last hidden layer.

$$\begin{aligned} \frac{\partial \varepsilon_{\mathrm{MSE}}}{\partial w_{ij}^{(L-1)}} &= \frac{\partial \varepsilon_{\mathrm{MSE}}}{\partial y_j^{(L-1)}} \cdot \frac{\partial y_j^{(L-1)}}{\partial \mathrm{net}_j^{(L-1)}} \cdot \frac{\partial \mathrm{net}_j^{(L-1)}}{\partial w_{ij}^{(L-1)}} \\ &= \frac{\partial \varepsilon_{\mathrm{MSE}}}{\partial y_j^{(L-1)}} \cdot f'(\mathrm{net}_j^{(L-1)}) \cdot y_i^{(L-1)} \end{aligned} \tag{4.41}$$

The following derivation shows that the differentiation of $\partial \varepsilon_{\mathrm{MSE}}$ w.r.t. $y_j^{(L-1)}$ can be computed as the sum of the sensitivity values $\delta_k^{(L)}$ of the layer above weighted by the weights $w_{jk}^{(L)}$:

$$\begin{aligned} \frac{\partial \varepsilon_{\mathrm{MSE}}}{\partial y_j^{(L-1)}} &= \frac{\partial}{\partial y_j^{(L-1)}} \left[ \frac{1}{2} \sum_{k=1}^{M^{(L)}} (t_k - y_k^{(L)})^2 \right] \\ &= -\sum_{k=1}^{M^{(L)}} (t_k - y_k^{(L)}) \frac{\partial y_k^{(L)}}{\partial y_j^{(L-1)}} \\ &= -\sum_{k=1}^{M^{(L)}} (t_k - y_k^{(L)}) \frac{\partial y_k^{(L)}}{\mathrm{net}_k^{(L)}} \cdot \frac{\mathrm{net}_k^{(L)}}{\partial y_j^{(L-1)}} \\ &= -\sum_{k=1}^{M^{(L)}} (t_k - y_k^{(L)}) f'(\mathrm{net}_k^{(L)}) \, w_{jk}^{(L)} \\ &= -\sum_{k=1}^{M^{(L)}} \delta_k^{(L)} w_{jk}^{(L)} \, . \end{aligned} \tag{4.42}$$

Defining the sensitivity $\delta_j^{(l)}$ for any hidden layer $l$, $0 < l < L$, in terms of the sensitivity values $\delta_k^{(l+1)}$ of the layer above as

$$\delta_j^{(l)} = f'(\mathrm{net}_j^{(l)}) \sum_{k=1}^{M^{(l+1)}} w_{jk}^{(l+1)} \delta_k^{(l+1)}, \tag{4.43}$$

the weights $w_{ij}^{(l)}$ can be updated with

$$\Delta w_{ij}^{(l)} = \eta \, \delta_j^{(l)} \, y_i^{(l)} \qquad (4.44)$$

beginning at the output layer and moving backwards through the hidden layers. With the backpropagation algorithm, a simple algorithm for training multilayer perceptrons is available.

## 4.2 Evaluation of Decoders

The last section shed some light on the functioning of the machine classifiers that are employed in the experiments of this thesis. In the next section, methods are presented to evaluate how well decoders actually perform in the given classification task. Decoders can be both human beings and automatic classifiers. Yet, the techniques used for evaluation are the same. In the following, the presentation is restricted to measures for category labels as these have been used to label the FAU Aibo Emotion Corpus.

### 4.2.1 Recognition Rate and Average Recall

It is obvious to use traditional evaluation methods used in machine learning to evaluate decoders. The total recognition rate (RR) is a widely used measure defined as the percentage of correctly classified samples:

$$\mathrm{RR} := \frac{1}{N} \sum_{\kappa=1}^{K} n_{\kappa\kappa} \cdot 100\,\% \ . \qquad (4.45)$$

$K$ is the number of classes, $n_{\kappa\kappa}$ are the number of cases where class $\Omega_\kappa$ is correctly classified as class $\Omega_\kappa$ (diagonal elements in the confusion matrix illustrated in Table 4.1), and $N$ is the total size of the sample set. The total recognition rate indicates how many correct decisions the classifier makes. In an application scenario with a forced decision and a $(0,1)$-cost function (see Chapter 4.1.1), the classifier which minimizes the costs maximizes the probability $p_c = 1 - p_e$ of a correct decision. Unfortunately, the recognition rate highly depends on the prior probabilities $p_\kappa = N_\kappa/N$ of the $K$ classes in the training set. A naïve classifier (in the sense of uninformed, clueless) which always decides in favor of the class $\Omega_\kappa$ with the highest prior probability $p_\kappa$ independently of the feature $c$ has a total recognition rate which is equal to $p_\kappa$. The effect is particularly high if the distribution of the classes is highly unbalanced as it is the case in emotion recognition experiments with real data. For example, if 84 % of the samples in the training set are neutral, already this naïve classifier attains a recognition rate of 84 %. Thus, high recognition rates do not necessarily imply a good classification performance.

*Recall* and *precision* are two measures which are specific for a single class $\Omega_\kappa$:

$$\mathrm{recall}_\kappa \ = \ \frac{n_{\kappa\kappa}}{\sum_{i=1}^{K} n_{\kappa i}} = \frac{n_{\kappa\kappa}}{N_\kappa} \ , \qquad (4.46)$$

$$\mathrm{precision}_\kappa \ = \ \frac{n_{\kappa\kappa}}{\sum_{i=1}^{K} n_{i\kappa}} \ . \qquad (4.47)$$

hypothesis

| | $\Omega_1$ | $\Omega_2$ | $\Omega_3$ | ... | $\Omega_K$ | $\sum$ |
|---|---|---|---|---|---|---|
| $\Omega_1$ | $n_{11}$ | $n_{12}$ | $n_{13}$ | ... | $n_{1K}$ | $N_1$ |
| $\Omega_2$ | $n_{21}$ | $n_{22}$ | $n_{23}$ | ... | $n_{2K}$ | $N_2$ |
| $\Omega_3$ | $n_{31}$ | $n_{32}$ | $n_{33}$ | ... | $n_{3K}$ | $N_3$ |
| $\vdots$ | $\vdots$ | $\vdots$ | $\vdots$ | $\ddots$ | $\vdots$ | $\vdots$ |
| $\Omega_K$ | $n_{K1}$ | $n_{K2}$ | $n_{K3}$ | ... | $n_{KK}$ | $N_K$ |
| $\sum$ | | | | | | $N$ |

(reference, left margin)

Table 4.1: Confusion matrix with absolute frequencies for a $K$-class problem

Recall is the fraction of cases belonging to class $\Omega_\kappa$ which are classified correctly as $\Omega_\kappa$ whereas precision is the fraction of cases being classified as $\Omega_\kappa$ which actually belong to class $\Omega_\kappa$.

The classwise averaged recognition rate (CL), defined as the (unweighted) average of the $K$ recall values, is a useful measure combining the advantages of the total recognition rate RR and the measures recall and precision: it is a single performance figure and it does not depend on the prior probabilities of the classes.

$$ \text{CL} := \frac{1}{K} \sum_{\kappa=1}^{K} \frac{n_{\kappa\kappa}}{N_\kappa} \cdot 100\,\% \tag{4.48} $$

A naïve classifier that always decides for the class $\Omega_\kappa$ with the highest prior probability $p_\kappa$ or randomly picks one of the $K$ classes has only a CL rate of $\frac{1}{K}$. If the prior probabilities $p_\kappa$ are the same for all $K$ classes,

$$ p_1 = p_2 = \ldots = p_K = \frac{1}{K}, $$

CL is equal to RR as $\forall \kappa : N_\kappa = \frac{N}{K}$. The weighted average of the $K$ recall values weighted with the prior probabilities $p_\kappa = \frac{N_\kappa}{N}$ is equal to the total recognition rate RR.

For the case of only two classes, the F-measure is defined as the harmonic mean of precision and recall and can also be used as one single performance measure:

$$ F := \frac{2}{\frac{1}{\text{precision}} + \frac{1}{\text{recall}}} = \frac{2 \cdot \text{precision} \cdot \text{recall}}{\text{precision} + \text{recall}} = \frac{2 \cdot n_{11}}{2 \cdot n_{11} + n_{12} + n_{21}} . \tag{4.49} $$

The presented performance measures evaluate the overall performance of a decoder or its classification performance for single classes, but they do not tell which classes the decoder mixes up. According to [Sche 03a], confusion patterns of human listener judges are very specific for each emotion and there is evidence that these patterns are similar even across different cultures. In [Bans 96] for example, hot anger is confused consistently only with cold anger and contempt. In general, similar emotions (similar on one or more dimensions, see Chapter 3.2) are more likely to be confused than others. Scherer states that confusions of a decoder are arguably even more interesting than the number of errors and confusion matrices of the type shown in Table 4.1 should be reported routinely in experiments on emotion recognition. This definitely also holds for machine classification experiments.

## 4.2.2 Entropy based Evaluation

The evaluation measures presented in the last section, including confusion matrices, assume that a sample belongs to exactly one class and that this class (called the reference or the ground truth) is known. A decision is correct if the reference class is chosen, all other decisions are incorrect. A distinction between the incorrect cases w. r. t. the severity of the confusion is not possible.

The more similar the emotions or emotion-related states in a speech corpus are, the less appropriate is the classification in white and black, in absolutely correct and totally wrong. A confusion of emotions of the same emotion family which differ only in their emotional intensity, like 'feeling distaste' and 'feeling disgust', is obviously less severe than a confusion of disgust and sadness, for example, or disgust and joy. Furthermore, individual differences in the assessment of emotional intensity render it impossible to define objective boundaries between emotional states which differ only slightly in their intensity. In a certain range between similar emotions, confusions are not only less severe but have to be accepted as correct. The same holds for blends of emotions where it is hard to decide which component prevails.

In contrast to the full-blown emotions usually portrayed in corpora of acted speech, speech corpora of natural emotions often include to a large extent weak emotions or blends of different emotions or emotion-related states. In most cases, the ground truth is not known. Because of their low intensity, weak emotions are likely to be confused with neutral.

In this thesis, an entropy based measure is presented which measures how well each decision of the decoder fits to the decisions of a group of reference labelers [Stei 05]. The decoder can be a machine classifier or a single human labeler. Henceforth, the other human labelers excluding the human decoder are denoted as reference labelers. The entropy based measure is especially suited for nominal classes. It neither requires prior knowledge of typical confusion patterns nor a distance measure for emotional states. The single decisions of the reference labelers are not transformed into a single decision for the whole group by majority vote. Each reference labeler decides for one emotional state out of a set of pre-defined states. The decisions of the reference labelers are then transformed into a soft decision label $l_{\mathrm{ref}}$ as shown in Figure 4.7. If the group of reference labelers is representative, the components of the vector $l_{\mathrm{ref}}$ contain the probabilities that the given sample belongs to the corresponding emotional state. Unambiguous samples will have one component set to one and all others set to zero. The example in Figure 4.7 shows a sample with emotion-related states taken from the FAU Aibo Emotion Corpus (for details see Chapter 5.3.7). The majority of the reference labelers (60 %) decides for the cover class *Anger*. The remaining reference labelers vary between *Emphatic* (30 %) and *Neutral* (10 %). None of the reference labelers opts for *Motherese*. As *Emphatic* can be interpreted as some kind of pre-stage of emotion (see p. 41), the sample obviously belongs to a state at the barrier between a non-emotional state in which the child already speaks in a pronounced, hyper-articulated way and the emotional state 'slight anger'.

In order to be able to compare a machine classifier to a human labeler later on, one of the $L$ human labelers is omitted. The soft label for sample $i$ of the remaining $L-1$ reference labelers without the human labeler $\bar{l}$ is denoted as $l_{\mathrm{ref}}(\bar{l}, i)$. The hard decision of the decoder (machine classifier or human labeler $\bar{l}$) is also transformed

| labeler | class |
|---------|-------|
| 1 | A |
| 2 | E |
| 3 | A |
| 4 | E |
| 5 | A |
| 6 | N |
| 7 | A |
| 8 | A |
| 9 | E |
| 10 | A |

$\rightarrow$

| A | E | N | M |
|---|---|---|---|
| 0.6 | 0.3 | 0.1 | 0.0 |

Figure 4.7: Conversion of the hard decisions of ten labelers into a soft reference label $l_{\mathrm{ref}}$. The four classes are *A*nger, *M*otherese, *E*mphatic, and *N*eutral

into a soft label, denoted as $l_{\mathrm{dec}}(i)$. The information entropy $H$ [Shan 48] of a soft decision vector $l$, defined as

$$H = -\sum_{k=1}^{K} l_k \cdot \log_2 l_k \quad \text{with} \quad 0 \cdot \log_2 0 = 0 \tag{4.50}$$

is a measure of the degree of agreement of the labelers. The entropy is equal to zero if all labelers agree on one emotion class and it reaches its maximum if all components of the vector have the same value which is then equal to $\frac{1}{K}$. The maximum depends on the number of classes and is equal to $\log_2 K$.

The decision of the decoder is added to the decisions of the reference labelers what will change the entropy value. If the decision of the decoder is the same as the majority vote of the reference labelers, the entropy will decrease (or remain zero if all labelers decide consentaneously for one class). The less probable the emotion class is which the decoder picked, the more the entropy will increase. The highest increase results from a decoder decision for a class which has not been picked by any reference labeler. The basic idea is to compare the influence on the entropy caused by a machine classifier with the influence caused by an average human labeler. In this comparison, both the reference label $l_{\mathrm{ref}}(\bar{\ell}, i)$ and the label of the decoder $l_{\mathrm{dec}}(i)$ are weighted equally to be independent of the number of reference labelers.

$$l(\bar{\ell}, i) = 0.5 \cdot l_{\mathrm{ref}}(\bar{\ell}, i) + 0.5 \cdot l_{\mathrm{dec}}(i) \tag{4.51}$$

The entropy of this combined soft decision label for a given sample $i$ is

$$H(\bar{\ell}, i) = -\sum_{k=1}^{K} l_k(\bar{\ell}, i) \cdot \log_2 l_k(\bar{\ell}, i) \ . \tag{4.52}$$

As one human labeler is omitted, the decoder (either the machine classifier or the omitted human labeler) is compared in a leave-one-labeler-out procedure to the remaining $L - 1$ reference labelers and the average entropy value is taken:

$$H(i) = \frac{1}{L} \sum_{\bar{\ell}=1}^{L} H(\bar{\ell}, i) \ . \tag{4.53}$$

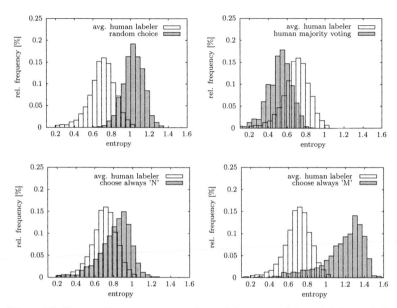

Figure 4.8: Entropy histograms: comparison of the average human labeler with different naïve classifiers (random choice, always *Neutral*, always *Motherese*) and the majority vote of the human labelers

Thereby, a machine classifier can be compared to the average human labeler of the group of human labelers. Finally, the entropy is averaged over all samples of the data set:

$$H_{\text{dec}} = \frac{1}{N} \sum_{i=1}^{N} H(i) \ . \tag{4.54}$$

Instead of calculating one single entropy value for the whole data, a histogram of the entropy values $H(i)$ can be plotted. Figure 4.8 shows the entropy histogram for the average human labeler in comparison to the histograms of four other decoders: a naïve decoder which randomly picks one of the four classes (random choice, top left), an artificial decoder which decides for the majority vote of the human labelers (human majority voting, top right), and two more naïve decoders which always choose *Neutral* (bottom left) and *Motherese* (bottom right), respectively. The figures are based on the labeling of the FAU Aibo Emotion Corpus [Stei 05]. The high mean entropy of the average human labeler ($H_{\text{dec}} = 0.721$) reflects the difficulty of labeling non-acted emotional speech data. The 'human majority voting'-decoder ($H_{\text{dec}} = 0.542$) clearly outperforms the average human labeler and marks the upper performance limit for any decoder. As to be expected, the three different naïve decoders do clearly worse than the average human labeler. Due to the high confusion of the emotional states with the neutral state, the decoder which always chooses *Neutral* ($H_{\text{dec}} = 0.843$)

outperforms the 'random choice'-decoder ($H_{\text{dec}} = 1.050$) and the 'always *Motherese*'-decoder ($H_{\text{dec}} = 1.196$).

## 4.3    Visualization Techniques

Humans lack the ability to visualize high-dimensional data and thus cannot discover its inherent structure. The problem is further aggravated if the data represents similarity or dissimilarity measures that generally miss the familiar properties of distances. In the following, two different techniques are presented which map $N$ points $\boldsymbol{c}^i$ from a high-dimensional space to a low-dimensional one with mostly only two or three dimensions:

$$\boldsymbol{c}^i \in \mathrm{R}^d \longrightarrow \boldsymbol{x}^i \in \mathrm{R}^{d'} \quad \text{with} \quad 1 \le i \le N \quad \text{and} \quad d' \ll d \ . \tag{4.55}$$

Both methods approximately preserve the inherent structure of the data, which finally can be visualized easily for $d' \le 3$.

### 4.3.1    Sammon Transformation

The *Sammon transformation* [Samm 69] is a nonlinear mapping such that the interpoint distances in the lower-dimensional space $d_{ij}$ between two points $\boldsymbol{x}^i$ and $\boldsymbol{x}^j$ approximate the distances $\delta_{ij}$ between the points $\boldsymbol{c}^i$ and $\boldsymbol{c}^j$ in the original high-dimensional space. It has been used successfully for a variety of problems, for example recently for the separation of different speaker groups (laryngectomized speakers with tracheoesophageal substitute voice, speakers with a hoarse and with a normal voice) in a two-dimensional space given the high-dimensional mixture weights of a speech recognizer based on semi-continuous hidden Markov models which have been adapted to the present speaker by HMM interpolation [Hade 06, Stei 03].

An error measure represents how well the present configuration of the $N$ points in the $d'$-dimensional space fits the $N$ points in the original $d$-dimensional space. The error $E_1$ is defined as follows:

$$E_1 = \frac{1}{\sum_{i<j} \delta_{ij}} \sum_{i<j}^{N} \frac{(\delta_{ij} - d_{ij})^2}{\delta_{ij}} \ . \tag{4.56}$$

Other error functions are also reasonable, e. g.

$$E_2 = \frac{\sum_{i<j} (\delta_{ij} - d_{ij})^2}{\sum_{i<j} \delta_{ij}^2} \quad \text{and} \tag{4.57}$$

$$E_3 = \sum_{i<j} \left( \frac{\delta_{ij} - d_{ij}}{\delta_{ij}} \right)^2 \ . \tag{4.58}$$

Since only the distances between points are involved, all of these error functions are invariant to rigid-body motions (translations, rotations) of the configuration. Furthermore, the normalizations make the minimum of the error functions invariant to dilations of the sample points. $E_2$ emphasizes large errors regardless of whether

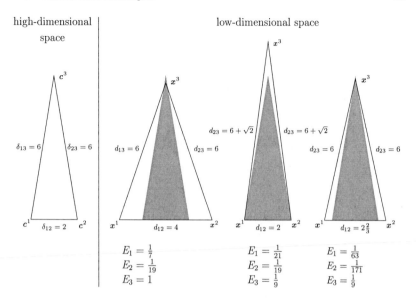

Figure 4.9: Illustration of the error functions $E_1$, $E_2$, and $E_3$

the distances $\delta_{ij}$ in the high-dimensional space are large or small. $E_3$ emphasizes large fractional errors only. $E_1$ is a compromise of both, emphasizing large errors as well as large fractional errors. In the left part of Figure 4.9, an example is given showing three points $c^1$, $c^2$, and $c^3$ and their high-dimensional distances $\delta_{12}$, $\delta_{13}$, and $\delta_{2,3}$. In the right part, three different mappings into the low-dimensional space are shown; all of them are not optimal. The error in terms of $E_2$ (squared error) is the same for the left and the middle mapping. Yet, the fractional error ($E_3$) is clearly smaller for the mapping in the middle since there, the error does not occur at the short edge but at the long edges of the triangle. According to the visual impression, the triangle in the middle represents the high-dimensional distances better than the left one. If the mapping in the middle is compared to the right one, the error $E_2$ is reduced while keeping $E_3$ constant. The error $E_1$ is reduced both from the left to the middle and from the middle to the right mapping.

The error function is a function in $N \cdot d'$ variables. The steepest descent procedure is used to search for the minimum of the error function. Using the definition of the Euclidian distance $d_{ij}$ between the points $x^i$ and $x^j$

$$d_{ij} = \sqrt{\sum_{k=1}^{d'}(x_k^i - x_k^j)^2} \,, \tag{4.59}$$

the gradient of the error function $E_1$ w.r.t. the $k^{\text{th}}$ component of point $\boldsymbol{x}^n$ is

$$\frac{\partial E_1}{\partial x_k^n} = \frac{-2}{\sum_{i<j}\delta_{ij}} \cdot \sum_{\substack{j=1,\\ j\neq n}}^{N} \left[\frac{\delta_{nj}-d_{nj}}{\delta_{nj}\,d_{nj}}\right] (x_k^n - x_k^j) \ . \tag{4.60}$$

An extension to the Sammon transformation to reduce the dependency on the recording conditions such as the use of different microphones is presented in [Maie 08].

### 4.3.2   Nonmetric Multidimensional Scaling

*Nonmetric multidimensional scaling* (NMDS) [Krus 64a, Krus 64b] is suited for problems where the quantities $\delta_{ij}$ are similarities (or dissimilarities) that miss the properties of distances and where only the rank order is important, but not the exact numerical values. In NMDS, the rank order of the distances $d_{ij}$ in the low-dimensional space approximates the rank order of the distances $\delta_{ij}$ in the original high-dimensional space. In the following, the quantities $\delta_{ij}$ are assumed to be dissimilarities with $\forall i, 1 \leq i \leq N : \delta_{ii} = 0$ and $\forall i \neq j : \delta_{ij} = \delta_{ji}$. The $M = N(N-1)/2$ quantities $\delta_{ij}$ are ordered in ascending order:

$$\delta_{i_1 j_1} \leq \delta_{i_2 j_2} \leq \ldots \leq \delta_{i_M j_M} \ . \tag{4.61}$$

*Any M numbers* $\hat{d}_{ij}$ for which the monotonicity constraint

$$\hat{d}_{i_1 j_1} \leq \hat{d}_{i_2 j_2} \leq \ldots \hat{d}_{i_M j_M} \tag{4.62}$$

holds is an ideal configuration. The stress function $S$ is a measure of the deviation of the present configuration from the given ideal configuration.

$$S(\boldsymbol{x}^1,\ldots,\boldsymbol{x}^N, \hat{d}_{i_1 j_1}, \ldots, \hat{d}_{i_M j_M}) = \sqrt{\frac{\sum_{i<j}(d_{ij}-\hat{d}_{ij})^2}{\sum_{i<j} d_{ij}^2}} \tag{4.63}$$

From all possible values $\hat{d}_{ij}$ which satisfy Equation 4.62 those values are chosen that minimize the stress for a fixed configuration $\boldsymbol{x}^1,\ldots,\boldsymbol{x}^N$.

$$S(\boldsymbol{x}^1,\ldots,\boldsymbol{x}^N) = \min_{\substack{\hat{d}_{ij} \text{ satisfying}\\ \text{Eq. } 4.62}} \sqrt{\frac{\sum_{i<j}(d_{ij}-\hat{d}_{ij})^2}{\sum_{i<j} d_{ij}^2}} \tag{4.64}$$

The situation is illustrated in the left part of Figure 4.10. Each star in the scatter diagram has abscissa $\delta_{ij}$ and ordinate $d_{ij}$. The corresponding ideal values $\hat{d}_{ij}$ are indicated with circles if they differ from the values $d_{ij}$ of the present configuration. Horizontal dashed lines indicate the deviation of the present configuration from the ideal one. $S(\boldsymbol{x}^1,\ldots,\boldsymbol{x}^N)$ is a function in $N \cdot d'$ parameters. Again, the steepest descent procedure is applied to search for a configuration which minimizes the stress function.

According to Equation 4.64, the ideal values $\hat{d}_{ij}$ have to be determined in each iteration step. This can be done by a rapid, efficient algorithm described in [Krus 64b].

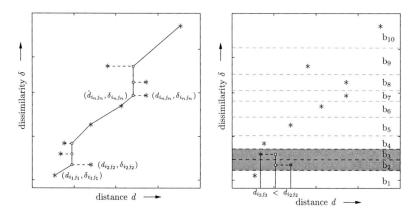

Figure 4.10: Nonmetric Dimensional Scaling: scatter diagram of the present configuration showing the deviation of the $d_{ij}$ from the ideal values $\hat{d}_{ij}$ (left) and illustration of the algorithm to find the ideal values $\hat{d}_{ij}$ (right)

The dissimilarities $\delta_{ij}$ are partitioned into consecutive blocks $b_1, \ldots, b_\mu$. Within each block $b$ the value $\hat{d}_b$ is constant and equal to the average of all values $d_{ij}$ in this block. The algorithm starts with the finest possible partition into blocks as illustrated in the right part of Figure 4.10, which consists of $M$ blocks, each block $b_m$ containing only a single dissimilarity $\delta_{i_m j_m}$. A block $b_m$ is called *up-satisfied* if $d_b < d_{b_{m+1}}$ and *down-satisfied* if $d_{b_{m-1}} < d_{b_m}$. The first and the last block are also up-satisfied and down-satisfied, respectively. At the beginning, the first block is *up-active*. At each stage, exactly one block is *active*, either *up-active* or *down-active*. An up-active block $b_m$ is compared to the next higher one and if block $b_m$ is not up-satisfied it is joined with block $b_{m+1}$. Thereby, the partition is changed and the number of blocks is decreased by one. If block $b_m$ is already up-satisfied, the partition remains unchanged. In both cases, block $b_m$ becomes down-active and is compared to the next lower one. If block $b_m$ is not down-satisfied, it is joined with block $b_{m-1}$. Then, block $b_m$ becomes up-active again. This alternation stops if block $b_m$ is both up- and down-satisfied and activity is then transferred to the next higher block. The algorithm terminates if the highest block is both up- and down-satisfied. Finally, the values $\hat{d}_{ij}$ are set to the values $d_b$ of the corresponding block.

The right part of Figure 4.10 shows the situation where block $b_1$ is both up- and down-satisfied. In the present stage of the algorithm, block $b_2$ becomes up-active and is compared to block $b_3$. Since $\hat{d}_{b_2} = d_{i_2 j_2}$ is smaller than $\hat{d}_{b_3} = d_{i_3 j_3}$, the monotonicity constraint is violated and block $b_2$ is not up-satisfied. The violation is removed by joining block $b_2$ with block $b_3$. The new value $\hat{d}_{b_2}$ of the new block $b_2$ is the average of $d_{i_2 j_2}$ and $d_{i_3 j_3}$ and illustrated with two circles in the scatter diagram. In the following stage, the new block will become down-active and will be compared to block $b_1$.

**Summary**   In this chapter, the fundamentals of machine classification are addressed. From a theoretical point of view, the optimal classifier is introduced. The mathematical fundamentals of Gaussian mixture models, linear discriminant analysis, and artificial neural networks are presented. These three classifiers cover different classification approaches and are used in the classification experiments of this thesis. Various measures like the total recognition rate, the precision and the recall of one class, the (unweighted) average recall of all classes, and the F-measure are given to evaluate the performance of a machine classifier or a human labeler. Furthermore, a new evaluation measure based on the entropy is introduced where confusions of the decoder are weighted accordingly to the decisions of the reference labelers for the particular segment under consideration. In order to visualize high-dimensional data, two techniques – the Sammon transformation and the nonmetric multidimensional scaling – are presented. Both techniques map points from a high-dimensional space onto points in a low-dimensional space such that the interpoint distances in the low-dimensional space approximate the distances between the points in the high-dimensional space. In contrast to the Sammon transformation, nonmetric dimensional scaling only preserves the rank order of the interpoint distances.

# Chapter 5

# FAU Aibo Emotion Corpus

This work aims at the automatic classification of emotion-related user states in an application-oriented scenario using speech as input modality. In order to avoid the disadvantages associated with emotion portrayals enumerated in Chapter 1.2, this work focuses on the investigation of speech data containing naturalistic emotions. Only a few databases of naturalistic emotions exist (s. Chapter 1.2). Moreover, many of these corpora are either not available for scientific research or are not appropriate for our purposes. The reasons are manifold: the small size of the corpus rendering machine learning impossible, the low number of subjects so that speaker independent systems are not possible, the focus on other input modalities than speech, etc. Hence, a new corpus of spontaneous speech in various emotion-related states, the FAU Aibo Emotion Corpus, has been recorded and is described in detail in this chapter. The description begins with the experimental design and the recording conditions.

## 5.1 Experimental Design and Recording

In 2002, the experimental setup of the FAU Aibo Emotion Corpus was designed with the goal to collect speech that is both spontaneous and emotional. The emotions ought to be as naturalistic as they can be in a staged recording scenario, with a preferably wide range of emotions. The collection of the data was funded by the European Community within the project PF-STAR (Preparing Future Multisensorial Interaction Research)[1] and was combined with the needs from another work package within PF-STAR we were involved in, namely the collection of speech data of children. Our PF-STAR partners from the School of Engineering[2] at the University of Birmingham reran parts of the Aibo recordings in a similar way so that a German and an English version of the FAU Aibo Emotion Corpus is available (cf. [Batl 04a]). The experiments in this thesis focus only on the German data.

In the chosen scenario, children play with the Sony robot Aibo[3] that is designed like a small dog. For our experiments, Sony placed the Aibo ERS-210A, shown in Figure 5.1, at our disposal. The ERS-210A belongs to the second generation of the Aibo robot series and includes wireless LAN movement control and voice and name

---

[1]http://pfstar.itc.it, last visited 01/12/2009
[2]http://www.eece.bham.ac.uk/, last visited 01/12/2009
[3]http://support.sony-europe.com/aibo/, last visited 01/12/2009

Figure 5.1: Sony Aibo ERS-210A, by courtesy of Sony Deutschland GmbH [Sony 06]

recognition of about 50 simple words. Various sensors allow Aibo to react to external stimuli. With its enhanced robot technology, Aibo can take its own decisions. The communication between Aibo and the child takes place by various means. By turning the head towards the child and ear movements or blinking LED lights, the impression that the child has Aibo's attention can be generated. In contrast, Aibo can ignore the child by turning or walking away. Furthermore, joy can be signaled by letting Aibo move its tail. Begging, for example, can be signaled by letting it sit down and move its paws.

The whole experiment consists of six parts: five rather simple object localization tasks where the child should direct Aibo to one out of two or three feeding dishes and the main experiment where the child should direct Aibo along a given parcours and let Aibo perform certain tasks at predefined places, e. g. let Aibo sit down, dance, or go to the three blue cups positioned in the parcours. The experiments are illustrated in Appendix A.1.1 and A.1.2. The parcours experiment took place between the third and the fourth object localization task. The children were told to talk to Aibo like they would talk to a real dog, especially to reprimand Aibo if it disobeys, or to praise it if it takes orders.

In Germany, the recordings were carried out at two different schools in Erlangen, the *Ohm-Gymnasium* (Ohm) and the *Montessori-Schule* (Mont). 51 children (30 female and 21 male pupils, see Table A.7 in Appendix A.2.1 for details) at the age of 10 to 13 took part in the experiments. The recording sessions took place in separate class rooms. Besides the child, the instructor, who told the child what to do, the controller, who stayed in the background pretending to control the video camera, and a third assistant, who helped to arrange the different scenarios, attended the recording session. During the recordings, they effaced themselves in order not to disturb the child. The wireless head set Shure UT 14/20 UHF series with the microphone WH20TQG was used in combination with the DAT recorder Tascam DA-P1 at a sampling rate of 48 kHz and a quantization of 16 bits. The audio data was transferred to a computer via a digital audio interface. Corresponding to the standard sampling rate in automatic speech recognition, the speech recordings were downsampled to 16 kHz. In addition to the audio recordings, the whole scene was recorded with a consumer video camera and a wide-angle lens at 25 fps in PAL resolution and

Figure 5.2: Experimental setup: object localization (left) and parcours (right)

interleaved mode. Figure 5.2 shows two takings from the video camera recordings at the *Montessori-Schule* during the experiments: on the left hand side the starting position of the second object localization experiment and on the right hand side the parcours experiment shortly after the beginning. In addition to the audio recordings with the close-talk microphone, the audio track of the video recordings contains the same utterances of the child under noisy and reverberated conditions. The evaluation of the effects of those conditions on the automatic classification of emotion is not part of this work, but has been investigated in [Schu 07c].

In Great Britain, only the parcours experiment was carried out. However, each child had to direct Aibo through the parcours twice: In the first run, Aibo follows the instructions of the child, in the second run, Aibo carries out its fixed, predetermined sequence of actions not taking into account what the child is saying. 30 pupils at the age of 4 to 14 of a school in Birmingham were recorded in a special multi-media studio in the *Centre for Educational Technology and Distant Learning (CETADL)* in the *Department of Electronic, Electrical and Computer Engineering (EECE)*. In addition to the Shure wireless head set a second wireless microphone, a Sennheiser ew100 range lapel microphone, clipped to the Shure head mount, in combination with a Sennheiser SK100 transmitter and EK100 receiver was used. The analog data was digitized with the external sound card Edirol UA-5 with USB interface at a sampling rate of 44.1 kHz and 16 bit quantization and stored directly on a computer hard disk. The data was downsampled to 16 kHz, too. The scene was recorded by three video cameres recording a view of the full face, a left angle and a rear angle top track view. Two video streams at a 352 x 288 resolution and a framerate of 25 fps exist; one of the full face view and one quad display stream incorporating the views of the three cameras and an informative view of the computer display.

Our experiments are Wizard-of-Oz experiments where Aibo was fully remote-controlled by the experimenter. Aibo's autonomous behavior and the integrated voice recognition function were disabled. Independently of the orders of the child, Aibo performed its actions in a fixed, predefined order (see Chapter 5.3.1 and Appendix A.1.1 and A.1.2) in order to be able to compare the behavior of the children towards Aibo. To evoke emotions, the children were put slightly under time pressure by telling them to direct Aibo as fast as possible through the parcours. At certain predefined situations in the course of the experiment, Aibo did not obey to evoke anger. The task to let Aibo dance was supposed to induce joy. In the object localization tasks, up to three feeding dishes are placed on the carpet. The child was told that one of them contains poison and that they have to make sure that Aibo does not go to this cup under any circumstances. Nevertheless, Aibo approaches exactly this cup in three of the five object localization tasks in order to elicit slight forms of fear or panic. Only in the first object localization task OL A, Aibo obeys. It was not intended to induce emotions but is meant to be some sort of "warm-up" to get acquainted with Aibo.

Although the Aibo scenario is a Wizard-of-Oz experiment, it differs from many other Wizard-of-Oz experiments in the respect that the participants did not pretend to be interested in the use of the system. For example, they did not have to book a flight although they actually did not need one. Instead, the children enjoyed very much playing with Aibo according to the impressions of the instructors and to the feedback of the children. The real purpose of the experiment, the elicitation of emotions, was not known to the children. None of the pupils realized that Aibo was remote-controlled.

## 5.2   Transliteration and Automatic Segmentation

For some emotion features, especially for linguistic features, but also for our prosodic features on the word level, the spoken sequence of words has to be known. It is obtained by a manual transliteration of the data. Besides complete words and word fragments, non-verbals like breath sounds, laughter, coughing, human and non-human noise, and vocal or nasal hesitations have been transliterated. The transliteration of the Aibo data has been revised during the subsequent emotion labeling steps. Since manual information is not available in a fully automatic system, the transliteration can be replaced by the most probable word chain obtained by an automatic speech recognition (ASR) system. The quality of the output depends on the quality of the speech recognizer, the audio quality of the data, and the correspondence between the actual test data and the data which has been used for training the ASR system. In any case, the recognized word chain will be partly erroneous with smaller or greater impacts on the subsequent emotion recognition module. As both the German and English version of the FAU Aibo Emotion Corpus are labeled on the word level, the correct wording is indispensable. The corresponding *word segmentation*, i. e. the information at which point of time a word begins and ends, respectively, is preferable for classification experiments on the word level in order to be able to calculate word level features for the correct region of the signal.

For easier handling of the German speech data, the recordings of each speaker are split into smaller audio files. The split is carried out automatically at pauses that are at least 1 s long. On the one hand, this heuristic threshold is supposed to guarantee that no split occurs during a single utterance of a child, on the other hand, it is warranted that the resulting audio files are not too long. It is assumed that the child is waiting for a reaction of the Aibo robot during the pause that follows the utterance. At this point in a conversation, the other conversational partner would take over. Hence, these units are often called *turns*. This term is adopted for the FAU Aibo Emotion Corpus. After the removal of larger pauses between turns, the German

```
BEGIN_LATTICE
  1  2  [-]        1.00     2    49 (AP (Z  - 2))
  2  3  Aibolein   1.00    50   141 (AP (Z  aI 50 b 77 o: 86 l 88 aI 102 n 135))
  3  4  [-]        1.00   142   170 (AP (Z  - 142))
  4  5  lauf       1.00   171   195 (AP (Z  l 171 aU 173 f 187))
  5  6  nach       1.00   196   222 (AP (Z  n 196 a: 205 x 213))
  6  7  rechts     1.00   223   303 (AP (Z  r 223 E 233 C 255 ts 274))
  7  8  [-]        1.00   304   304 (AP (Z  - 304))
END_LATTICE
```

Figure 5.3: Example of a word hypothesis graph for the utterance "Aibolein, lauf nach rechts!" ("Cute little Aibo, move to the right!"). A description of the WHG format is given in the text

FAU Aibo Emotion Corpus consists of 8.9 hours of speech and 48,401 words in 13,642 turns. On average, a turn is 3.5 words long. The lexicon contains 1,147 entries. A list of the most frequently used words is given in Table A.11 in Appendix A.2.8.

The segmentation is obtained by a forced time alignment of the spoken word sequence to the audio data using the ASR system that has been developed within our research group. To achieve the best segmentation results that are possible, the ASR system is trained on the FAU Aibo Emotion Corpus. A recent description of our system can be found in [Stem 05]. It is based on standard MFCC features that are calculated every 10 ms for frames that are 16 ms long (256 samples at a sampling rate of 16 kHz). Words are modeled using context dependent polyphones which are a generalization of the well-known triphones and allow larger contexts to be modeled. The size of the context depends on the frequencies with which a polyphone is observed during the training phase. The polyphones are modeled with semi-continuous hidden Markov models. The output probability density functions are Gaussian mixture models with full covariance matrices. The multi-codebook approach as described in [Hack 03] is applied: Two separate codebooks, each consisting of 250 Gaussian densities, are used for static and dynamic MFCC features. The result of the forced alignment is a *word hypothesis graph* (WHG) as shown in Figure 5.3. For each word of the spoken word sequence and for pauses between words, which are denoted as [-], the WHG contains one line with the following information: the number of the logical start node and the logical end node, the word itself, the a posteriori score of the recognizer, which is 1.0 in the case of a forced alignment, the frame number where the word begins and the frame number where it ends, and acoustic-prosodic information (AP). In our case, the acoustic-prosodic information contains the time alignment (Zuordnung, engl. *alignment*) of the phonemes, i. e. the frame number where a phoneme begins. Due to implementation issues, the frame numbering starts with 2. Details of the extendable WHG format are given in [Noth 93].

For the German Aibo data, the noisy and reverberated data of the video camera has been segmented using the segmentation information of the close-talk microphone data in order to obtain the same number of turns and turns containing the same utterances. Unfortunately, the recordings of the DAT recorder and those of the video camera are not totally synchronous. As time goes on both audio streams diverge.

Although all turns do contain the same utterances, the utterances do not necessarily start at the same frame in the audio files.

The British FAU Aibo Emotion Corpus has been transliterated manually as well. Due to the remarkably smaller size of the British version of the corpus, the audio files of each speaker are split manually into turns such that a turn contains only a single command. Again, larger pauses between the turns have been removed. Thereafter, the corpus consists of 1.3 hours of speech and 8,474 words in 5,302 turns. On average, a turn is only 1.6 words long and thus less than half as long as a turn in the German corpus. The size of the lexicon of the British version is remarkably smaller as well. With 236 entries, its size is only one fifth of the one of the German version. Due to the instructions that might have been slightly different for the British children, the British pupils regard Aibo much more as a machine than as a pet. Their speaking style is characterized primarily by short commands resulting in smaller turns and a smaller size of the vocabulary that is used. In Table A.12 in Appendix A.2.8, a list of the words that are used most frequently in the British version can be found. Whereas 'Aibo' is the word used most often by the German children, it is used rather seldom by the British pupils (rank 17).

## 5.3   Annotation

The outstanding qualities of the FAU Aibo Emotion Corpus – besides the type of the emotional data itself – are its annotations. On the German FAU Aibo Emotion Corpus and partly also on the British version, a variety of annotations and manual corrections has been carried out. Some of them are rather time-consuming and hence, quite unique for a large corpus like this one. The turns of the children have been aligned to Aibo's pre-defined behavior, the automatic segmentation and the automatically calculated values of the fundamental frequency have been manually corrected, and the data has been labeled with part-of-speech tags, syntactic and prosodic labels, and emotion categories. The emotion labels on the word level are used to assign emotion labels on higher levels such as the chunk and the turn level.

### 5.3.1   Alignment to Aibo's Behavior

Aibo's actions are pre-defined and independent of the commands of the child. The detailed description of Aibo's behavior is given in Appendix A. Table A.1 lists Aibo's actions in the parcours experiment, tables A.2, A.3, A.4, A.5, and A.6 list the plots for the five object localization tasks OL A, OL B, OL C, OL D, and OL E.

For the parcours experiment of the German FAU Aibo Emotion Corpus, the turns have been manually aligned to the plot of Aibo's actions which can be categorized into *co-operative* actions (+C), *non-cooperative* actions (-C), and *non-verbal* actions (NV). Furthermore, it is annotated when Aibo reaches certain landmarks in the parcours (POS). Figure 5.4 shows the alignment of the first turns in the parcours experiment of child Ohm_18. The child addresses Aibo, Aibo reacts by showing its greeting gesture and the child continues to ask Aibo to get up and to walk forward. At first, Aibo obeys and the child praises Aibo, but then, Aibo stops and then even starts to walk backwards. The child calls on Aibo not to walk backwards but to walk forward.

| Ohm_18_049: | Aibo steh auf komm Aibo aufstehen |
| | *Aibo get up come on Aibo get up* |
| Ohm_18_050: | ja fein aufstehen lauf mal g'radeaus ja g'radeaus |
| | *yes fine get up walk forward yes forward* |

NV: gesture 'Hi'

| Ohm_18_051: | ja g'radeaus aufstehen hopp aufstehen |
| | *yes forward get up get up* |

+C: gets up
+C: goes forward

| Ohm_18_052: | ja lauf mal *z ja lauf mal fein gut *gema |
| | *yes go on *t yes go on fine well *do* |
| Ohm_18_053: | ganz *fa |
| | *very *fi* |

-C: stops

| Ohm_18_054: | nein Aibo g'radeaus |
| | *no Aibo straight forward* |

-C: goes backwards

| Ohm_18_055: | nein auch nicht rückwärts stopp Aibolein |
| | *no not backwards either stop little Aibo* |
| Ohm_18_056: | g'radeaus |
| | *straight forward* |

Figure 5.4: Alignment of the turns to the pre-defined plot of Aibo's actions (NV: non-verbal action, C+: co-operative action, C-: non-cooperative action of Aibo); an example taken from the beginning of the parcours experiment

As Aibo's non-cooperative behavior was intended to produce anger whereas certain non-verbal actions were, for example, intended to elicit joy, the alignment allows to study the direct influence of Aibo's behavior on the emotional state of the child.

## 5.3.2 Manually Corrected Segmentation

The word segmentation obtained by a forced alignment yields acceptable results. Nevertheless, the segmentation certainly contains errors to some degree which will influence the emotion feature calculation on the word level and by that probably also the performance of the emotion classification module. So far, it is unknown how big the actual influence is. In order to find out, the segmentation of the German FAU Aibo Emotion Corpus has been manually corrected using our tool *eLabel* which has been developed especially with the purpose of processing the large number of turns in the FAU Aibo Emotion Corpus efficiently without the need to load and save the single audio and transcription files manually for each turn. The tool displays the waveform of the audio file, the transcription, and the spectrogram which is very important to identify the word boundaries. Fricatives, for example, are clearly visible in the spectrogram even if the signal energy being displayed in the waveform is close to zero (see Figure 5.5). However, identifying the exact word boundaries is not that simple as one might expect. Although a close-talk microphone is used, reverberation makes it hard to determine the end of a word. The influence of reverberation can be seen in the spectrogram of the word *g'radeaus* ('gra:|d@|?aUs, *straight forward*) in Figure 5.5.

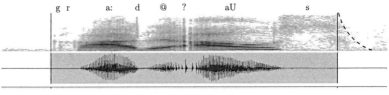

g r      a:   d   @   ?      aU            s

g'radeaus

Figure 5.5: Manual correction of the word segmentation: the word boundaries, especially at the end of a word, are not clear-cut as illustrated by the manually inserted dashed line

At the end of the word, the energy in different energy bands first diminishes in the higher frequency bands before it diminishes gradually also in the lower bands. Finally, the signal turns into noise. The tool eLabel highlights the word boundaries both in the waveform and in the spectrogram. They can be easily adjusted in steps of one frame (10 ms) using the arrow keys. The control via the keyboard facilitates an effortless operation to process a large amount of data. Screenshots of the tool eLabel can be found in Appendix C.

The correlation between the word durations of the manually corrected segmentation $l_{\mathrm{manu}}$ and the durations $l_{\mathrm{auto}}$ obtained by the forced alignment of the spoken word chain is very high (correlation value of 0.93). The two-dimensional histogram in Figure 5.6 shows the frequencies of pairs $(l_{\mathrm{manu}}, l_{\mathrm{auto}})$ on a logarithmic gray scale. The average word duration in the automatic segmentation is 36.8 frames. It is 3.4 frames longer than the average word duration in the manually corrected segmentation. This is due to the fact that the speech aligner avoids small pauses between words.

Let $t_{\mathrm{s,manu}}$ and $t_{\mathrm{e,manu}}$ be the left and the right word boundary of the manually corrected segmentation in terms of frames, and $t_{\mathrm{s,auto}}$ and $t_{\mathrm{e,auto}}$ be the ones of the forced alignment. Then, the signed segmentation error at the beginning of the word is $\Delta t_{\mathrm{s}} = t_{\mathrm{s,auto}} - t_{\mathrm{s,manu}}$, the error at the end of the word is $\Delta t_{\mathrm{e}} = t_{\mathrm{e,auto}} - t_{\mathrm{e,manu}}$. The total absolute segmentation error $\Delta t$ of the word is defined as $\Delta t = |\Delta t_{\mathrm{s}}| + |\Delta t_{\mathrm{e}}|$. The histograms in Figure 5.7 show how many words are wrongly segmented by the forced alignment in dependency of the size of the segmentation error. The left figure shows the histogram of the total segmentation error $\Delta t$, the right figure the two histograms of the segmentation errors $\Delta t_{\mathrm{s}}$ and $\Delta t_{\mathrm{e}}$ at the beginning of the word and the end, respectively. On average, a word in the forced alignment begins 1.5 frames too early and end 2.0 frames too late.

In order to have a closer look at the occurring segmentation errors, they are categorized into six groups which are illustrated in Figure 5.8. Errors of type s3 and s6 indicate that the automatically segmented word is either too short (s3) or too long (s6). Automatically segmented words that are shifted slightly to the left on the time axis, i. e. words that begin and end too early but where the automatic and the manual segmentation do overlap to some degree, are of type s2. Those words that are shifted to the right are of type s4. In the case of no overlap between the automatic and manual segmentation, the words are of type s1 or s5 depending on whether

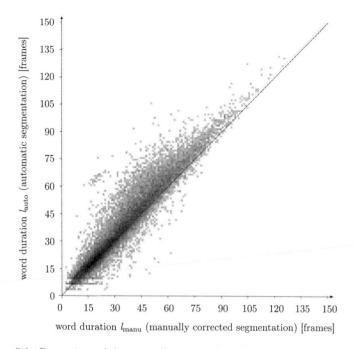

Figure 5.6: Comparison of the manually corrected word segmentation with the automatic segmentation obtained by forced alignment of the spoken word chain. The histogram frequencies are displayed on a logarithmic gray scale

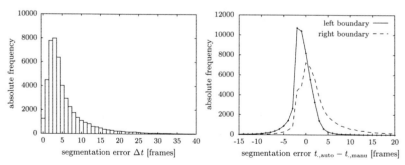

Figure 5.7: Histograms of the total segmentation error $\Delta t$ (left) and the segmentation error at the beginning $\Delta t_\mathrm{s}$ and the end $\Delta t_\mathrm{e}$ of the word (right)

the automatically segmented words appear before ($\mathfrak{s}1$) or after ($\mathfrak{s}5$) the manually segmented one. The frequencies of the different error types are given in Table 5.1. Deviations of at most three frames at both word boundaries are tolerated. Using this

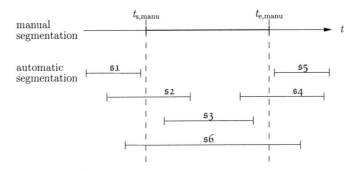

Figure 5.8: Different types of segmentation errors

| type of error | ꜱ1 | ꜱ2 | ꜱ3 | ꜱ4 | ꜱ5 | ꜱ6 | $\sum$ |
|---|---|---|---|---|---|---|---|
| frequency | 300 | 2,598 | 1,133 | 6,249 | 149 | 8,427 | 18,856 |
|  | 0.6 % | 5.4 % | 2.3 % | 12.9 % | 0.3 % | 17.4 % | 39.0 % |

Table 5.1: Frequencies of different types of segmentation errors

threshold, the segmentation of 39.0 % of all words in the corpus is incorrect. In most cases (17.4 %) the automatically segmented words are too long (error type ꜱ6) what is due to the fact that the speech aligner avoids small pauses between words. In about 1 % of the cases, the words are completely misplaced by the automatic alignment (types ꜱ1 and ꜱ5).

Due to the size of the FAU Aibo Emotion Corpus, it is impossible to manually correct the alignment of the phonemes within a single word. A forced alignment of each word providing the start and end frames has been carried out and new word hypothesis graphs have been created. Our speech recognition system is based on polyphones which are modelled with linear HMMs. In general, each HMM consists of three or four states. Polyphones with the '@' phoneme in the nucleus are the only exception. They are modeled by an HMM of only one state. In contrast to Bakis or left-right models, linear HMMs do not allow to skip certain states. Instead, each HMM state has to be entered at least once in the decoding. Thus, the minimal duration of a word is given by the total number of HMM states of the pertaining polyphones. Words like "and", for example, can only be aligned if the duration of the word is at least nine frames long. These circumstances led to the fact that a few words could not be aligned according to the manual segmentation. To solve the problem, the phoneme models in our system have been extended by parallel alternatives which consist of two or only one state. For details of our system ISADORA, please see [Schu 95]. Still it is not possible to skip whole phonemes. Figure 5.9 shows two histograms of the phoneme durations over all phonemes obtained by the forced alignment. The left histogram emerged from the original HMM models. The '@' phoneme is the only one that can be one or two frames long. Most phonemes are three frames long. Words that could not be aligned are missing. The right histogram shows the distribution of the phoneme durations obtained by a forced alignment with HMM models that can

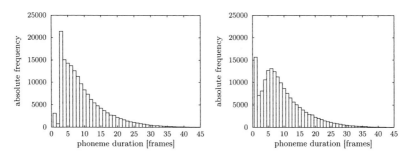

Figure 5.9: Phoneme durations obtained by forced alignment of the words using the manually corrected segmentation. Left: each phoneme is modeled by an HMM with three or four states (except the phoneme '@'). Right: additionally to the standard models, phoneme models consist of alternatives containing less states

also have only one or two states. Obviously, many phonemes are shorter than three frames if given the possibility. This is an interesting by-product as in speech recognition of read and spontaneous speech, the best recognition performance is generally achieved with models of three or four states.

### 5.3.3 Manually Corrected $F_0$

Prosodic features play a major role in emotion recognition. They model suprasegmental characteristics of the speech, amongst others the contour of the pitch within a single word or over the whole turn. The acoustic correlate of the perceived pitch is the fundamental frequency $F_0$. For a long time, much effort has been put into the development of robust $F_0$ extraction algorithms. An overview up to 2003 over various techniques is given in [Gerh 03]. So far, it is still an open question to what extent $F_0$ extraction errors influence the performance of emotion recognition systems based on state-of-the-art prosodic features. For this reason, the $F_0$ values of a certain part of the German FAU Aibo Emotion Corpus, the Aibo turn set (3,996 turns, see Chapter 5.4), have been manually corrected by a phonetician [Stei 08]. As a starting position, the $F_0$ has been calculated automatically using the freely available and well established $F_0$ algorithm of the popular *Entropic Signal Processing System* (ESPS) toolkit which is often used for benchmarking. Due to the large amount of data ($> 10^6$ frames), it is impossible to examine the $F_0$ value of each frame. The manual determination of the length of each period is totally out of the scope of what can be done with a reasonable effort. Hence, the focus is set on the manual correction of obvious errors like voiced/unvoiced errors, octave jumps, or other gross errors. Besides real errors of the pitch extraction algorithm, irregularities in the speech production exist which actually change the fundamental frequency of the signal and can be perceived as suprasegmental irritations modulated onto the pitch contour, but which are not perceived as jumps up or down [Batl 07a, Batl 93]. Since the manual correction is geared to human perception, a better term of 'correction' would be 'smoothed and adjusted to human perception'. We use the term *laryngealization* for various types of

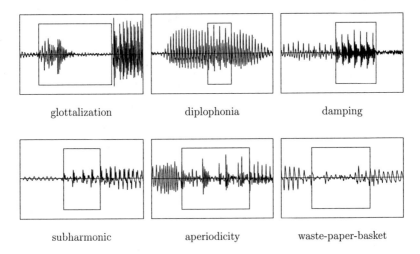

glottalization            diplophonia            damping

subharmonic            aperiodicity            waste-paper-basket

Figure 5.10: Prototypical examples of five different types of laryngealizations and the waste-paper-basket type; from [Batl 93]

irregular voiced stretches of speech. In [Batl 93], five types of laryngealizations have been established: glottalization, diplophonia, damping, subharmonic, and aperiodicity. Prototypical examples of these types are illustrated in Figure 5.10.

The manual correction mostly dealt with the following phenomena:

**(1) octave jumps:** The ESPS $F_0$ has been corrected by one octave jump up, in some rare cases also two octave jumps up, or one octave jump down. This concerns rather smooth curves which had to be transposed. In most cases, it is a matter of irregular phonation where the extraction algorithm modelled pitch rather 'close to the signal' instead of 'close to perception'. In a few cases, however, no clear sign of laryngealization can be observed. Sometimes, the context and/or the perception had to decide whether an octave jump has to be corrected or not. If the whole word is laryngealized and the impression is low pitch throughout, then laryngealization is not modulated onto pitch and the pitch was kept unchanged.

**(2) smoothing at irregularities:** The ESPS curve is not smooth but irregular due to laryngealizations or voiceless parts which ESPS wrongly classified as voiced. Here, often the $F_0$ values between the context to the left and the context to the right were interpolated in order to result in a smoothed curve. In case of voiceless parts, the $F_0$ values were set to zero.

**(3) other phenomena** like irregularities at transitions which are not necessarily due to irregular phonation: Smoothing at transitions is admittedly a bit delicate – when should it be done if the phenomenon is well known, e. g. in the case of higher $F_0$ values after voiceless consonants. Sometimes, the context and/or the perception had to decide whether an octave jump had to be corrected or not. A typical problem is a hiatus, i. e. the lack of a consonant separating two vowels in separate syllables. The perception is rather no pitch movement but 'something' modulated onto the

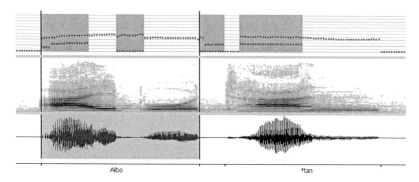

Figure 5.11: Manual $F_0$ correction for the utterance "Aibo, *tanz!" (*Aibo, *dance!*).
Word fragments are marked with a '*' in the transliteration. An explanation of the
$F_0$ values being displayed is given in the text

pitch curve. In these cases, various $F_0$ extraction errors can occur: the $F_0$ values may
be set to zero, i. e. the segment is classified as voiceless, octave jumps up or down
may occur, the $F_0$ values may be fully irregular, or values from low to higher may
occur. Here, the $F_0$ was sometimes interpolated, sometimes doubled, or sometimes
not corrected (in the case from 'low to higher'). Sometimes, clear criteria for the
one or the other solution could not be found, at least not with a reasonable effort.
In voiced-unvoiced-voiced sequences within a word, e. g. in the word "Aibo", the
plosive sometimes was set to voiceless even if voiced would have been possible – $F_0$
postprocessing sometimes interpolates in such cases anyway. In some rare cases, it
had to be "educated guessing" and was not really based on strong criteria.

Figure 5.11 shows an example with $F_0$ correction: below, the time signal, in the
middle, the spectrogram, and above, the $F_0$ values ($0-600$ Hz) per frame à 10 ms.
Manually corrected $F_0$ values are displayed with gray, filled circles. The color of the
background is set to gray if ESPS and manually corrected $F_0$ values differ. The first
part (the [a] in [aI]) of /Aibo/ is clearly laryngealized: first glottalization, then
diplophonia, and in the last irregular part, aperiodicity. The intervocalic plosive [b]
was set to voiceless (note that this is regular in south German dialects). Without
using the 'magnifying glass' to scale up the time signal, the [a] in /tanz/ does not
display clear signs of irregular phonation.

To illustrate which types of $F_0$ extraction errors occur how often, a two-dimensional
histogram of the pairs ($F_{0,\text{manu}}$, $F_{0,\text{auto}}$) is given in Figure 5.12. The frequencies of
these pairs are displayed on a logarithmic gray scale in order to make less frequent
errors visible as well. Cases where both ESPS and the human corrector decided
for voiceless, i. e. pairs $(0, 0)$, are discarded in the histogram due to their very high
frequency. The histogram shows that the $F_0$ extraction errors can be categorized
into various types of errors. They are denominated with $f1$ to $f7$ and are defined
in Table 5.2. Since only obvious errors have been corrected, the $F_0$ values of most
frames (94.3 %, see Table 5.3) have been kept unchanged resulting in the dark diag-

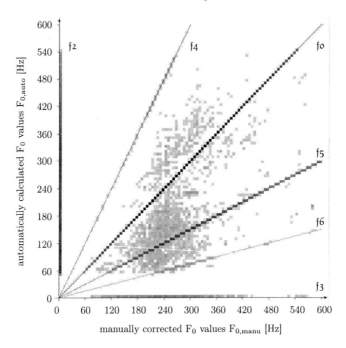

Figure 5.12: Comparison of the automatically calculated and the manually corrected $F_0$ values. The frequencies in the histogram are displayed on a logarithmic gray scale

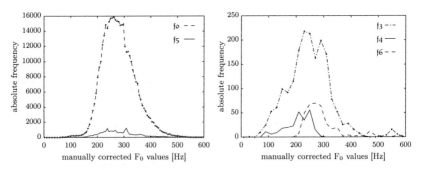

Figure 5.13: Histograms of correct $F_0$ values (ʃo) and octave errors of type ʃ5 (left) and unvoiced errors (ʃ3) and octave errors of type ʃ4 and ʃ6 (right)

onal (ʃo) in the histogram. Voiced errors (ʃ2), i.e. $F_0$ values which are considered to be voiceless by the human corrector and voiced by ESPS, result in the vertical straight line. Unvoiced errors (ʃ3), i.e. $F_0$ values which are wrongly considered to be voiceless by ESPS, yield the horizontal straight line. Three more straight lines result

| symbol | short description | long description |
|--------|-------------------|-----------------|
| ʃo | identical | $F_0$ value calculated by ESPS is not changed by the manual correction |
| ʃ1 | minor error | deviation of the ESPS $F_0$ value from the manually corrected $F_0$ value is less than 10 % |
| ʃ2 | voiced error | ESPS calculates a $F_0$ value for a frame which is considered to be unvoiced by the manual correction |
| ʃ3 | unvoiced error | a frame which is considered to be voiced by the manual correction is marked as unvoiced by ESPS |
| ʃ4 | octave error ↑ | ESPS $F_0$ value is twice the manually corrected $F_0$ value with a tolerance of 10 % |
| ʃ5 | octave error ↓ | ESPS $F_0$ value is half the manually corrected $F_0$ value with a tolerance of 10 % |
| ʃ6 | octave error ↓↓ | ESPS $F_0$ value is one fourth of the manually corrected $F_0$ value with a tolerance of 10 % |
| ʃ7 | other gross error | deviation of the ESPS $F_0$ value of more than 10 % but not one of the octave jumps mentioned above |

Table 5.2: Description of different $F_0$ error types

| type of error | | evaluation | | |
|---------------|--|------------|--|--|
| | | whole turn | | only within words |
| ʃo | identical | 1,050,450 | 94.3 % | 574,485 | 93.7 % |
| ʃ1 | minor errors | 455 | 0.0 % | 452 | 0.1 % |
| ʃ2 | voiced errors | 32,774 | 2.9 % | 8,804 | 1.4 % |
| ʃ3 | unvoiced errors | 1,884 | 0.2 % | 1,877 | 0.3 % |
| ʃ4 | octave errors ↑ | 247 | 0.0 % | 239 | 0.0 % |
| ʃ5 | octave errors ↓ | 23,718 | 2.1 % | 23,498 | 3.8 % |
| ʃ6 | octave errors ↓↓ | 375 | 0.0 % | 364 | 0.1 % |
| ʃ7 | other gross errors | 3,634 | 0.3 % | 3,559 | 0.6 % |

Table 5.3: Frequencies of the different $F_0$ error types on the Aibo turn set; evaluation on the whole turn or only within words

from one (ʃ5) or two (ʃ6) octave jumps down (one half and one fourth of the manually corrected $F_0$ value, respectively) or one octave jump up (ʃ(4), ESPS $F_0$ value is twice the manually corrected one). Hence, the angles of these lines with the horizontal line are $\arctan(\frac{1}{2}) \approx 26.6°$, $\arctan(\frac{1}{4}) \approx 14.0°$, and $\arctan(2) \approx 63.4°$, respectively. Other gross $F_0$ errors are located between these lines. One-dimensional histograms for identical $F_0$ values (ʃo) and the error types ʃ3 to ʃ6 are shown in Figure 5.13.

The frequencies of the different error types are given in Table 5.3. Numbers are given for the evaluation on the whole turns and for the evaluation only within words. As our prosodic features are word based, $F_0$ values outside words (45 % of all frames)

are irrelevant for our feature extraction. The comparison reveals that – as expected
– almost all $F_0$ errors occur within words. Only voiced errors appear mostly outside
words (73 %). Within words, octave errors of type ʃ5 (one octave jump down) make
up the largest part of the $F_0$ errors. Octave jumps up (ʃ4) are rare since in most cases,
they are prevented by the upper $F_0$ limit of the $F_0$ extraction algorithm. Only $F_0$
values below 300 Hz are candidates for octave jumps up, but deep male voices are not
included in the corpus since the male pupils are before their puberty vocal change.
The average $F_0$ values for male and female pupils is nearly the same: 281.2 Hz for male
and 280.9 Hz for female pupils. Figure A.5 in Appendix A.2.5 shows the distribution
of the manually corrected $F_0$ values on the Aibo turn set (3,996 turns) for which the
manual correction has been performed. The table also lists a few minor errors defined
as deviations of less than 10 %. As explained above, minor errors were not in the focus
of our manual correction. Anyway, state-of-the-art $F_0$ features only model the rough
contour of the fundamental frequency. Thus, minor errors are highly unlikely to
influence the emotion recognition.

Again, our tool eLabel was used to process the data set efficiently. eLabel offers
two possibilities to determine the fundamental frequency for a single frame: the first
method is to manually define periods within the frame. The program then calculates
the average frequency of these periods and assigns this value to the frame. The second
opportunity is to manually select the maximum of the auto-correlation function which
eLabel is able to plot. eLabel offers various window lengths and windowing functions.
To fix errors efficiently, eLabel offers to set the $F_0$ values for single frames or for a
selection of frames to zero (errors of type ʃ2), to double or halve the values (errors of
type ʃ4, ʃ5, and ʃ6), or to interpolate values between the selected ones. eLabel shows
both the original $F_0$ values by ESPS and the manually corrected ones. Screenshots
can be found in Appendix C.

### 5.3.4  Part-of-Speech Tags

All entries of the German Aibo lexicon, which consists of all word forms occurring in
the German FAU Aibo Emotion Corpus, are annotated manually with part-of-speech
(POS) tags. In general, a word has to be examined in its syntactic context in order
to annotate the correct POS label. Depending on its position in a sentence, one and
the same word can have different POS tags. For our purpose, we use a set of only
six coarse lexical and morphological main word classes (see [Batl 03a]) and annotate
the isolated words of the lexicon without examining their context. If in doubt, we
refer to the transliteration. In the case of near-homographs, for example, the initial
letter (upper or lower case) can tell apart noun from adjective. Nevertheless, this
approach will yield erroneous results in some cases. We believe that for our purposes
where the vocabulary is very limited the effects are neglectable. Sentences can also be
annotated by automatic POS taggers using more than six POS categories. Due to the
rather simple structure of the sentences in the FAU Aibo Emotion Corpus and to the
fact that the corpus contains spontaneous speech with sometimes non-grammatical
utterances, the use of those POS taggers with more POS classes seems not to be
beneficial.

| POS | description | frequencies | | | |
|---|---|---|---|---|---|
| | | types | | tokens | |
| NOUN | nouns, proper names, fragments of a noun or proper name | 165 | 14.4% | 8,275 | 17.0% |
| API | inflected adjectives (attributive), fragments (¬ noun) | 64 | 5.6% | 354 | 0.7% |
| APN | participles (present/past, not inflected), adjectives (not inflected) | 104 | 9.0% | 1,584 | 3.2% |
| VERB | (all other) verbs, infinitives (or 1st or 3rd person plural) | 222 | 19.4% | 13,197 | 27.3% |
| AUX | auxiliaries, copulative verbs | 50 | 4.4% | 474 | 1.0% |
| PAJ | articles, pronouns, particles (adverbs, prepositions, conjunctions), interjections | 542 | 47.2% | 24,517 | 50.7% |
| | | 1,147 | 100.0% | 48,401 | 100.0% |

Table 5.4: Description of the part-of-speech (POS) tags and their frequencies for the lexicon (types) and in the transliteration (token) of the German FAU Aibo Emotion Corpus

We use one class for nouns, proper names, and fragments of both of them (NOUN), one for inflected adjectives and word fragments excluding fragments of nouns (API), one for not inflected adjectives and not inflected present and past participles (APN), one for non-copulative verbs and infinitives including verbs in the first or third person plural (VERB), one for auxiliaries and copulative verbs (AUX), and finally one for articles, pronouns, interjections, and particles like adverbs, propositions, and conjunctions (PAJ). An overview in table form is given in Table 5.4. This table also includes the frequencies of these six POS classes within the lexicon (types) and within the German FAU Aibo Emotion Corpus (tokens). Concerning types, the most frequent POS class is PAJ (47.2%) followed by VERB (19.4%) and NOUN (14.4%). The other three classes AUX, APN, and API play only a minor role. In the case of tokens, this situation becomes even clearer: PAJ, VERB, and NOUN make up 95% of all words in the corpus.

## 5.3.5 Syntactic Labels and Splitting into Chunks

As mentioned in Chapter 5.2, the speech recordings of the children have been split automatically into smaller units – the turns – at pauses that are at least 1 s long. To be able to capture even quick changes of the emotional state within single turns, the emotional state is annotated on the word level (see Chapter 5.3.7). These labels on the word level can be mapped onto labels for larger segments like turns (see Chapter 5.3.8) without the need to relabel the whole data. Nevertheless, the optimal unit for emotion analysis is neither the word nor a long unit like a turn but is some intermediate, syntactically and semantically meaningful chunk (see [Batl 03a] for a study on appointment scheduling dialogs in a Wizard-of-Oz scenario).

| type | description | example |
|------|-------------|---------|
| s3 | boundary between two main clauses | geh ein Stückchen nach links s3 geh nach links (*turn a little bit to the left* s3 *go to the left*) |
| s2 | co-ordination of main/ subordinate clauses, boundary between main and subordinate clause | steh auf s2 und geh nach links (*get up* s2 *and go to the left*) |
| s1 | 'sentence-initial' particle or imperative "komm" | komm s1 lauf vorwärts (*come on* s1 *go forwards*) |
| p3 | boundary after/between free phrases/particles | okay p3 jetzt wieder aufstehen (*okay* p3 *now get up again*) |
| d2 | dislocation to the right or left | lauf vorwärts d2 noch weiter (*forwards* d2 *keep on going*) |
| v2 | after vocative | Aibo v2 steh auf (*Aibo* v2 *get up*) |
| v1 | before vocative | lauf weiter v1 Aibo (*keep on walking* v1 *Aibo*) |
| v2v1 | between vocatives | böser Aibo v2v1 Aibo v2 steh wieder auf (*bad Aibo* v2v1 *Aibo* v2 *get up again*) |
| eot | end-of-turn, functions the same way as s3/p3 | jetzt steh wieder auf eot dreh dich um eot (*now get up again* eot *turn around* eot) |
| f1 | no syntactic boundary at the end of the turn | lauf nach f1 (*go to* f1) |

Table 5.5: Description of the syntactic boundaries annotated for the German FAU Aibo Emotion Corpus and prototypical examples

This is especially true for our scenario where no real dialog between conversational partners exists: only the child is speaking, Aibo is only acting. Using only the speech channel, the different turns are hard to identify since a 'tidy' stimulus-response sequence cannot be observed. Aibo's action during or slightly before or after a child's utterance is not conveyed via this channel. Many pauses of varying length can be found. They are either pauses segmenting into different dialog acts (the child is waiting for Aibo's actions before he/she reacts to them) or simple hesitation pauses. Longer pauses like those that are longer than 1 s are more likely to separate different turns. Another peculiarity of the FAU Aibo Emotion Corpus is the speaking style which, besides some 'well-formed' utterances, is dominated by a mixture of short sentences and one-word commands. Neither 'integrating' prosody as in the case of reading, nor 'isolating' prosody as in the case of TV reporters can be observed. Therefore, hybrid syntactic-prosodic criteria are used for segmenting into chunks: higher syntactic boundaries always trigger chunking, lower syntactic boundaries only in combination with pauses that are at least 500 ms long. By that, vocatives that simply function as 'relators' can be distinguished from vocatives with specific illocutions like '*Hi, I'm talking to you*' or '*Now I'm, getting angry*' [Batl 09]. Since there is a rather high correlation between prosodic, syntactic, and dialog act boundaries (see [Batl 98]), chunk triggering based on prosodic boundaries alone might not result

| syntactic | pause duration | | | | | | | | $\sum$ |
|---|---|---|---|---|---|---|---|---|---|
| boundary | P1 | | P2 | | P3 | | P4 | | |
| s3 | 801 | 44.0% | 407 | 22.4% | 340 | 18.7% | 273 | 15.0% | 1,821 |
| s2 | 165 | 83.8% | 10 | 5.1% | 12 | 6.1% | 10 | 5.1% | 197 |
| s1 | 328 | 75.2% | 48 | 11.0% | 32 | 7.3% | 28 | 6.4% | 436 |
| p3 | 885 | 59.8% | 276 | 18.7% | 183 | 12.4% | 135 | 9.1% | 1,479 |
| d2 | 56 | 80.0% | 5 | 7.1% | 7 | 10.0% | 2 | 2.9% | 70 |
| v2 | 3,278 | 74.8% | 498 | 11.4% | 376 | 8.6% | 228 | 5.2% | 4,380 |
| v1 | 3,226 | 84.3% | 217 | 5.7% | 204 | 5.3% | 178 | 4.7% | 3,825 |
| v2v1 | 20 | 10.2% | 49 | 24.9% | 59 | 29.9% | 69 | 35.0% | 197 |
| eot | | | | | | | | | 13,642 |
| f1 | | | | | | | | | 17 |

Table 5.6: Frequencies of the annotated syntactic boundaries for the German FAU Aibo Emotion Corpus. P1: pause duration $l_{\text{pause}} < 250\,\text{ms}$; P2: $250\,\text{ms} \leq l_{\text{pause}} < 500\,\text{ms}$; P3: $500\,\text{ms} \leq l_{\text{pause}} < 750\,\text{ms}$; P4: $750\,\text{ms} \leq l_{\text{pause}} < 1,000\,\text{ms}$. Gray rows and columns indicate chunk triggering boundaries

in a (much) worse classification performance. From the point of view of an end-to-end processing system where some modules are based on syntactic segments whereas other modules process prosodic segments, the segmentation using both syntactic and prosodic criteria results in smaller segments but simplifies the time alignment of the prosodic and linguistic units which is in general needed at some later stage in the system.

The whole German FAU Aibo Emotion Corpus has been annotated with syntactic labels along the lines of [Batl 98]. The set of labels has been reduced and adapted to the lower linguistic variety of our data. The syntactic labels are summarized in Table 5.5 together with a brief description and examples. We annotated syntactic boundaries between two main clauses (s3), between co-ordinated main or subordinate clauses and between a main clause and a subordinate clause (s2) as well as boundaries after free phrases or particles or between a sequence of free phrases or particles (p3). Furthermore, there are labels for dislocations to the left or to the right (d2), for vocatives (post vocative v2, prae vocative v1, between two vocatives v2v1), and for the particle "komm" (*come on*) at the beginning of a sentence (s1). In our scenario, "komm" is obviously rather a particle ("komm" in the meaning of "come on") than a 'real' imperative ("komm" in the meaning of "come to me").

The label f1 signals that the end of a turn (label eot) does not correspond to a syntactic boundary. Fortunately, this happens only in a very few cases as the frequencies of the syntactic labels given in Table 5.6 indicate. The cross-tabulation in Table 5.6 reveals how long the pauses are at syntactic boundaries. The pause durations $l_{\text{pause}}$ are quantized into four categories P1 to P4 in steps of 250 ms.

The following heuristic is used to split turns into chunks: A turn is split at the syntactic boundaries s3 and p3 as the emerging chunks behave like full-fledged sentences. Furthermore, turns are split between consecutive vocatives (v2v1) since the emotional states of both vocatives can be different: 'dreh dich nach links Aibo v2v1 Aibo' (*turn to the left Aibo* v2v1 *Aibo*). The child asks Aibo to turn to the

| unit of analysis | description |
|---|---|
| words | entries of the lexicon of the speech recognizer such as<br>• single words: 'Aibo'<br>• short forms: 'ist's' instead of 'ist es'<br>• dialectal forms: 'des' instead of 'das',<br>• word fragments: '*fei' instead of 'feiner' |
| turns | the audio file of a speaker is split automatically into turns at pauses $\geq 1\,$s |
| chunks | syntactically and semantically meaningful, intermediate unit between words and turns obtained by splitting turns at manually labeled higher syntactic boundaries and at lower syntactic boundaries in combination with pauses $\geq 500\,$ms |

Table 5.7: Units of analysis: definition of words, turns, and chunks

left and as Aibo does not obey, the child calls Aibo's name again to enforce his/her command. The way of speaking changes from a neutral style at the beginning to a reprimanding or angry way at the second vocative. In addition, we split at large pauses, i. e. pauses that are at least 500 ms long (P3 and P4). The chunk triggering boundaries are highlighted in Table 5.6. The definitions of the three different levels of analysis – the word, the turn, and the chunk level – are summarized in Table 5.7.

### 5.3.6  Prosodic Labels

It can be assumed that the children change their way of speaking if they want to persuade Aibo to take orders, to reprimand Aibo if it does not obey or to reward Aibo for its obedient behavior. For this reason, prosodic peculiarities have been annotated for the German FAU Aibo Emotion Corpus by an experienced labeler. The annotations are along the same lines as the annotations for the SympaFly database [Batl 03b, Batl 04b] and for the emotional Wizard-of-Oz data in the Verbmobil project [Batl 03a]. Eleven different phenomena are annotated on the word level: strong emphasis of particular syllables, careful, hyper-clear articulation of words, unusual lengthening of syllables, insertion of extra syllables, shift of the accent position to another syllable, unusual pauses within or between words or phrases as well as extra long pauses where the child is waiting for Aibo to fulfil the given command, speech distortions due to laughter, loud speech and shouting, and vocatives that are produced in a prosodically peculiar way. The prosodic phenomena and their description are summarized in Table 5.8. More than one label can be attributed to the same word. A cross-tabulation of the prosodic peculiarities and the emotion categories, which are described in the following chapter, can be found in Chapter 5.3.9.

The frequencies of these eleven prosodic labels for the German FAU Aibo Emotion Corpus are given in Table 5.9. About 20 % of the words are annotated with one or more prosodic labels. The most frequent prosodic phenomena are *emphasis* (37.7 % of all prosodic labels), followed by *unusual lengthening of syllables* (31.4 %) and *hyper-clear articulation* (21.4 %). The other phenomena are rather rare (less than 2.5 %). In 11.6 % of the cases where a word is labeled as prosodically peculiar, more than

| prosodic label | description |
|---|---|
| CLEAR_ART | careful, very clear articulation; avoidance of contractions, deletions, etc. |
| EMPHASIS | strong emphasis on particular syllables |
| SHOUTING | shouting |
| ACC_SHIFT | shift of accent position, for instance /Aibo/ [aɪˈboː] |
| LENGTH_SYLL | unusual, pronounced lengthening of syllables |
| INS_SYLL | insertion of syllables, for instance /stop/ [ˈStoː|hOp] |
| PAUSE_LONG | very long pauses (child is waiting for Aibo to fulfil a command) |
| PAUSE_WORD | pauses between words inside syntactic/semantic units; for instance, between preposition, article, and noun |
| PAUSE_SYLL | pauses within a word, between syllables |
| LAUGHTER | speech distorted by laughter |
| VOCATIVE | prosodically peculiar vocative (only for the words *Aibo* and *Aibolein*) |

Table 5.8: Description of the prosodic labels

| prosodic label | frequency | |
|---|---|---|
| words with prosodic peculiarities | 10,341 | 21.4 % |
| words without prosodic peculiarities | 38,060 | 78.6 % |
| CLEAR_ART | 2,482 | 21.4 % |
| EMPHASIS | 4,371 | 37.7 % |
| SHOUTING | 180 | 1.6 % |
| ACC_SHIFT | 11 | 0.1 % |
| LENGTH_SYLL | 3,636 | 31.4 % |
| INS_SYLL | 85 | 0.7 % |
| PAUSE_LONG | 174 | 1.5 % |
| PAUSE_WORD | 267 | 2.3 % |
| PAUSE_SYLL | 34 | 0.3 % |
| LAUGHTER | 77 | 0.7 % |
| VOCATIVE | 273 | 2.4 % |

Table 5.9: Number of words in the German FAU Aibo Emotion Corpus that are annotated with the respective prosodic label

one prosodic label is annotated. The most frequent combinations of prosodic labels are *emphasis* combined with *unusual lengthening of syllables* (536 cases), *emphasis* combined with *hyper-clear articulation* (218 cases), and a combination of *unusual lengthening of syllables* and *hyper-clear articulation* (110 cases). Other combinations are clearly less frequent: *unusual lengthening of syllables* and *vocative* (39 cases), *emphasis* and *pauses between words* (31 cases), *unusual lengthening of syllables* and *shouting* (30 cases), *hyper-clear articulation* and *pauses between words* (28 cases), etc.

## 5.3.7   Emotion Labels for Words

While playing with the Sony robot Aibo, the emotion-related user state of the children changes over time. This is expressed in changes of the voice and the speech of the children. As we are only interested in the vocal changes and not in the underlying emotional state itself, it does not matter whether the child actually is emotional or only deliberately changes its voice to make Aibo react in a certain way. The labeling is based on the speech of the children only. Neither antecedent conditions like Aibo's behavior, nor body movements and gestures, or facial expressions of the children in the case of the British FAU Aibo Emotion Corpus, have been used for the purpose of labeling since this information will not be available to the automatic classification system either in our experiments.

For the German FAU Aibo Emotion Corpus, five human labelers (advanced students of linguistics) have been employed who listened to the utterances of each child in sequential (not randomized) order and labeled independently from each other each word using category labels. The labelers had to decide for exactly one of the given categories. The context information has an effect on the decision a labeler makes [Caul 00]. By giving the opportunity to listen to the whole turn, the surrounding context within one turn was made available. Furthermore, the preceding turns are known to the labelers. Although the approach to label emotions on the word level is unique and very time-consuming, we opted for it as the emotion-related user states can change rather quickly, even within single turns. That way, the problem that turns are labeled as a whole with only one category but in fact do contain more than one emotion-related user state is avoided. However, this approach does not exclude the opportunity to merge words of the same category to larger units or to map emotion labels on the word level onto labels for fixed units of larger size like, for example, whole turns.

The categories that have been utilized have been obtained in advance by inspection of the data. Besides *neutral*, which is the default user state, the following ten other categories are used: *angry, touchy/irritated, joyful, surprised, bored, helpless, motherese, reprimanding, emphatic*, and a category *other* for all remaining phenomena which are rare and not covered by the other classes. Whereas the first five categories describe emotional states in a narrower sense of emotion, the latter describe typical user states (e. g. helpless) and behavioral patterns (motherese, reprimanding) in this scenario which are not emotions proper but emotion-related. The categories are listed and described in Table 5.10. Certainly, these categories do not represent emotions of children in general, but we claim that they are adequate for modeling the behavior of the children in this specific scenario.

The state *emphatic* has to be commented on especially (see [Batl 05a]): As already mentioned in Chapter 3.1, any marked deviation from a neutral speaking style can (but need not) be taken as a possible indication of some (starting) trouble in communication [Batl 03a]. If a user gets the impression that the machine does not understand him, he will try different strategies like the use of repetitions, re-formulations, other wordings, or simply a pronounced, marked speaking style. Such a speaking style does not necessarily mean that the state of the user is not neutral anymore but the probability that the user state will be changing soon is significantly higher. Of course, this speaking style can also be caused by other circumstances. It can be due to

| user state | description |
|---|---|
| joyful (J) | the child enjoys Aibo's action and/or notices that something is funny |
| surprised (S) | the child is (positively) surprised, because obviously she/he did not expect Aibo to react that way |
| motherese (M) | the child addresses Aibo in the way mothers/parents address their babies (also called 'infant-directed speech') – either because Aibo is well-behaving or because the child wants Aibo to obey; this is the positive equivalent to *reprimanding* |
| neutral (N) | default user state, not belonging to any other category; not labeled explicitly |
| other (O) | not neutral but not belonging to any of the other categories, i.e. some other spurious emotions |
| bored (B) | the child is (momentarily) not interested in the interaction with Aibo |
| emphatic (E) | the child speaks in a pronounced, accentuated, sometimes hyper-articulated way but without showing any emotion |
| helpless (H) | the child hesitates, seems not to know what to tell Aibo next; can be marked by disfluencies and/or filled pauses |
| touchy (T) (irritated) | the child is slightly irritated; pre-stage of anger |
| reprimanding (R) | the child is reproachful, reprimanding, 'wags the finger'; this is the negative equivalent of *motherese* |
| angry (A) | the child is clearly angry, annoyed, speaks in a loud voice |

Table 5.10: Category labels describing the emotion-related user states of the children in the FAU Aibo Emotion Corpus; ordered from positive to negative valence

user idiosyncrasy or caused by the conversation with a computer ('computer talk'), a child, a non-native person, or an elderly person who is hard of hearing. Besides modeling emphasis as an indication of arising problems in communication, there are two other – practical – arguments for the annotation of *emphatic*: Firstly, it is to a large extent a prosodic phenomenon and thus, it can be modeled and classified with prosodic features. Secondly, if the labelers are allowed to label *emphatic*, it might be less likely that they confuse it with other user states.

For the German FAU Aibo Emotion Corpus, Table 5.11 lists the frequencies of the eleven user states separately for each of the five labelers. As expected, the predominant portion of these raw labels is *neutral* (71 % on average over all labelers). It is followed by *emphatic* with only 17 % on average. *Motherese* is with 4.3 % of all raw labels on third place, followed by *reprimanding* with 2.4 %. Only in a few cases, the children got (slightly) angry or were joyful (both 0.6 %). The other states occurred even less frequently.

Not only the differences between the categories but also the differences between the labelers are high. Labeler No. 1 and No. 5 labeled about 90 % of the words as neutral, labeler No. 2 only 35 %. On the other hand, labeler No. 2 is the one with the

| user state | labeler | | | | | total frequency | |
|---|---|---|---|---|---|---|---|
| | No. 1 | No. 2 | No. 3 | No. 4 | No. 5 | abs. | rel. |
| neutral (N) | 43,417 | 17,173 | 30,908 | 36,857 | 44,220 | 172,575 | 71.3 % |
| emphatic (E) | 2,279 | 22,916 | 10,792 | 3,594 | 361 | 39,942 | 16.5 % |
| motherese (M) | 767 | 3,560 | 2,297 | 2,241 | 1,548 | 10,413 | 4.3 % |
| touchy (T) | 244 | 1,962 | 3,130 | 780 | 1,300 | 7,416 | 3.1 % |
| reprimanding (R) | 1,049 | 1,396 | 152 | 2,611 | 716 | 5,924 | 2.4 % |
| angry (A) | 210 | 413 | 189 | 740 | 42 | 1,594 | 0.6 % |
| joyful (J) | 259 | 679 | 171 | 289 | 89 | 1,487 | 0.6 % |
| bored (B) | 111 | 134 | 223 | 593 | 92 | 1,153 | 0.5 % |
| hesitant (H) | 4 | 162 | 217 | 480 | 17 | 880 | 0.4 % |
| other (O) | 60 | 5 | 292 | 213 | 14 | 584 | 0.2 % |
| surprised (S) | 1 | 1 | 30 | 3 | 2 | 37 | 0.0 % |

Table 5.11: Distribution of the eleven user states for each single labeler for the whole German FAU Aibo Emotion Corpus (48,401 words) ordered by the total frequency of the user states

highest proportion of *emphatic* (47 %). In contrast, labeler No. 5 decided for *emphatic* in less than 1 %. For the other categories, the situation is similar.

Although the inter-labeler agreement seems to be bad, it would be wrong to blame the labelers or the system of category labels that has been used, nor is the data 'bad'. It just shows that the addressed problem is a very complicated one – not only for machines but also for human beings. It might be well possible to use the decisions of only one labeler to train a machine classifier. The machine would then try to decide exactly the same way this single human does. If the information of more labelers is available, one can only gain, either by training the classifier so that it decides as the majority of the labelers does or by focusing on more prototypical examples by selecting samples of high agreement. There are reasons why the inter-labeler agreement is that low: Labeling with categories forces the labeler to choose exactly one category. This decision has to be made independently of the intensity of the emotional state. In the case of the FAU Aibo Emotion Corpus, the emotional or emotion-related states that can be observed are rather weak compared to the full-blown emotions one might be used to from emotion portrayals. Hence, the choice of one category is much more difficult and the emotional/emotion-related states are much more likely to be confused with neutral. The problem is even aggravated by the fact that humans have their individual thresholds up to which they rate the state of another person as (still) neutral and above which they consider the state as (already) emotional. In a similar way, it is hard to tell the exact transition from a neutral to a marked, pronounced speaking style. It gets even harder if this speaking style does not indicate a change in the user state but is just the speaking style the child uses all the time to talk to Aibo. Nevertheless, this is the data one gets from a realistic scenario and humans can perceive little changes in the states of a person, although these changes are not always perceived in the same way by different humans. If one wants to employ machines for emotion recognition in real scenarios, one has to address these problems.

| user state | labeler | | | total frequency | |
|---|---|---|---|---|---|
|  | No. 1 | No. 4 | No. 5 | abs. | rel. |
| neutral (N) | 6,874 | 5,299 | 8,198 | 20,371 | 80.1 % |
| emphatic (E) | 991 | 1,906 | 49 | 2,946 | 11.6 % |
| reprimanding (R) | 351 | 714 | 41 | 1,106 | 4.4 % |
| motherese (M) | 82 | 141 | 66 | 289 | 1.1 % |
| hesitant (H) | 31 | 104 | 21 | 156 | 0.6 % |
| angry (A) | 89 | 58 | 3 | 150 | 0.6 % |
| bored (B) | 5 | 120 | 13 | 138 | 0.5 % |
| touchy (T) | 32 | 37 | 53 | 122 | 0.5 % |
| joyful (J) | 17 | 31 | 13 | 61 | 0.2 % |
| other (O) | 2 | 64 | 17 | 83 | 0.3 % |
| surprised (S) | 0 | 0 | 0 | 0 | 0.0 % |

Table 5.12: Distribution of the eleven user states for each single labeler for the whole British FAU Aibo Emotion Corpus (8,474 words) ordered by the total frequency of the user states

The British FAU Aibo Emotion Corpus has been labeled by only three of the five labelers who have labeled the German version. The same set of categories has been used. In Table 5.12, the frequencies of the emotion labels are given for each labeler. Again, there is a similar picture: The frequencies of the states differ to some degree and the order of the most frequent states has changed a bit: *neutral* outweighs by far the other states (80 % of all raw labels). *Emphatic* is on second place (11.6 %), followed by *reprimanding* (4.4 %) and *motherese* (only 1.1 %).

If more than one labeler is available, it is common to combine the single decisions of the participating labelers by taking the majority vote as reference label. The majority vote represents the decision of the average labeler and is more robust against 'outliers' of single labelers. The numbers are given in Table 5.13 and Table 5.14 for the German and the British FAU Aibo Emotion Corpus, respectively. The tables also contain information about how many labelers agree on the majority label. If four out of five labelers agree, the agreement is 0.8. For the German FAU Aibo Emotion Corpus, this is the case in 40.9 % of the words where the majority vote is *neutral*. The majority does not have to be an absolute majority, i. e. an agreement of two out of five labelers is possible (e. g. A, E, A, N, R). There are also cases where no clear majority exists because the same two categories occur twice (e. g. A, T, T, E, A) or in rare cases, five different categories were chosen. These cases are denoted with '–' in the tables.

In order to be able to train a machine classifier, each of the classes which are to be separated by the machine has to be observed with a reasonably high frequency in the training data. This practical reason necessitates the mapping of the rare categories *bored*, *hesitant*, and *surprised* onto the category *Other*. Furthermore, the three categories *reprimanding*, *touchy*, and *angry* are mapped onto *Anger*. These categories are frequently confused what justifies this mapping to some degree but it must be very clear that this new class is a cover class subsuming not only different types of anger but also other emotion-related states, namely touchy/irritated and

| user state | frequency | | agreement of the five labelers | | | |
|---|---|---|---|---|---|---|
| | | | 0.4 | 0.6 | 0.8 | 1.0 |
| neutral (N) | 39,975 | 82.6 % | 2.0 % | 26.1 % | 40.3 % | 31.6 % |
| emphatic (E) | 2,807 | 5.8 % | 9.9 % | 68.1 % | 19.6 % | 2.4 % |
| motherese (M) | 1,311 | 2.7 % | 3.9 % | 56.1 % | 38.8 % | 1.2 % |
| reprimanding (R) | 463 | 1.0 % | 33.0 % | 51.8 % | 11.4 % | 3.7 % |
| touchy (T) | 419 | 0.9 % | 46.3 % | 48.4 % | 5.0 % | 0.2 % |
| angry (A) | 134 | 0.3 % | 37.3 % | 53.7 % | 9.0 % | 0.0 % |
| joyful (J) | 109 | 0.2 % | 7.3 % | 74.3 % | 18.3 % | 0.0 % |
| bored (B) | 16 | 0.0 % | 31.3 % | 50.0 % | 18.8 % | 0.0 % |
| other (O) | 10 | 0.0 % | 70.0 % | 30.0 % | 0.0 % | 0.0 % |
| hesitant (H) | 4 | 0.0 % | 25.0 % | 75.0 % | 0.0 % | 0.0 % |
| surprised (S) | 0 | 0.0 % | | | | |
| – | 3,153 | 6.5 % | | | | |
| all | 48,401 | 100.0 % | 9.6 % | 28.2 % | 35.7 % | 26.3 % |

Table 5.13: Distribution of the user state labels according to the majority voting of the five labelers in the whole German FAU Aibo Emotion Corpus ordered by the frequency of the user state

| user state | frequency | | agreement of the three labelers | |
|---|---|---|---|---|
| | | | 0.66 | 1.0 |
| neutral (N) | 7,171 | 84.6 % | 32.1 % | 67.9 % |
| emphatic (E) | 631 | 7.4 % | 97.1 % | 2.9 % |
| reprimanding (R) | 127 | 1.5 % | 93.7 % | 6.3 % |
| motherese (M) | 55 | 0.6 % | 70.9 % | 29.1 % |
| angry (A) | 23 | 0.3 % | 95.7 % | 4.3 % |
| hesitant (H) | 20 | 0.2 % | 95.0 % | 5.0 % |
| joyful (J) | 11 | 0.1 % | 72.7 % | 27.3 % |
| touchy (T) | 7 | 0.1 % | 85.7 % | 14.3 % |
| bored (B) | 0 | 0.0 % | | |
| other (O) | 0 | 0.0 % | | |
| surprised (S) | 0 | 0.0 % | | |
| – | 429 | 5.1 % | | |
| all | 8,474 | 100.0 % | 36.9 % | 58.0 % |

Table 5.14: Distribution of the user state labels according to the majority voting of the three labelers in the whole British FAU Aibo Emotion Corpus ordered by the frequency of the user state

reprimanding. The mapping onto cover classes is summarized in Table 5.15. The abbreviations of the six cover classes are given in bold face to distinguish them from the original emotion-related user state categories.

The frequencies of the majority vote for the cover classes are given in Table 5.16 and Table 5.17 for the German and the British FAU Aibo Emotion Corpus, respectively. The labels are mapped before the majority voting, resulting in 1,718 words

| user state label | cover class |
|---|---|
| angry (A)<br>touchy (T)<br>reprimanding (R) | **Anger** |
| emphatic (E) | **Emphatic** |
| neutral (N) | **Neutral** |
| motherese (M) | **Motherese** |
| joyful (J) | **Joyful** |
| bored (B)<br>hesitant (H)<br>surprised (S)<br>other (O) | **Other** |

Table 5.15: Mapping of the eleven user state labels onto six cover classes (given in bold face)

| cover class | frequency | | agreement of the five labelers | | | |
|---|---|---|---|---|---|---|
| | | | 0.4 | 0.6 | 0.8 | 1.0 |
| Neutral | 39,408 | 81.4 % | 0.6 % | 26.4 % | 40.9 % | 32.1 % |
| Emphatic | 2,605 | 5.4 % | 3.0 % | 73.4 % | 21.1 % | 2.6 % |
| Anger | 1,718 | 3.5 % | 4.2 % | 57.1 % | 27.5 % | 11.1 % |
| Motherese | 1,300 | 2.7 % | 3.1 % | 56.5 % | 39.2 % | 1.2 % |
| Joyful | 107 | 0.2 % | 5.6 % | 75.7 % | 18.7 % | 0.0 % |
| Other | 45 | 0.1 % | 33.3 % | 53.3 % | 8.9 % | 4.4 % |
| – | 3,218 | 6.6 % | | | | |
| all | 48,401 | 100.0 % | 7.6 % | 29.2 % | 36.5 % | 26.7 % |

Table 5.16: Distribution of the six cover classes according to the majority voting of the five labelers in the whole German FAU Aibo Emotion Corpus ordered by the frequency of the cover classes

of the cover class *Anger* for the German FAU Aibo Emotion Corpus. This number is much more than the sum (1,016) of the original labels *angry* (134), *reprimanding* (463), and *touchy* (419) given in Table 5.13. It has been mentioned before that the speaking style of the British children is characterized primarily by short commands as they are typical for controlling machines whereas the German pupils often address Aibo more like a real dog. The proportion of *Motherese* in the British corpus (0.6 %) is clearly lower as for the German corpus (2.7 %); only 55 cases of *Motherese* can be observed in the British data. Thus, only the three cover classes *Anger*, *Emphasis*, and *Neutral* occur frequently enough to be used for classification experiments. Hence, classification experiments are carried out only on the German FAU Aibo Emotion Corpus. The analysis of the confusions of the human labers (see Chapter 5.5) suggest that there are no principal differences between the German and the British emotion-related states.

|              |           |         | agreement of the three labelers | |
| cover class  | frequency | | 0.66    | 1.0     |
|--------------|-----------|---------|---------|---------|
| Neutral      | 7,171     | 84.6 %  | 32.1 %  | 67.9 %  |
| Emphatic     | 631       | 7.4 %   | 97.1 %  | 2.9 %   |
| Anger        | 214       | 2.5 %   | 86.9 %  | 13.1 %  |
| Motherese    | 55        | 0.6 %   | 70.9 %  | 29.1 %  |
| Joyful       | 11        | 0.1 %   | 72.7 %  | 27.3 %  |
| Other        | 30        | 0.4 %   | 80.0 %  | 20.0 %  |
| –            | 362       | 4.3 %   |         |         |
| all          | 8,474     | 100.0 % | 37.4 %  | 58.3 %  |

Table 5.17: Distribution of the six cover classes according to the majority voting of the three labelers in the whole British FAU Aibo Emotion Corpus ordered by the frequency of the cover classes

## 5.3.8   Emotion Labels for Larger Units

If the emotion labels are annotated on the word level, they can be used to determine an emotion label for larger units like turns (see Chapter 5.2) or chunks (see Chapter 5.3.5).

It turned out that a simple majority vote on the raw labels (the decisions of the single labelers for each word in the turn or chunk) does not necessarily yield a meaningful label for the whole sequence. A whole turn which, for example, consists of two main clauses – one clause which is labeled as *Neutral* and one slightly shorter clause which is labeled as *Anger* by the majority – would be labeled as *Neutral*. A chunk consisting of five words, two of them clearly labeled as *Motherese*, three of them being *Neutral*, can be reasonably labeled as *Motherese* although the majority of raw labels yields a different result. Thus, the mapping of labels from the word level onto higher units is not that clear as one might expect. A more practical problem of a simple majority vote is that the sparse data problem, which already exists on the word level, is even aggravated on higher levels since the dominating choice of the label *neutral* on the word level yields an even higher proportion of *neutral* chunks and turns.

The structogram in Figure 5.14 illustrates the heuristic algorithm used for mapping emotion labels from the word level to the turn and the chunk level. The algorithm uses the raw labels on the word level mapped onto the cover classes *Neutral*, *Emphatic*, *Anger*, and *Motherese* (see Table 5.15). Because of their low frequency, labels of the remaining two cover classes *Joyful* and *Other* are ignored. Let $h(\cdot)$ be the number of raw labels for the respective cover class, $s.$ denotes the sum of the raw labels for the cover classes given in the index. The resultant chunk label is stored in the variable $l$.

If the proportion of raw labels for *Neutral* is above a threshold $\theta_N$, the whole unit is considered to be *Neutral*. This threshold depends on the length of the unit; it has to be higher for turns than for chunks. For turns, it has been set to 70 %, for chunks to 60 %.

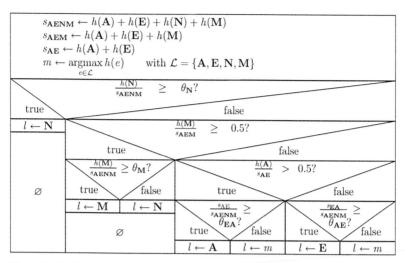

Figure 5.14: Mapping of the cover classes on the word level onto the chunk level ($\theta_{\mathbf{N}} = 0.6$, $\theta_{\mathbf{M}} = 0.4$, $\theta_{\mathbf{AE}} = 0.5$) and the turn level ($\theta_{\mathbf{N}} = 0.7$, $\theta_{\mathbf{M}} = 0.0$, $\theta_{\mathbf{AE}} = 0.0$)

If this threshold is not reached, the frequency of the raw labels *Motherese* is compared to the sum of the frequencies of *Emphatic* and *Anger* which are pooled since *emphatic* is considered as a possible pre-stage of *anger*. If *Motherese* prevails, the turn or the chunk is labeled as *Motherese*, provided that the relative frequency of *Motherese* w. r. t. the other three cover classes is above a certain threshold $\theta_{\mathbf{M}}$. If not, the whole unit is considered to be *Neutral*.

If *Motherese* does not prevail, the frequency of *Emphatic* is compared to the one of *Anger*. The label of the whole unit is the one of the prevailing class, again provided that the relative frequency of this class w. r. t. the other three cover classes is above a threshold $\theta_{\mathbf{EA}}$. For the mapping onto the chunk level, $\theta_{\mathbf{M}}$ is set to 40 % and $\theta_{\mathbf{EA}}$ to 50 %. These thresholds are set heuristically by checking the results of the algorithm for a random subset of chunks. On the turn level, a more simple algorithm has been used where both thresholds are set to zero. If the frequencies of the raw labels of *Anger* and *Emphatic* are equal, *Anger* wins on the turn level.

## 5.3.9 Cross-tabulation of POS/Prosodic Labels and Emotion Categories

Part-of-speech tags (POS, Chapter 5.3.4) can only be used successfully for emotion recognition if the distributions of the POS tags differ significantly for different emotion categories. The cross-tabulation in Table A.9 in Appendix A.2.6 contrasts the six POS classes NOUN, API, APN, VERB, AUX, and PAJ with the emotion cover classes *Anger*, *Emphatic*, *Neutral*, and *Motherese*. To be complete, the rare cover classes *Joyful* and *Other* are included, as well as those cases where the majority vote of

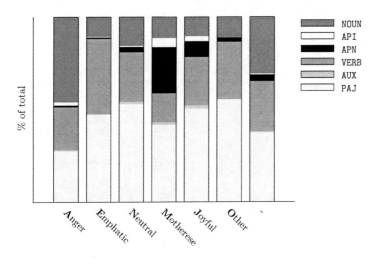

Figure 5.15: Distribution of the part-of-speech tags for different emotion categories

the five labelers is ambiguous (–). POS tags and emotion cover classes on the word level are contrasted for the whole German FAU Aibo Emotion Corpus. The POS distributions for the different emotion cover classes are depicted in Figure 5.15. Clear differences between these distributions can be observed illustrating the high impact of the rather coarse taxonomy of part-of-speech tags. *Emphatic* is characterized mainly by a high proportion of verbs (VERB) and particles (PAJ), but a low proportion of nouns (NOUN). Almost no adjectives (API, APN) are used. In this state, the children use short commands such as "Geh (VERB) nach (PAJ) links (PAJ)!" (*Go to the left!*) or "Setz (VERB) dich (PAJ) wieder (PAJ) hin (PAJ)!" (*Sit down again!*). *Anger* displays the largest proportion of nouns. As in the state *Emphatic*, the children use many short commands characterized by verbs and particles, but they reinforce their commands very often by addressing Aibo by its name (*Aibo, sit down!*) leading to the high proportion of nouns. Adjectives are used rarely; the most widely used adjective is 'böser' (*bad*). In contrast, *Motherese* (*good boy*) is characterized by a remarkably high proportion of adjectives (API, APN). In this state, the children praise Aibo for its obedient behavior using adjectives such as 'fein', 'brav', and 'gut' (all synonyms for *good*). Figure A.6 in Appendix A.2.6 depicts the same cross-tabulation from a different point of view: it shows the distributions of the emotion cover classes for different POS tags. If an adjective (APN, API) is observed, the most probable emotion cover class the observed word belongs to is still *Neutral* due to its high a priori probability in the whole corpus, although *Motherese* is characterized by the highest proportion of adjectives.

Along the same lines, a cross-tabulation for prosodic labels and emotion cover classes is given in Table A.10 in Appendix A.2.7. The eleven prosodic phenomena defined in Table 5.8 are contrasted with the emotion cover classes. As a single word

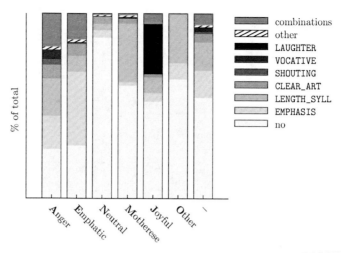

Figure 5.16: Distribution of the prosodic labels for different emotion categories

can be annotated with more than one prosodic label, the occurrence of exactly one
prosodic peculiarity and combinations of prosodic labels are distinguished. Again,
clear differences between the distributions of the prosodic labels can be observed.
As to be expected, most of the words belonging to *Neutral* (86.9 %) are not annotated with any prosodic label. Nevertheless, strong emphasis on particular syllables (EMPHASIS, 4.1 %), unusual, pronounced lengthening of syllables (LENGTH_SYLL,
3.3 %), and careful, very clear articulation (CLEAR_ART, 4.0 %), or combinations of
them (0.6 %) can be observed to some degree for *Neutral* words, too. The proportion of words that are annotated with at least one prosodic label increases from
*Neutral* (13.1 %), to *Motherese* (39.1 %) and *Joyful* (47.7 %), and finally to *Emphatic*
(71.5 %) and *Anger* (73.5 %). Hence, a large proportion of the words belonging to
*Emphatic* and *Anger* are marked prosodically. *Emphatic* is mainly characterized by
its high proportion of EMPHASIS (40.0 %). To some degree, unusual lengthening of
syllables (LENGTH_SYLL, 8.6 %) and very clear articulation (CLEAR_ART, 6.4 %) can be
observed. Frequently, combinations of prosodic labels (14.1 %) are annotated. The
highest proportion of such combinations is annotated for *Anger* (18.0 %). *Anger*
is characterized by the occurrence of many different prosodic peculiarities such as
EMPHASIS (18.0 %), LENGTH_SYLL (20.2 %), CLEAR_ART (7.5 %), prosodically peculiar
vocatives (VOCATIVE, 5.2 %) and shouting (SHOUTING, 2.9 %). Hence, states with a
higher emotional intensity are characterized by a larger number of different prosodic
peculiarities as well as a larger number of combinations. *Motherese* is primarily characterized by its high proportion of LENGTH_SYLL (31.8 %). Frequently, the words 'ja',
'fein', 'feiner', 'brav', 'braver', 'gut', 'ganz', and 'so' are lengthened (a translation of
the words is given in Table A.11). Other prosodic labels or combinations are rare.
*Joyful* is mainly characterized by the large proportion of words that are distorted
by laughter (LAUGHTER, 27.1 %). The distributions of the emotion cover classes for

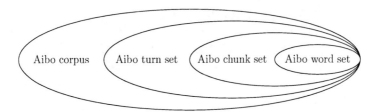

Figure 5.17: Data sets of the German FAU Aibo Emotion Corpus used in the experiments

| data set | number of words | taken from | |
|---|---|---|---|
| | | # chunks | # turns |
| Aibo corpus | 48,401 | 18,216 | 13,642 |
| Aibo word set | 6,070 | 4,543 | 3,996 |
| Aibo chunk set | 13,217 | 4,543 | 3,996 |
| Aibo turn set | 17,618 | 6,413 | 3,996 |

Table 5.18: Data sets of the German FAU Aibo Emotion Corpus used in the experiments

different prosodic labels are depicted in Figure A.7 in Appendix A.2.7. The figure shows, for example, that if a word distorted by laughter is observed, it belongs to *Joyful* in 46.0 % of the cases, but in 41.3 % of the cases, it is labeled as *Neutral*.

## 5.4   Data Selection

The experiments described in this thesis (see Chapter 7) are conducted on the German FAU Aibo Emotion Corpus. *Neutral* outweighs the other cover classes by far. In order to train a machine classifier, the classes in the training set should be roughly balanced. This holds especially for artificial neural networks. A balanced training set can be achieved either by upsampling the samples of less frequent classes or by downsampling the samples of frequent classes. If the data is upsampled, the size of the training set is drastically enlarged – 81.4 % of the data is *Neutral* – resulting in a massively delayed training process. However, no new information about less frequent classes is obtained as the samples are only copied. In contrast, if the samples of frequent classes are downsampled, the training set is kept compact, but some information that is available for frequent classes is not used. We decided for the latter approach.

For classification experiments on the word level, the *Aibo word set* is defined. It is a subset of 6,070 words of the original 48,401 words. The words in this subset are labeled as belonging to one of the four cover classes *Motherese*, *Neutral*, *Emphatic*, and *Anger*. Words belonging to any of the two other cover classes *Joyful* and *Other* are omitted due to their low frequency. Only words have been selected where all five labelers decided for one of the four cover classes and at least three of them agreed. This resulted in 1,223 words labeled by the majority as *Motherese* and 1,557 words labeled as *Anger*. Both *Emphatic* and *Neutral* are downsampled to 1,645 words

| cover class | frequency | | | | | |
|---|---|---|---|---|---|---|
| | Aibo turn set | | Aibo chunk set | | Aibo word set | |
| Anger | 868 | 21.7% | 914 | 20.1% | 1,557 | 25.7% |
| Emphatic | 1,349 | 33.8% | 1,045 | 23.0% | 1,645 | 27.1% |
| Neutral | 1,282 | 32.1% | 1,998 | 44.0% | 1,645 | 27.1% |
| Motherese | 497 | 12.4% | 586 | 12.9% | 1,223 | 20.1% |
| all | 3,996 | 100.0% | 4,543 | 100.0% | 6,070 | 100.0% |

Table 5.19: Distribution of the labels on the turn level (Aibo turn set), on the chunk level (Aibo chunk set), and on the word level (Aibo word set)

| | 1 | 2 | 3 | 4 | 5 |
|---|---|---|---|---|---|
| 1 | 1.0 | 0.49 | 0.52 | 0.52 | 0.42 |
| 2 | | 1.0 | 0.78 | 0.76 | 0.46 |
| 3 | | | 1.0 | 0.78 | 0.53 |
| 4 | | | | 1.0 | 0.58 |
| 5 | | | | | 1.0 |

Table 5.20: Weighted kappa values for pairs of labelers on the Aibo word set

each by randomly picking samples of the respective class. It is important to mention that in doing so the distribution of the agreement of the five labelers is preserved, i. e. the selection did not favor prototypical samples where all five labelers agreed. Although this would make the automatic classification easier and result in a higher recognition performance, it would be a further deviation of the circumstances in a real application.

For experiments on larger units, two more data sets are defined: the *Aibo chunk set* and the *Aibo turn set*. The *Aibo chunk set* contains those chunks which consist of at least one word of the *Aibo word set* resulting in 4,543 chunks and 13,217 words in total. Along the same lines, the *Aibo turn set* is defined as the set of those turns which contain at least one word of the *Aibo word set* resulting in 3,996 turns containing 17,618 words in total. The 3,996 turns are split into 6,413 different chunks. As illustrated in Figure 5.17, the *Aibo word set* is a subset of the *Aibo chunk set* which itself is a subset of the *Aibo turn set*. The three different subsets are summarized w. r. t. the number of words, chunks, and turns once more in Table 5.18. In Table 5.19, the distribution of the four emotion cover classes *Anger*, *Emphatic*, *Neutral*, and *Motherese* is given for the word, the chunk, and the turn level. The mapping of the labels from the word level onto chunk and turn level labels (Chapter 5.3.8) results in a less balanced distribution of the four cover classes on the chunk and turn level.

In Table 5.20, weighted kappa values (see Chapter 3.5.2) are given for the *Aibo word set*. In order to use a weight function, the categories have to be arranged on a linear scale such that the distances can be interpreted meaningfully as dissimilarities. The function defined in Equation 3.8 based on the squared differences is used. As *Anger* and *Motherese* are quite opposite, 1 is assigned to the former and 4 to the latter. *Neutral* is arranged between them and assigned the number 3. *Emphatic* as some sort of pre-stage of *Anger* is arranged between *Neutral* and *Anger* and given the number 2. The numbers in Table 5.20 show that labelers 2, 3, and 4 agree very

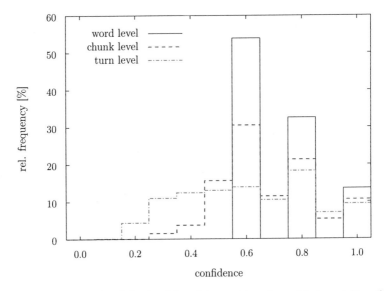

Figure 5.18:  Histogram of the 'confidence' (proportion of raw labels matching the label for the whole unit) of the labels on the word level (Aibo word set), on the chunk level (Aibo chunk set), and on the turn level (Aibo turn set)

well. For these three labelers, the weighted kappa value is 0.77 compared to 0.56 for all five labelers. For the majority vote, it is sufficient if only three of them agree.

To assess the quality of single labels on the different levels, the proportion of raw labels, i. e. the original decisions of the five labelers on the word level, matching the label for the whole unit is computed. Figure 5.18 shows histograms of this 'confidence' measure for the word, the chunk, and the turn level. The confidence is evaluated on the Aibo word set, Aibo chunk set, and Aibo turn set, respectively. The highest confidence values are obtained on the word level. The distribution of the confidence values shifts to lower values from the word to the chunk and to the turn level.

## 5.5   Data-driven Dimensions of Emotion

On the basis of dimensional emotion theories (Chapter 2.2.2), emotions can be described in terms of a few dimensions (see Chapter 3.2, *Dimensional Labeling*). The most widely used dimensions are *valence* and *arousal*. This two-dimensional space is suited to represent prototypical, full-blown emotions. Yet, naturally occurring emotional/emotion-related states that can be observed in real application scenarios differ strongly from those full-blown emotions and it is an open question whether *valence* and *arousal* are the two most appropriate dimensions to model these states. Therefore, we derive dimensions in a data-driven approach based on confusion matrices of human labelers. The confusion of one class with another is interpreted as

| emotion category | | A | T | R | E | N | M | J | words |
|---|---|---|---|---|---|---|---|---|---|
| | | **43.3** | 13.0 | 12.9 | 12.1 | 18.1 | 0.1 | 0.0 | 134 |
| | angry (A) | | | | | | | | |
| majority vote | touchy (T) | 4.5 | **42.9** | 11.7 | 13.7 | 23.5 | 1.0 | 0.1 | 419 |
| | reprimanding (R) | 3.8 | 15.7 | **45.8** | 14.0 | 18.2 | 1.3 | 0.1 | 463 |
| | emphatic (E) | 1.3 | 5.8 | 6.7 | **53.6** | 29.9 | 1.2 | 0.5 | 2,807 |
| | neutral (N) | 0.4 | 2.2 | 1.5 | 13.9 | **77.8** | 2.7 | 0.5 | 39,975 |
| | motherese (M) | 0.0 | 0.8 | 1.4 | 4.9 | 30.4 | **61.1** | 0.9 | 1,311 |
| | joyful (J) | 0.1 | 0.6 | 1.1 | 7.3 | 32.4 | 2.0 | **54.2** | 109 |

Table 5.21: Confusion matrix in percent of the five labelers for the German FAU Aibo Emotion Corpus. The entries of the rare categories *helpless*, *bored*, *surprised*, and *other* are not displayed

similarity measure. Non-metric dimensional scaling (NMDS, Chapter 4.3.2) is used to arrange the emotion categories in a one- or two-dimensional space such that the distances in the low-dimensional space match the similarities given in the confusion matrix. That way, highly similar states are arranged close to each other whereas dissimilar states are located far away from each other. Alternatively, the similarities can be obtained from the results of machine classification experiments like in [Truo 07] or by calculating Euclidean distances between feature vectors for acoustic or linguistic features like the mean MFCC feature vectors for one emotion category over all utterances/words [Batl 08b]. As far as we know, both approaches – the one based on confusion matrices of human labelers and the one based on distances between feature vectors – are applied for the first time for this purpose.

We focus on the methodologically interesting 7-class problem *angry, touchy, reprimanding, emphatic, neutral, motherese*, and *joyful* [Batl 05a, Batl 08b]. The other four remaining categories *helpless, bored, surprised*, and *other* are omitted because of their low frequency in the German FAU Aibo Emotion Corpus. For the British FAU Aibo Emotion Corpus, the same set of categories is investigated. The confusion matrices for the German and the British FAU Aibo Emotion Corpus are given in Table 5.21 and Table 5.22, respectively. The majority vote of the human labelers is taken as reference label. In some cases, the majority vote is not unique because two categories get both two votes (2+2+1, occurring 3,070 times in the German FAU Aibo Emotion Corpus) or because all labelers decide for different categories (1+1+1+1+1 and 1+1+1, respectively, occurring 81 times in the German version and 429 times in the British corpus). In these cases, each of the possible majority votes is taken once as reference for which the other raw labels are entered as confusions into the matrix. Hence, these words appear more than once (up to the number of labelers) in the matrix putting more emphasis on these non-prototypical cases.

The two-dimensional NMDS results for the 7-class problem are shown for both the German and British corpus in Figure 5.19. They are obtained with the ALSCAL procedure of the statistical package SPSS. To assess the quality of the NMDS results, Kruskal's stress $S$ (Equation 4.64) and the squared correlation RSQ are given in the figures. For a more intuitive graphical representation, the figures are transformed by translation, scaling, rotation, and reflexion such that *neutral* is located in the origin of the coordinate system, whereas *motherese* is located in the first, *angry* in

| | emotion category | A | T | R | E | N | M | J | words |
|---|---|---|---|---|---|---|---|---|---|
| majority vote | angry (A) | **41.8** | 5.0 | 8.9 | 16.3 | 28.0 | 0.0 | 0.0 | 23 |
| | touchy (T) | 5.6 | **37.4** | 17.4 | 16.4 | 17.4 | 0.5 | 0.0 | 7 |
| | reprimanding (R) | 1.8 | 3.1 | **44.3** | 19.4 | 29.1 | 1.2 | 0.1 | 127 |
| | emphatic (E) | 1.6 | 1.2 | 8.4 | **55.7** | 31.1 | 0.4 | 0.1 | 631 |
| | neutral (N) | 0.4 | 0.3 | 3.5 | 7.2 | **86.4** | 0.7 | 0.2 | 7,171 |
| | motherese (M) | 0.0 | 0.4 | 6.4 | 3.2 | 24.8 | **58.5** | 2.1 | 55 |
| | joyful (J) | 0.0 | 0.0 | 1.7 | 6.7 | 25.0 | 8.3 | **56.7** | 11 |

Table 5.22: Confusion matrix in percent of the three labelers for the British FAU Aibo Emotion Corpus. Along the lines of Table 5.21, the entries for the other emotion categories are not displayed

the third, and *joyful* in the fourth quadrant. The figures are scaled to the region $[-1,+1][-1,+1]$ using the same factor on both axis. Regarding the German FAU Aibo Emotion Corpus, the first, most important direction is the direction from *west* to *east*, which can be clearly interpreted as *valence*: from negative (*angry*, *reprimanding*, and *touchy*) in the *west* over *neutral* to positive (*motherese* and *joyful*) in the *east*. However, the second dimension from *north* to *south* cannot be interpreted as the traditional dimension *arousal*. Although *angry* and *joyful* represent high, *emphatic* medium, and *neutral* no arousal, *motherese* and *reprimanding* cannot be interpreted as having lower arousal than *neutral*. Moreover, by listening to the data it is not justifiable that *joyful* in our scenario represents more pronounced arousal than *angry*. Rather the opposite can be observed. Interpersonal *intimacy* is partly entailed in the second dimension – *motherese* and *reprimanding* characterize a more intimate speech register [Batl 06a] than *emphatic* and *neutral* – but *angry* and *joyful* cannot be interpreted as less intimate than neutral. Instead, the second dimension can be interpreted in more general terms as *orientation* towards the speaker himself/herself or towards the conversational partner (in our case Aibo), as *dialog* aspect (monolog vs. dialog), as *social* aspect, or as *interaction* (*−interaction* vs. *+interaction*). For the Aibo scenario, we decided in favor of the term *interaction*. In other contexts, the other names might be more adequate. The states *angry* (negative valence) and *joyful* (positive valence) both represent *−interaction* since subjects can be in these states even if they are alone. In contrast, *reprimanding* (negative valence) and *motherese* (positive valence) require a conversational partner to be addressed (*+interaction*). The two dimensions *valence* and *interaction* can also be found in the British corpus.

The left figure in Figure 5.20 shows the one-dimensional NMDS solution for the 7-class problem of the German FAU Aibo Emotion Corpus. Obviously, the remaining dimension is *valence*. But the markedly higher stress and lower RSQ values compared to the two-dimensional solution indicate that the second dimension clearly constributes to interpretation. For the computation of weighted kappa, the distances in this one-dimensional space can be used to weight confusions of the labelers. The one-dimensional NMDS solution confirms the arrangement of the four cover classes ***Anger***, ***Emphatic***, ***Neutral***, and ***Motherese*** in exactly this order (see Chapter 5.4). The two-dimensional NMDS solution for these four cover classes on the Aibo word set of the German corpus is depicted in the right figure in Figure 5.20. Again, the

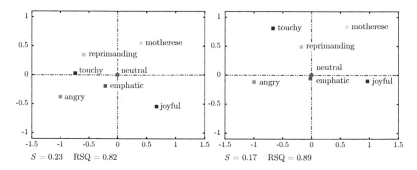

Figure 5.19: 2-dimensional NMDS solutions for the 7-class problem based on confusion matrices of the labelers for the German (left) and the British (right) FAU Aibo Emotion Corpus

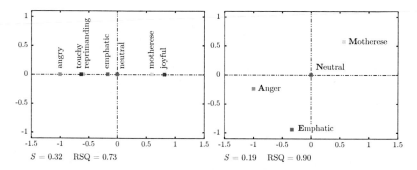

Figure 5.20: 1-dimensional NMDS solution for the 7-class problem (left) and 2-dimensional solution for the 4-class problem of emotion cover classes (right), both based on confusion matrices of the labelers for the German FAU Aibo Emotion Corpus

most important dimension is *valence*. Yet, the second dimension is hard to interpret since *reprimanding* is subsumed under *Anger* and *Joyful* is not included in the Aibo word set since the frequency of *Joyful* is too low for classification experiments. There are only four items; hence, this two-dimensional solution is not stable.

As mentioned above, distances between feature vectors can be used instead of confusion matrices of labelers. This approach is dealt with in Chapter 6, *Features for Emotion Recognition from Speech*. For a more extensive examination of the subject including dimensions derived from another type of data, namely the SympaFly corpus, please see [Batl08b].

# 5.6   Initiative CEICES

CEICES (Combining Efforts for Improving Automatic Classification of Emotional User States) is an initiative originated by our research group under the guidance of the European Network of Excellence HUMAINE (2004-2007). The goal of CEICES is to force co-operation in the area of automatic emotion recognition from speech by bringing together people from different sites with excellence in this area of research.

HUMAINE has been planned as an interdisciplinary network to facilitate the exchange between all the different branches of science working in the vast field of emotion research. The backgrounds of the partners participating in CEICES reflect this diversity: they come, for example, from a general engineering background, from automatic speech recognition, from speech pathology, and from basic research such as phonetics and psychology. Moreover, sites from outside HUMAINE have been invited to take part in this co-operation. Please see Appendix A.3.1 for a list of the CEICES members. The different traditions affect the tools that the CEICES members use as well as the types of their features. Linguistic information, for example, is typically only used by sites having some expertise in speech recognition. Features modeling aspects of intonation theories are normally only used by sites coming from basic (phonetic) research. The idea behind CEICES was to combine this heterogeneous expertise by gathering the features that are extracted at the partner sites. By that, the diversity of state-of-the-art features for emotion recognition can be covered to a large extent. Of course, the sheer number of features is not a virtue in itself, automatically paying off in classification performance. The results in [Batl 06b] document that one site using 'only' 32 features produces a classification performance in the same range as other sites using more than 1,000 features. But chances are that relevant features are not missed. Apart from the goal to increase the classification performance, the available set of features is suited to investigate the topic which types of features contribute the most to the recognition of emotion [Batl 09, Schu 07b, Schu 07c].

The originator site provides speech files, a phonetic lexicon, manually corrected word segmentation and manually corrected $F_0$ values, a segmentation into chunks, emotional labels on the word, the chunk, and the turn level, a definition of train and test samples, etc. All partners committed themselves to share their extracted feature values with all the other partners. In addition, the partners provide information about the format the features are stored in, which feature models which acoustic or linguistic phenomenon, which classifier was used to achieve the reported classification performance, etc. For details, please see the text of the CEICES contract in Appendix A.3.2. Thus, each site can assess the features provided by the other sites, together with their own features, aiming at a repertoire of optimal features.

In order to be able to compare different types of features across different sites, an agreed-upon machine readable representation of the extracted features has been defined within CEICES. For details, please see [Batl 09].

Up to now, the following publications have been published within the framework of CEICES: [Batl 09, Batl 08a, Sepp 08a, Sepp 08b, Schu 08, Batl 07b, Schu 07c, Schu 07b, Batl 06b]. Major achievements being relevant for this thesis are presented in 7.4.

**Summary** The FAU Aibo Emotion Corpus is a speech corpus with naturally occurring emotion-related states of children that is suited for classification experiments. In this chapter, the experimental design and the recording conditions are described. A lot of time-consuming and exceptional annotations such as the manual correction of the word segmentation and the $F_0$ values have been carried out on the data. Different types of segmentation and $F_0$ errors which might have an impact on the subsequent feature calculation are identified and quantified. Emotion categories are labeled on the word level. In addition, larger units are defined using syntactic and prosodic criteria and algorithms are presented to map emotion categories from the word level onto the chunk and the turn level. It is shown that the distribution of part-of-speech tags and prosodic labels differs to a large extent for different emotion categories. As most of the words are *neutral*, different subsets of the German FAU Aibo Emotion Corpus are defined which are more balanced and thus better suited for the classification experiments described in Chapter 7. The two dimensions *valence* and *interaction* are derived in a data-driven approach from the confusion matrix of the human labelers. By that, the second dimension differs from *activation* and *perceived control* which are generally proposed in psychological studies. The chapter closes introducing our initiative CEICES where state-of-the-art features from the participating sites are gathered to evaluate different types of feature w.r.t. their importance for emotion recognition. The evaluation is based on the speech corpus presented here. Important results are presented in Chapter 7.4.

# Chapter 6

# Features for Emotion Recognition from Speech

In Chapter 1.2, *State-of-the-Art*, an overview is given over acoustic and linguistic features that are currently being used successfully for emotion recognition from speech. These features can be categorized into acoustic and linguistic features. The acoustic features can be divided into prosodic features, spectral features, and voice quality features. In this chapter, those features are described that are evaluated in the experiments of this thesis. The implemented features cover all four groups of features. Our prosodic features are described in Chapter 6.1, the spectral features in Chapter 6.2, and the voice quality features in Chapter 6.3. The linguistic features are addressed in Chapter 6.4. In Chapter 6.5, the emotion-related states are correlated with Aibo's behavior which is known to be co-operative or non-cooperative for a given turn. The experimental results are described in Chapter 7.

## 6.1 Features of the Erlangen Prosody Module

The Erlangen Prosody Module has been originally designed to detect prosodic events such as phrase boundaries, phrase accents, and sentence mood in order to improve the automatic processing of speech [Warn 03, Gall 02, Noth 02, Komp 97, Kies 97, Noth 91, Noth 88]. The Erlangen Prosody Module has been an integral component of the German Verbmobil project [Batl 00c, Batl 00a, Noth 00] and the SmartKom project [Zeis 06]. Our prosodic features have also been used successfully for emotion recognition [Hube 02, Batl 00b, Batl 00c].

Many research groups rely on the discriminative power of prosodic features. Mostly, these features are calculated for the whole speech segment, i. e. the whole chunk or the whole turn in the case of the FAU Aibo Emotion Corpus. In contrast, our prosodic features are calculated for each word separately and are thus suited for the subsequent classification on the word level. Besides the speech signal itself, the Erlangen Prosody Module requires information about which words are contained in the speech segment and when these words begin and end. The word hypothesis graph (WHG, s. Chapter 5.2) provides this information. The basis is the sequence of words that are actually spoken, which is obtained by a manual transliteration of the audio data. In a fully automatic system, the actually spoken word chain has to be replaced by the recognized sequence of words obtained by an automatic speech recognizer. For this thesis, the problem of speech recognition and the one of recognizing emotions are separated and only the latter one is considered. In a fully automatic system, the recognition of emotions with features of the Erlangen Prosody Module will profit necessarily from future improvements in automatic speech recognition. The experimental results shown here are an upper limit for a perfect automatic speech recognition. Yet, there is another reason why the actually spoken word chain is used, which is even more important if the emotion-related state is classified on the word level: the FAU Aibo Emotion Corpus is labeled on the word level which requires that the sequence of actually spoken words is known. These emotion labels that are assigned to the actually spoken words cannot be assigned to the automatically recognized words since an actually spoken word and an automatically recognized one may cover different time periods. On the turn and the chunk level, automatic speech recognition can be applied if the segment boundaries are kept constant. Results within CEICES [Schu 07c] are reported in Chapter 7.4.

The features of the Erlangen Prosody Module model the contour of the fundamental frequency and the short-term energy, aspects of temporal lengthening of words, and the duration of pauses. In total, the Erlangen Prosody Module computes 100 prosodic features for each word: 26 $F_0$ based features, 33 energy based features, 33 duration based features, and 8 features based on pauses.

Besides its main purpose to calculate prosodic features, the Erlangen Prosody Module can also be used to calculate some non-prosodic features such as jitter and shimmer features, which are described in the section on voice quality features (s. Chapter 6.3.1), and part-of-speech features, which are described in the section on linguistic features (s. Chapter 6.4.2). In the following four subsections of this section, a detailed description of the prosodic features is given.

### 6.1.1  $F_0$ based Features

The $F_0$ based features model the contour of the (logarithmic) fundamental frequency as it is illustrated in Figure 6.1. In detail, the contour is described by the slope of the regression line, the error that occurs if the contour is approximated by this line, the maximum and the minimum of the fundamental frequency, and the $F_0$ onset and the $F_0$ offset, i.e. the $F_0$ values at the first voiced frame and the last voiced frame, respectively. Furthermore, the average of the $F_0$ values within one word is included. The position of both extrema and the positions of the on- and the offset are temporal measures specifying the distance from a given reference point that is defined as the end of the current word. In the experiments, these temporal features are treated separately or in combination with the duration based features described in Chapter 6.1.3.

Many algorithms exist to extract the fundamental frequency. The quality of the $F_0$ algorithm that is used might have an impact on the quality of the $F_0$ features. In the experiments of this thesis, the RAPT algorithm [Talk 95], which is implemented in ESPS, and an algorithm by Medan [Meda 91] and Bagshaw [Bags 93] that has been modified by M. Nutt [Zeis 09] are compared. Furthermore, the $F_0$ contour of the ESPS algorithm has been manually corrected in terms of 'smoothed and adjusted

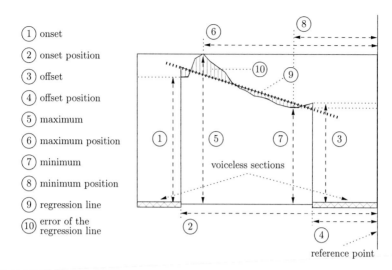

Figure 6.1: Features of the Erlangen Prosody Module after [Buck 99b]

to human perception' (s. Chapter 5.3.3). In comparing automatic algorithms and manual correction, the impact of the automatic extraction errors on the performance of the emotion recognition can be evaluated.

The feature vector for the word under consideration is extended by the features of the words constituting the left and the right context. A context of at most two words to the left and two words to the right is considered since former experiments have shown that larger context sizes do not improve the classification performance [Batl 00a]. Reasons that are pointed out are either the fact that a larger context does not contain relevant information to model the local events, or the rather limited size of the training data that has been used in the Verbmobil project. Regarding the size of the FAU Aibo Emotion Corpus, the latter reason certainly holds for the experiments in this thesis as well. Table 6.2 shows which features are calculated for which context [Hube 02, Kies 97]. The slope of the regression line and the corresponding approximation error is also calculated for speech segments covering two words. Furthermore, the mean $F_0$ value for the whole turn is included. In total, 26 $F_0$ based features are extracted for each word.

## 6.1.2 Energy based Features

Similar to the $F_0$ based features, the energy based features model the contour of the short-term energy of each frame (frames of 16 ms duration, time shift of 10 ms). Certain statistics like the minimum, which is always zero or close to zero, and the on- and the offset do not make any sense and are excluded [Kies 97]. In contrast, the position of the minimum may make sense very well. Again, the positions of the

| feature | context | | | | |
|---|---|---|---|---|---|
| | −2 | −1 | 0 | +1 | +2 |
| maximum | | • | • | • | |
| minimum | | • | • | • | |
| mean | | • | • | • | |
| | whole turn | | | | |
| onset | | | • | • | |
| offset | | • | • | | |
| regression coefficient | | • | • | • | |
| | | | • | | |
| | • | | | | • |
| regression error | | • | • | • | |
| | | | • | | |
| | • | | | | • |

Figure 6.2: 26 local $F_0$ based features and their context of computation

extrema are treated as duration features. In addition, the energy of the whole word is included: once as its absolute value and once in a normalized form.

The normalized energy of a word is based on the work of Wightman [Wigh 92]. The energy factor $\tau_{\text{en}}$ specifies how much louder or softer the speaker produces the words in an interval $I$ compared to an average speaker. In the Erlangen Prosody Module, the interval $I$ is equal to the whole audio file, i. e. one turn in the case of the FAU Aibo Emotion Corpus.

$$\tau_{\text{en}}(I) := \frac{1}{\#I} \sum_{w \in I} \frac{\text{en}(w)}{\mu_{\text{en}}(w)} \qquad (6.1)$$

$\text{en}(w)$ denotes the energy of the word $w$. The statistics $\mu_{\text{en}}(w)$ and $\sigma_{\text{en}}(w)$ are the average energy of the word $w$ produced by an average speaker and the corresponding standard deviation, respectively. Both statistics are estimated on the German FAU Aibo Emotion Corpus in a leave-one-speaker-out procedure (s. Chapter 7) such that the data of the test speaker is not used for the estimation. If the frequency of the given word is too small to obtain robust estimates of the statistics, they can be approximated based on the energy statistics of the syllables or phonemes that the word consists of. The energy factor $\tau_{\text{en}}$ is added to the feature vector and is constant for all words within one turn. Furthermore, the factor $\tau_{\text{en}}$ is used to scale the expected energy $\mu_{\text{en}}(w)$ of the word $w$ in order to adapt the expected energy to the energy level of the whole turn. The difference $\text{en}(w) - \tau_{\text{en}}(I)\mu_{\text{en}}(w)$ in the numerator of Equation 6.2 is the deviation of the energy of the current word from its expected energy. In order to get rid of the speech sound dependent variation, this deviation is normalized with the standard deviation $\sigma_{\text{en}}(w)$ which is also scaled by the factor $\tau_{\text{en}}$. The resulting feature $\zeta_{\text{en}}(J, I)$ for single words – in this case the interval $J$ consists of only the current word – or for larger contexts is defined as follows:

$$\zeta_{\text{en}}(J, I) := \frac{1}{\#J} \sum_{w \in J} \frac{\text{en}(w) - \tau_{\text{en}}(I)\mu_{\text{en}}(w)}{\tau_{\text{en}}(I)\sigma_{\text{en}}(w)} \; . \qquad (6.2)$$

| feature | context | | | | |
|---|---|---|---|---|---|
| | −2 | −1 | 0 | +1 | +2 |
| maximum | | • | • | • | |
| mean | | • | • | • | |
| | | • | | | • |
| | • | | | • | |
| regression coefficient | | • | • | • | |
| | | | • | | |
| | • | | | | • |
| regression error | | • | • | • | |
| | | | • | | |
| | • | | | | • |
| absolute energy of a word | | • | • | • | |
| | • | | | • | |
| normalized energy $\zeta_{\mathrm{en}}$ | | • | • | • | |
| | • | | | • | |
| $\tau_{\mathrm{en}}$ | whole turn | | | | |

Figure 6.3: 33 local energy based features and their context of computation

As for $F_0$ based features, features describing the context of the word are included resulting in 33 energy based features. Table 6.3 illustrates which features are calculated for which context.

## 6.1.3   Duration based Features

Duration based features model aspects of temporal lengthening of words. Besides the absolute duration of a word, two normalized forms are added to the feature vector. The first normalization is rather simple and normalizes the duration of a word by the number of syllables the word consists of. The second normalization is along the same lines as for the energy normalization. The factor $\tau_{\mathrm{dur}}$ is the speaking rate. For its computation, only 'en' has to be substituted by 'dur' in Equation 6.1. $\mathrm{dur}(w)$ denotes the duration of the word $w$. The statistics $\mu_{\mathrm{dur}}(w)$ and $\sigma_{\mathrm{dur}}(w)$ are the average duration of word $w$ produced by an average speaker and the corresponding standard deviation, respectively. Again, both statistics are estimated on the FAU Aibo Emotion Corpus in a leave-out-speaker-out procedure using only the data of the 50 speakers that are not used for testing. Analogously to Equation 6.2, the normalized duration $\zeta_{\mathrm{dur}}(I, J)$ is computed for single words or larger contexts $J$.

Table 6.4 shows which features are computed for which contexts resulting in a 17-dimensional feature vector. In addition, there are 16 features describing the positions of the $F_0$ and energy extrema as it has been mentioned in the previous two sections. All in all, there are 33 duration based features.

| feature | context | | | | |
|---|---|---|---|---|---|
| | $-2$ | $-1$ | $0$ | $+1$ | $+2$ |
| absolute duration of a word | | • | • | • | |
| | • | | | | • |
| duration of a word normalized | | • | • | • | |
| with the number of syllables | • | | | | • |
| normalized duration $\zeta_{\text{dur}}$ | | • | • | • | |
| | | | • | | |
| | • | | | | • |
| speaking rate $\tau_{\text{dur}}$ | whole turn | | | | |
| position of the $F_0$ maximum | | • | • | • | |
| position of the $F_0$ minimum | | • | • | • | |
| position of the $F_0$ onset | | | • | • | |
| position of the $F_0$ offset | | • | • | | |
| position of the energy maximum | | • | • | • | |
| position of the energy minimum | | • | • | • | |

Figure 6.4: 33 local duration based features and their context of computation

| feature | | context | | | | |
|---|---|---|---|---|---|---|
| | | $-2$ | $-1$ | $0$ | $+1$ | $+2$ |
| filled pauses | before the word | | • | • | | |
| | after the word | | | • | • | |
| silent pauses | before the word | | • | • | | |
| | after the word | | | • | • | |

Figure 6.5: 8 local features based on pauses and their context of computation

## 6.1.4   Features based on Pauses

The features in this group measure the duration of the pauses which might be before or after the word. Filled pauses (e. g. "uhm", "uh", ...) and silent pauses are distinguished. In Table 6.5, the various contexts are listed for which these features are calculated. In total, eight features based on pauses are extracted.

## 6.1.5   Features for Larger Units

To obtain features for larger segments such as chunks and turns, the varying number of words within one turn or chunk has to be handled. A simple concatenation of the features on the word level would result in feature vectors of varying length which are not suited for classification. Hence, features on turn/chunk level are obtained by averaging the features on word level. Furthermore, the standard deviation is added as well as the maximum and the minimum of the feature values within the segment. Inevitably, this approach increases the number of features by a factor of four. Fortunately, the features describing the context can be discarded. The features $\tau_{\text{en}}$, $\tau_{\text{dur}}$ and the average fundamental frequency for the whole turn are constant for all words within one turn and can be added as they are. Eventually, there are 29

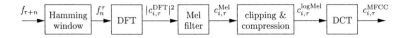

Figure 6.6: Steps to compute the Mel frequency cepstral coefficients

$F_0$ based features, 25 energy based features, 37 duration based features (24 features describing the position of the $F_0$ and energy extrema and 13 original duration based features), and 16 features based on pauses. All in all, the feature vector for turns and chunks consists of 107 prosodic features. Approximately, this matches the number of prosodic features on the word level (100). However, the proportions of the four groups of features differ. If larger units are classified, the number of samples available for training and testing the classifier decreases: The Aibo word set consists of 6,070 samples (words), the Aibo chunk set of 4,543 samples (chunks), and the Aibo turn set of only 3,996 samples (turns). Details are given in Table 5.18.

## 6.2 Spectral Features

The features of this group are based on the spectral short-term analysis. The Mel frequency cepstral coefficients (MFCC) are the standard features in speech recognition. They have been designed to discriminate phones and to represent what is spoken in a very compact way. Other information like the information how something is spoken should be removed. The computation of the MFCC features consists of several steps, which are illustrated in Figure 6.6. In each steps, the dimension of the feature vector is reduced: the 256 samples of the speech signal, a frame typically consists of, are finally reduced to only 12 MFCC coefficients. Despite this large reduction of information and despite the design goal to remove as much of the information how something is spoken, MFCC features have been used successfully for emotion recognition. One reason certainly is that long-term MFCC features model linguistic information. Nevertheless, features of earlier stages in the computation of the MFCC features with less reduction should contain more information about the emotional state of the speaker and might be more appropriate for emotion classification. In the following, the individual steps in the computation of the MFCC features are described. In the experiments in Chapter 7, the 128 coefficients of the Discrete Fourier Transformation and the 22 logarithmic Mel frequency coefficients are compared to the 12 MFCC coefficients. Formants describing the resonance frequencies of the vocal tract are another type of spectral features, which are described at the end of this chapter.

### 6.2.1 DFT Features

Speech signals are non-stationary signals whose spectral properties change at least from one phone to another. Hence, the spectral analysis is performed on small periods of the discrete speech signal $f_n$, which are about 5-30 ms long. Within these so-called *windows* or *frames*, the signal can be assumed to be approximately stationary. In

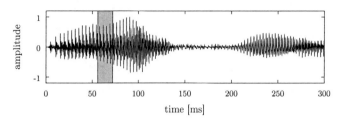

Figure 6.7: Speech signal of the word "Aibo"

automatic speech recognition, a frame is typically 16 ms long corresponding to $N_\text{s} = 256$ samples at a sampling rate of 16 kHz. For computational reasons, it is beneficial if $N_\text{s}$ is a power of 2. Every 10 ms, a new frame is analyzed so that consecutive frames overlap. Figure 6.7 shows a speech signal of 300 ms duration where the word "Aibo" is spoken. A single frame of 16 ms duration is highlighted.

For each frame, the power spectrum is computed using the Discrete Fourier Transformation (DFT). The DFT assumes that the discrete and time limited signal is periodically continued. To avoid discontinuities at the beginning and the end of the frame, the amplitude of the signal is extenuated towards the borders of the window by applying a window function $w_n$. Let $f_n^\tau$ denote the samples of a frame that starts at sample $\tau$ after the application of the window function $w_n$:

$$f_n^\tau := \begin{cases} f_{\tau+n} \cdot w_n & 0 \le n < N_\text{s} \\ 0 & \text{otherwise} \end{cases} . \tag{6.3}$$

The window function $w_n$ is centered around $\tau + \frac{N_\text{s}-1}{2}$. Various window functions such as the Hamming window, the Hann window, the Gauss window, or the Blackman window are common. For this work, the Hamming window is used which is defined as follows:

$$w_n^{\text{Hamming}} := \begin{cases} 0.54 - 0.46 \cos\left(\frac{2\pi n}{N_\text{s}}\right) & 0 \le n < N_\text{s} \\ 0 & \text{otherwise} \end{cases} . \tag{6.4}$$

Figure 6.8 shows the samples of the frame highlighted in Figure 6.7 and the window function of the Hamming window. The samples of the frame after the application of the Hamming window are shown in the left part of Figure 6.9.

Instead of the Discrete Fourier Transformation, the Fast Hartley Transformation (FHT) [Brac 84] is implemented. The FHT is a fast implementation of the Discrete Hartley Transformation (DHT), a Fourier related transformation transforming an input of real numbers into an output of real numbers without the involvement of complex numbers. The DHT coefficients are defined as follows:

$$c_{i,\tau}^{\text{DHT}} := \sum_{n=0}^{N_\text{s}-1} f_n^\tau \left[ \cos\left(\frac{2\pi n i}{N_\text{s}}\right) + \sin\left(\frac{2\pi n i}{N_\text{s}}\right) \right] , \quad i = 0, 1, \ldots, N_\text{s} - 1 . \tag{6.5}$$

The first coefficient $c_{0,\tau}^{\text{DHT}}$ is the mean of the amplitude values of the signal, which is often called *DC offset*. It is identical to the first DFT coefficient $c_{0,\tau}^{\text{DFT}}$. The other

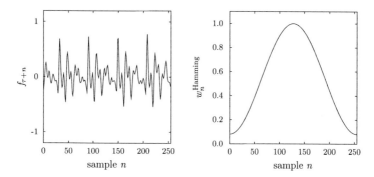

Figure 6.8: Speech frame of 256 samples starting at sample $\tau$ (left) and Hamming window (right)

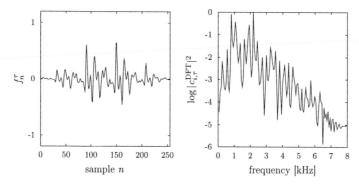

Figure 6.9: Amplitudes of the speech frame after application of the Hamming window (left) and power spectrum of the speech frame (right)

DFT coefficients $c_{i,\tau}^{\mathrm{DFT}}$, $i = 1, \ldots, N_{\mathrm{s}}/2$, are complex numbers and can be obtained from the real-valued DHT coefficients using the following relationship:

$$\mathrm{Re}(c_{i,\tau}^{\mathrm{DFT}}) = \frac{1}{2}\big(c_{i,\tau}^{\mathrm{DHT}} + c_{N_{\mathrm{s}}-i,\tau}^{\mathrm{DHT}}\big) , \tag{6.6}$$

$$\mathrm{Im}(c_{i,\tau}^{\mathrm{DFT}}) = \frac{1}{2}\big(c_{N_{\mathrm{s}}-i,\tau}^{\mathrm{DHT}} - c_{i,\tau}^{\mathrm{DHT}}\big) . \tag{6.7}$$

The phase of the speech signal does not contribute to the discrimination of phones. Furthermore, the phase is highly affected by reverberation. Hence, the power spectrum is used to eliminate the phase information:

$$|c_{i,\tau}^{\mathrm{DFT}}|^2 = \frac{1}{2}\Big((c_{i,\tau}^{\mathrm{DHT}})^2 + (c_{N_{\mathrm{s}}-i,\tau}^{\mathrm{DHT}})^2\Big) , \quad i = 0, 1, \ldots, \frac{N_{\mathrm{s}}}{2} . \tag{6.8}$$

Hence, the dimension of the feature vector is reduced from 256 sample to only $\frac{N_{\mathrm{s}}}{2} + 1 = 129$ features. The right plot in Figure 6.9 shows the spectrum of the windowed

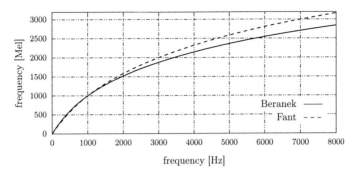

Figure 6.10: Mel scales proposed by Beranek [Bera 49] and Fant [Fant 68]

speech signal that is depicted in the left part of the figure. The first local maximum represents the fundamental frequency, which is about 275 Hz in this case. The other local maxima are the harmonics, which are multiples of the fundamental frequency. Certain frequency bands are emphasized due to resonance frequencies of the vocal tract. These frequencies are known as formants and described in more detail in Chapter 6.2.4. Especially, the frequencies around the second and the third harmonic and around the sixth and the seventh harmonic are significantly higher than the surrounding harmonics due to the first and the second formant, respectively.

## 6.2.2 Mel Features

The Mel scale reflects the non-linear relationship between the frequency of a tone and the perceived pitch. In experiments by Stevens et al. , tones scattered throughout the audible range were presented at a constant loudness level of 60 dB to observers who had to adjust the frequency of a second tone until it sounded just half as high in pitch as the standard tone [Stev 37]. At a frequency of 1000 Hz, the unit of the frequency and the unit of the perceived pitch are equal: $1000\,\text{Hz} \,\hat{=}\, 1000\,\text{Mel}$. Several quite similar equations describe this non-linear relationship between Hz and Mel found in the experiments by Stevens, e. g. the equation by Beranek [Bera 49]

$$f_{\text{Beranek}} = 1127.01048 \cdot \ln\left(1 + \frac{f_{\text{Hz}}}{700}\right) \qquad (6.9)$$

or the one proposed by Fant [Fant 68]

$$f_{\text{Fant}} = \frac{1000}{\ln(2)} \cdot \ln\left(1 + \frac{f_{\text{Hz}}}{1000}\right) \ . \qquad (6.10)$$

Both curves are plotted in Figure 6.10. The transformation of the frequency is approximated by applying a bank of $N_{\text{filter}}$ filters [Riec 95]:

$$c_{i,\tau}^{\text{Mel}} = \sum_{j=1}^{N_{\text{s}}/2} w_{i,j}^{\triangle} \cdot |c_{j,\tau}^{\text{DFT}}|^2 \ , \quad i = 1, 2, \ldots, N_{\text{filter}} \ . \qquad (6.11)$$

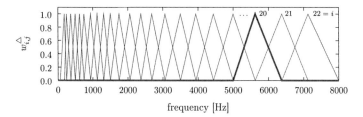

Figure 6.11: Mel filter bank consisting of 22 triangular filters covering a frequency range of 80 Hz to 8 kHz. The coefficients $w_{20,j}^{\triangle}$ of the 20th filter are highlighted

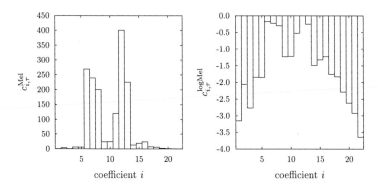

Figure 6.12: Mel spectrum (left) and log-Mel spectrum of the speech frame (right)

The filters are designed for a higher resolution at lower frequencies. For higher frequencies, the number of filters decreases and the filters cover a wider range of frequency bands. This models the decreasing frequency resolution for higher frequencies of the human auditory system. The weighted summation of adjacent frequency coefficients removes the harmonic structure of the spectrum as it can be seen from the Mel spectrum shown in the left figure of Figure 6.12. Furthermore, the number of coefficients is reduced from $N_s/2 + 1 = 129$ to $N_{\text{filter}}$. For this work, $N_{\text{filter}} = 22$ triangular filters are used. They are depicted in Figure 6.11.

Approximately, the Mel spectrum coefficients $c_{i,\tau}^{\text{Mel}}$ are distributed log-normally. For a classification with Gaussian mixture models (s. Chapter 4.1.2), this is not favorable if the number of mixtures is low. Hence, the Mel spectrum coefficients are compressed by taking the logarithm. In order to prevent numerical problems if the logarithm is taken of values that are close to zero, the Mel spectrum coefficients are clipped to the interval $[\epsilon; 1]$ prior to the compression:

$$c_{i,\tau}^{\text{normMel}} = \begin{cases} \dfrac{c_{i,\tau}^{\text{Mel}}}{\max\limits_{j} c_{j,\tau}^{\text{Mel}}} & c_{i,\tau}^{\text{Mel}} > \epsilon \max\limits_{j} c_{j,\tau}^{\text{Mel}} \\ \epsilon & \text{otherwise} \end{cases} , \quad i = 1, 2, \ldots, N_{\text{filter}} . \tag{6.12}$$

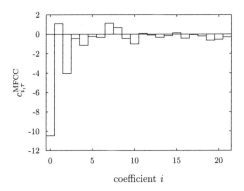

Figure 6.13: Mel frequency cepstral coefficients (MFCC)

In the experiments, $\epsilon$ is set to 0.000001. Finally, the compressed Mel spectrum coefficients $c_{i,\tau}^{\mathrm{logMel}}$ are obtained by:

$$c_{i,\tau}^{\mathrm{logMel}} = \log_{10}\left(c_{i,\tau}^{\mathrm{normMel}}\right) , \quad i = 1, 2, \ldots, N_{\mathrm{filter}} . \tag{6.13}$$

The compressed Mel spectrum is shown in the right part of Figure 6.12.

### 6.2.3  MFCC Features

The output of consecutive Mel filters is correlated. With a suitable linear transformation the dimension of the feature vector can be reduced further. Because of fewer parameters that have to be estimated, the models of a statistical classifier can be trained more robustly and the time to train the models is significantly shorter.

The Mel frequency cepstral coefficients (MFCC) have been proposed by Davis and Mermelstein [Davi 80]. The Discrete Cosine Transformation (DCT) is applied to the log-Mel spectrum:

$$c_{i,\tau}^{\mathrm{MFCC}} := \sqrt{\frac{2}{N_{\mathrm{filter}}}} \sum_{j=1}^{N_{\mathrm{filter}}} c_{j,\tau}^{\mathrm{logMel}} \cdot \cos\left(\frac{i(j - \frac{1}{2})\pi}{N_{\mathrm{filter}}}\right) , \quad i = 0, 1, \ldots, N_{\mathrm{filter}} - 1 . \tag{6.14}$$

The DCT is a Fourier related transformation that can be applied to real data with even symmetry. The output of the DFT of the speech signal meets these requirements. Hence, the spectrum of the log-Mel spectrum is computed. The domain is called *cepstrum*, a term made up by reversing the letters of the first syllable of 'spectrum'. Only the first 12 MFCC coefficients are taken discarding the coefficients that represent higher frequencies. The MFCC coefficients are depicted in Figure 6.13. The Discrete Cosine Transformation decorrelates the log-Mel coefficients similar to the principal component analysis (PCA) [Ahme 74] but with the advantage of a constant transformation matrix and without the need to compute the eigenvectors of the data.

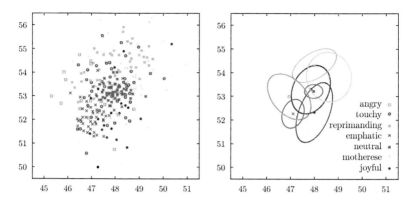

Figure 6.14: Clustering of seven emotional-related states using the Sammon transformation, based on distances between MFCC feature vectors averaged per speaker and emotion-related state

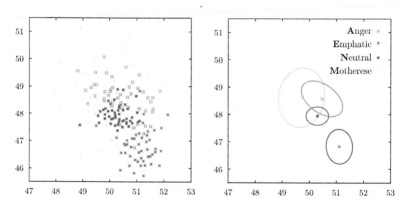

Figure 6.15: Clustering of four emotion cover classes using the Sammon transformation, based on distances between MFCC feature vectors averaged per speaker and emotion cover class

The first MFCC coefficient $c_{0,\tau}^{\mathrm{MFCC}}$ is substituted by the logarithm of the short-time energy $c_{\tau}^{\mathrm{en}}$ defined as the sum of all Mel spectrum coefficients:

$$c_{\tau}^{\mathrm{en}} = \log_{10} \left( \sum_{i=1}^{N_{\mathrm{filter}}} c_{i,\tau}^{\mathrm{Mel}} \right) . \tag{6.15}$$

In order to reduce the impact that changes of the environmental conditions such as noise, room, microphone, or speaker characteristics have on the MFCC features, techniques like the *cepstral mean substraction* (CMS) are applied where a pre-computed mean of the MFCC feature vector is substracted. An extension, which is used in our implementation, is the *dynamic adaptive cepstral substraction* (DACS) where the pre-computed mean is updated while new frames are processed. Only frames that actually contain speech are used for the adaptation of the mean.

The MFCC coefficients $c_{i,\tau}^{\mathrm{MFCC}}$ are called *static* features as they describe the spectral properties within one frame where the signal is approximately stationary. The feature vector is extended by *dynamic* features, which describe the behavior of the static features over time. For this purpose, the first and sometimes also the second derivative of the static features are calculated. These features are often called $\Delta$ and $\Delta\Delta$ features, respectively. For this work, only $\Delta$ features are investigated. The first derivative is approximated by the slope of the regression line [Furu 86] that is fitted to the MFCC feature vectors of five consecutive frames:

$$c_{i,\tau}^{\Delta\mathrm{MFCC}} = \frac{\sum_{j=-2}^{2} j \cdot c_{i,\tau+j}^{\mathrm{MFCC}}}{\sum_{j=-2}^{2} j^2} \ . \tag{6.16}$$

MFCC features have proven to be suited for emotion recognition. This is substantiated by the experimental results on the FAU Aibo Emotion Corpus reported in Chapter 7. The Sammon transformation (s. Chapter 4.3.1) is used to visualize the influence of the emotional state on the long-term average MFCC features. For this purpose, the average MFCC feature vector for each speaker and for each emotion-related user state is computed. Only the twelve static MFCC features are used. The Sammon transformation arranges the long-term MFCC feature vectors in a two-dimensional space such that the Euclidean distances between the points in the two-dimensional space approximate the distances between the feature vectors in the original 12-dimensional space. Figure 6.14 shows the arrangement for the seven classes *angry, touchy, reprimanding, emphatic, neutral, motherese,* and *joyful*. Each point in the left figure represents the long-term average MFCC feature vector of one speaker in a particular emotion-related state. The features are calculated on the whole German FAU Aibo Emotion Corpus. Although the number of classes is quite high and the features are transformed to only a two-dimensional space, the points that correspond to the same emotion-related state cluster quite well. This is especially true for *neutral* and *emphatic* whose clusters are very compact. The cluster of *motherese* is not as compact as the ones of *neutral* and *emphatic*, but *motherese* can still be distinguished from *neutral* and *emphatic* quite well. The clusters of other states overlap to a higher degree. For a better illustration, the distribution of the points of the same emotion-related user state is modeled with a two-dimensional Gaussian probability density function. The mean and the covariance matrix of each class are depicted in the right figure of Figure 6.14. Along the same lines, Figure 6.15 shows the arrangement of the four cover classes *Anger, Emphatic, Neutral,* and *Motherese.* Remember that *Anger* subsumes the three different states *angry, touchy,* and *reprimanding.* The data of the cover classes *Joyful* and *Other* are omitted. Again, the clusters of *Neutral* and *Emphatic* are very compact and well separated. The cluster of *Motherese* is larger and overlaps with the one of *Neutral* and the one of *Anger* to some degree.

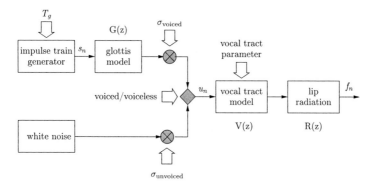

Figure 6.16: Fant's source-filter model after [Schu 95]

## 6.2.4   Formant based Features

Fant's source-filter model [Fant 60] illustrated in Figure 6.16 models the process of speech production as a series of linear, time invariant systems. The discrete speech signal can be obtained by the convolution $f_n = u_n \star v_n \star r_n$. The following equation holds for the $z$-transform of the speech signal:

$$F(z) = U(z) \cdot V(z) \cdot R(z) . \tag{6.17}$$

The complete transmission function for voiced sounds is $H(z) = \sigma_{\text{voiced}} \cdot G(z) \cdot V(z) \cdot R(z)$. $G(z)$ is the $z$-transform of the glottis model, $V(z)$ the one of the vocal tract and $R(z)$ models the radiation at the lips.

In order to model the resonance characteristics of the vocal tract, the vocal tract is modeled in a simplified way by an acoustic tube of the length $L$ consisting of $M$ cylindrical segments as illustrated in Figure 6.17. The nasal tract and losses at the wall of the vocal tract are not modeled. All segments have the same length $l = L/M$ but different cross sectional areas $A_i$, $1 \leq i \leq M$. The typical length of the vocal tract is about $L = 170\,\text{mm}$ for adults. In the direction of the tube, a planar propagation of the signal can be assumed since the length of the cylindrical segments is far below the wave length of speech signals [Schu 95]. The acoustic flow in the forward and the backward direction can be computed iteratively from the reflexion coefficients

$$k_i = \frac{A_i - A_{i+1}}{A_i + A_{i+1}} , \quad 0 \leq i \leq M . \tag{6.18}$$

The area $A_0$ of the "outside world" cylinder in front of the lips is set to infinity; then $k_0$ is 1. The area of the terminator at the glottis does not affect the resonance characteristics and can be chosen arbitrarily. The propagation of the signal is disturbed only at equidistant points of time due to the change of the diameter of the tube at the transition from one cylinder to another. Hence, a simple term results for the $z$-transform of the vocal tract:

$$V(z) = \frac{\prod_{i=0}(1 + k_i)}{1 - \sum_{i=1}^{M} a_i z^{-i}} . \tag{6.19}$$

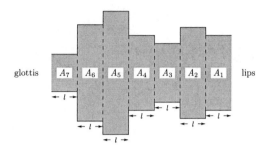

Figure 6.17: Vocal tract model: acoustic tube without loss consisting of cylindrical segments of equal length after [Schu 95]

The polynomial coefficients $a_i = a_i^{(M)}$ in the denominator can be computed iteratively:

$$a_i^{(m)} = \begin{cases} 1 & i = 0 \\ a_i^{(m-1)} + k_m\, a_{m-i}^{(m-1)} & i < 1 < m \\ k_m & i = m \end{cases} \quad . \tag{6.20}$$

The function $V(z)$ has $M/2$ pairs of complex conjugate poles where the polynomial in the denominator is equal to zero:

$$1 - \sum_{i=1}^{M} a_i z^{-i} = \prod_{i=1}^{M/2} \left(1 - 2e^{-c_i T}\cos(b_i T)z^{-1} + e^{-2c_i T}z^{-2}\right) . \tag{6.21}$$

These poles are the resonances of the vocal tract well-known as *formants*. They are characterized by their center frequencies $F_i = b_i/(2\pi)$ and their bandwidths $B_i = c_i/(2\pi)$. The formants characterize the current shape of the vocal tract while a phone is being produced. They are independent of the perceived pitch. Yet, they do depend on the length of the vocal tract and hence, depend on the age and the gender of the speaker. Significant differences in the position of the first two formants between adults and children have been found [Stem 05]. Nevertheless, the first two formants are sufficient to identify vowels. Algorithms that determine the formants by finding the poles of $V(z)$ are called *root extraction methods*.

Other algorithms, called *spectral peak picking methods*, extract the local maxima of a smoothed spectrum such as the one obtained by linear prediction coding (LPC). The LP spectrum is shown in Figure 6.18. LPC assumes that the samples of a stationary period of the signal can be predicted by a linear combination of the preceding $N_{LP}$ samples:

$$\hat{f}_n^\tau = -\sum_{j=1}^{N_{LP}} \alpha_j \cdot f_{n-j}^\tau . \tag{6.22}$$

$N_{LP}$ is called the prediction order; $\alpha_j$, $1 \le j \le N_{LP}$, denote the LP coefficients. There will be a deviation between the predicted value $\hat{f}_n^\tau$ and the actual value $f_n^\tau$:

$$e_n^\tau = f_n^\tau - \hat{f}_n^\tau = \sum_{j=0}^{N_{LP}} \alpha_j \cdot f_{n-j}^\tau \quad \text{with} \quad \alpha_0 = 1 . \tag{6.23}$$

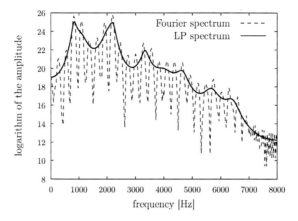

Figure 6.18: Log-Fourier and log-LP spectrum ($N_{\mathrm{LP}} = 20$) of the speech frame

The LP coefficients $\alpha_1, \ldots, \alpha_{N_{\mathrm{LP}}}$ are determined such that the accumulated squared error

$$\epsilon_{\mathrm{LP}} = \sum_{j=N_{\mathrm{s}}}^{N_{\mathrm{s}}-1} (e_n^\tau)^2 = \sum_{j=N_{\mathrm{s}}}^{N_{\mathrm{s}}-1} \left( \sum_{j=0}^{N_{\mathrm{LP}}} \alpha_j \cdot f_{n-j}^\tau \right)^2 \tag{6.24}$$

is minimized. Again, $N_{\mathrm{s}}$ is the number of samples in the speech frame. The error $\epsilon_{\mathrm{LP}}$ can be rewritten in a more compact form as a linear combination of quadratic functions:

$$\epsilon_{\mathrm{LP}} = \sum_{j=0}^{N_{\mathrm{LP}}} \sum_{k=0}^{N_{\mathrm{LP}}} \alpha_j \phi_{jk}^\tau \alpha_k \quad \text{with} \quad \phi_{jk}^\tau = \sum_{n=0}^{N_{\mathrm{s}}-1} f_{n-j}^\tau f_{n-k}^\tau \ . \tag{6.25}$$

Hence, $\epsilon_{\mathrm{LP}}$ has a unique minimum which can be found by setting the partial derivatives $\partial \epsilon_{\mathrm{LP}} / \partial \alpha_k = \sum_{j=0}^{N_{\mathrm{LP}}} \alpha_j \phi_{jk}^\tau$ to zero. This results in a system of $N_{\mathrm{LP}}$ linear equations:

$$\sum_{j=1}^{N_{\mathrm{LP}}} \alpha_j \phi_{jk}^\tau = -\phi_{jk}^\tau, \quad 1 \le k \le N_{\mathrm{LP}} \ . \tag{6.26}$$

Instead of solving this system, the LP coefficients can be determined in a faster way using the *covariance method* or the *autocorrelation method*. The first one in based on a Cholesky decomposition of the symmetric matrix $\boldsymbol{\phi}^\tau$, the latter one uses the autocorrelation function $r$ to compute the components of $\boldsymbol{\phi}^\tau$:

$$\phi_{jk}^\tau = r_{|j-k|}^\tau \tag{6.27}$$

and benefits from the form of $\boldsymbol{\phi}^\tau$, which is a Toeplitz matrix (constant elements on each descending diagonal from left to right). In this case, the system of equations can be solved with the Levinson-Durbin recursion [Levi 47, Durb 60]. In order to compute the LP spectrum, the LP coefficients are zero padded before applying the Discrete Fourier Transformation. Finally, the local maxima of the spectrum are determined.

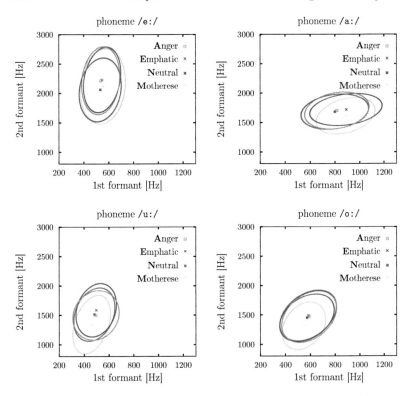

Figure 6.19: Distribution of the center frequencies of the first and the second formant for the long vowels /e:/, /a:/, /u:/, and /o:/ and for the emotion cover classes *Anger*, *Emphatic*, *Neutral*, and *Motherese*

The number of local maxima strongly depends on the prediction order $N_{\mathrm{LP}}$. If the order is too low, one local maximum models more than one formant. If $N_{\mathrm{LP}}$ is too high, the local maxima model the harmonic structure. Generally, good results are obtained if $N_{\mathrm{LP}}$ is set to $f_s + 4$; $f_s$ is the sampling frequency given in kHz.

In the experiments, the first four formants and their bandwidths are used. They are extracted using the formant extractor of ESPS, which is incorporated in the software WaveSurfer. The algorithm is based on the root extraction method. In order to find the most probable poles related to actual formants, a modified Viterbi algorithm is used. In [Kim 06], the ESPS algorithm is attested sufficiently good performance in most cases.

Figure 6.19 shows the influence of the four cover classes *Anger*, *Emphatic*, *Neutral*, and *Motherese* on the position of the first and the second formant for the long vowels /e:/, /a:/, /u:/, and /o:/. For each combination of vowel and emotional state, the average of the first and second formant has been computed. In order to be able to average the values of the formants for single phones, a time alignment on the phone level is necessary. It is obtained by a forced alignment of the manually transliterated words using the start and end frames of the manual correction of the segmentation. The distribution of the center frequencies of the first and the second formant is modeled with a two-dimensional Gaussian probability density function which is depicted by the mean and the covariance. It can be seen that the emotional state has some influence on the first and the second formant. The average center frequency of the first formant of the vowel /a:/, for example, is about 90 Hz higher if the vowel is produced in the state *Emphatic* compared to *Neutral*. If the vowel /u:/ is produced in the state *Motherese*, for example, the average center frequency of the second formant decreases by 170 Hz compared to *Neutral*. Nevertheless, the variance due to different speaker characteristics and due to co-articulation effects is much higher.

## 6.3 Voice Quality Features

Voice quality features characterize the source signal which emerges from the oscillation of the vocal cords. The source signal can be estimated by inverse filtering of the speech signal canceling the effects of the vocal tract. As pointed out in Chapter 1.2, inverse filtering techniques tend to perform least well especially for many non-modal voice qualities due to phases of the glottal cycle that are not completely closed and due to errors of the automatic extraction of the formants. For this thesis, only voice quality features are investigated that are obtained directly from the speech signal, namely jitter and shimmer, the harmonics-to-noise ratio, and a feature that is based on the Teager energy profile of multiple critical frequency bands.

### 6.3.1 Jitter and Shimmer

The term *jitter* denotes cycle-to-cycle variations of the fundamental frequency. Here, an approximation of the first derivative of the fundamental frequency is used:

$$\text{jitter}(i) = \frac{|\text{F}_0(i+1) - \text{F}_0(i)|}{\text{F}_0(i)} \ . \tag{6.28}$$

These variations are not perceived as changes of the pitch but as changes of the voice quality. Along the same lines, the term *shimmer* denotes variations of the energy from one cycle to another:

$$\text{shimmer}(i) = \frac{|\text{en}(i+1) - \text{en}(i)|}{\text{en}(i)} \ . \tag{6.29}$$

Cycle-to-cycle variations require that the fundamental frequency is calculated for consecutive periods and not as the average $\text{F}_0$ for a whole frame of constant length. The PDDP (**p**eriod **d**etection by means of **d**ynamic **p**rogramming) algorithm described in [Kies 97] is applied. In a first step, segments of voiced speech are located and estimates of the average fundamental frequency in these segments are computed. Then, the possible candidates for the period boundaries are located at positive zero crossings of the signal. Characteristics like the integral or the extrema in the segments from one positive zero crossing to the next one are computed and can be used to reduce the number of candidates by eliminating irrelevant candidates like those with negative integral. Within a voiced segment, hypotheses of periods are generated: Each positive zero crossing can be the starting point of several periods. The period length is limited to an interval that is defined by the average fundamental frequency estimated for the whole voiced segment and the maximal relative deviation from this value that is permitted. Dynamic programming (DP) is used to find the optimal path in the graph of hypotheses. Two types of cost functions are defined: cost functions that characterize the period itself and cost functions that characterize the similarity of consecutive periods. Several heuristic cost functions are defined in [Kies 97]. They are combined to a single cost function by an artificial neutral network classifier which has been trained on manually labeled positions of periods. For a more detailed description of the algorithm, please see [Kies 97].

Features for words are obtained by averaging the jitter and shimmer values over all detected periods within the given word. Additionally, the feature vector is extended by the standard deviation of the jitter and shimmer values. Features for turns and chunks are obtained along the same lines as for the prosodic features (s. Chapter 6.1.5).

## 6.3.2   Harmonics-to-Noise Ratio

The *harmonics-to-noise ratio* [Boer 93] is a measure for the degree of periodicity of a voiced signal, which can be found from the relative height of the maximum of the *autocorrelation function*. The autocorrelation function $r_f$ is computed for short speech frames to assure that the speech signal is approximately stationary:

$$r_f(x) := \sum_{n=0}^{N_s-1} f_n^\tau \cdot f_{n+x}^\tau \ . \qquad (6.30)$$

The function has a global maximum at the lag $x = 0$. If the function $f$ is periodic with the fundamental frequency $F_0 = \frac{1}{T_0}$, the length of the frame is a multiple of $T_0$, and the windowed signal $f_n^\tau$ is continued periodically, there will be other *global* maxima at positions $i \cdot T_0$ for every integer $i$. If this is not the case, there can be still local maxima. The signal is said to have at least a periodic part if the highest local maximum is at lag $x_{\max}$ and its height $r_f(x_{\max})$ is large enough. The *harmonic strength* $R_0 = r_f'(x_{\max})$ is a number between 0 and 1 and results from the *normalized autocorrelation function* $r_f'$

$$r_f'(x) := \frac{r_f(x)}{r_f(0)} \qquad (6.31)$$

at lag $x_{\max}$. If noise $n_n$ is added to a periodic signal $h_n$ of period $T_0$ and $n_n$ and $h_n$ are uncorrelated, the autocorrelation function of the resulting signal $f_n$ at zero lag is $r_f(0) = r_h(0) + r_n(0)$. If white noise is added, a local maximum can be found at lag $x_{\max} = T_0$ with height $r_f(x_{\max}) = r_h(T_0) = r_h(0)$. The autocorrelation function at zero lag equals the power of the signal. Hence, the normalized autocorrelation at lag

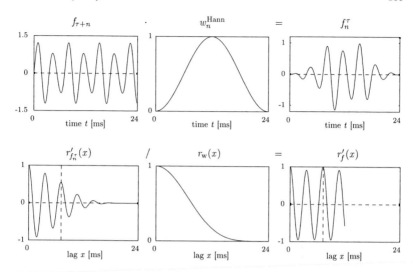

Figure 6.20: First line: speech segment before (left) and after (right) the application of the Hann window (middle). Second line: autocorrelation (ac) function of the windowed signal (left), ac function of the Hann window (middle) and ac function of the windowed signal divided by the one of the window; after [Boer 93]

$x_{\max}$ represents the relative power of the periodic (or *harmonic*) component of the signal whereas its complement represents the relative power of the noise component:

$$r_f'(x_{\max}) = \frac{r_h(0)}{r_f(0)} \; ; \qquad 1 - r_f'(x_{\max}) = \frac{r_n(0)}{r_f(0)} \; . \tag{6.32}$$

This leads to the definition of the logarithmic *harmonics-to-noise ratio* (HNR):

$$\mathrm{HNR} = 10 \cdot \log_{10} \frac{r_f'(x_{\max})}{1 - r_f'(x_{\max})} \; . \tag{6.33}$$

In the experiments of this thesis, the HNR is computed using the speech analysis tool Praat[1]. A detailed description of the implemented HNR algorithm is given in [Boer 93]. A Gaussian window, which has been shown to be superior in comparison to a rectangular, Hamming, and Hann window, is applied to the speech segment prior to the calculation of the autocorrelation function. An unintended side effect of any window is that the autocorrelation function is extenuated smoothly to zero as the autocorrelation index increases. Hence, the local maximum with the highest peak does not always correspond to the fundamental frequency. This effect is avoided if the autocorrelation function of the windowed signal is divided by the autocorrelation function of the window as it is demonstrated in Figure 6.20 where a Hann window has been used. The HNR estimation requires a precise estimate of the lag $x_{\max}$. To

---

[1]http://www.fon.hum.uva.nl/praat/, last visited 01/12/2009

increase the resolution of the sampled autocorrelation function, a sinc interpolation is applied prior to the detection of the local maxima. For each frame, several $F_0$ candidates and their harmonic strength values are computed which form a graph. The Viterbi algorithm is used to find the globally best path with the lowest costs. The cost function is chosen such that transitions from voiced to unvoiced frames and vice versa, and octave jumps are penalized. Furthermore, high harmonic strength values are favored. On the word, the turn, and the chunk level, the mean HNR values, averaged over all voiced frames, and the standard deviation are used as features.

### 6.3.3   Teager Energy Profile based Features

The Teager energy operator is based on the observation that the energy of a simple oscillation is proportional not only to the square of the amplitude but also to the square of the frequency of the oscillation [Kais 90]. In a simple mechanical system where a mass $m$ is attached to a linear spring of force constant $k$, the motion of the mass is described by a harmonic motion $x(t) = A\cos(\omega t + \phi)$. $A$ is the amplitude of the oscillation, $\omega$ the angular frequency, which is equal to $2\pi f$ and to $\sqrt{k/m}$, and $\phi$ an arbitrary initial phase. The total energy $E$ of the system is the sum of the potential energy in the spring and the kinetic energy of the mass:

$$E = \frac{1}{2}k\,x^2 + \frac{1}{2}m\dot{x}^2 = \frac{1}{2}m\,\omega^2 A^2 \ . \tag{6.34}$$

The energy $E$ is proportional to both the square of the amplitude $A$ and the square of the angular frequency $\omega$: $E \propto \omega^2 A^2$.

Let $x_n$ be the discrete samples of the oscillation $x_n = A\cos(\Omega n + \phi)$. The digital frequency $\Omega$ given in radians/samples is equal to $2\pi f/f_s$ where $f_s$ is the sampling frequency. The function $x_n$ depends on the three parameters $A$, $\Omega$, and $\phi$, which can be obtained from three samples of the function $x_n$, e. g., the three consecutive, equally-spaced samples $x_{n-1}$, $x_n$, and $x_{n+1}$. The product $x_{n-1}\cdot x_{n+1}$ can be transformed using the trigonometric identities $\cos(\alpha + \beta) \cdot \cos(\alpha - \beta) = \frac{1}{2}[\cos(2\alpha) + \cos(2\beta)]$ and $\cos(2\alpha) = 2\cos^2(\alpha) - 1 = 1 - 2\sin^2(\alpha)$ into:

$$
\begin{aligned}
x_{n-1} \cdot x_{n+1} &= A^2 \cos\big(\Omega(n-1) + \phi\big)\sin\big(\Omega(n+1) + \phi\big) & (6.35)\\
&= \frac{A^2}{2}\Big[\cos\big(2(\Omega n + \phi)\big) + \cos(2\phi)\Big] & (6.36)\\
&= A^2 \cos^2(\Omega n + \phi) - A^2 \sin^2(\Omega) & (6.37)\\
&= x_n^2 - A^2 \sin^2(\Omega) \ . & (6.38)
\end{aligned}
$$

For small values of $\Omega$, the sine of $\Omega$ is approximately equal to $\Omega$. This leads to the definition of the Teager energy operator (TEO) with the desired properties:

$$\Psi(x_n) = (x_n)^2 - x_{n-1}\cdot x_{n+1} \approx A^2\Omega^2 \ . \tag{6.39}$$

The TEO is a very local operator, which is computed for each sample of the signal and not for whole frames. Note that for harmonic oscillations $x_n = A\cos(\Omega n + \phi)$, the TEO output is constant. More properties of this operator are described in [Kais 93]. Its output is called the *Teager energy profile* (TEP). It is depicted in Figure 6.21 for

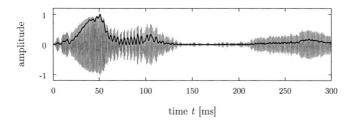

time $t$ [ms]

Figure 6.21: Teager energy profile of a bandpass filtered speech signal

a bandpass filtered speech signal. The speech signal is filtered with a Gabor filter centered at 1 kHz and a bandwidth of 160 Hz. The TEP is normalized such that the maximum of the profile is 1.

Linear speech production models assume that the airflow propagates in the vocal tract as a plane wave and that this pulsatory flow is the source of the sound production. In contrast, studies by Teager [Teag 80, Teag 83, Teag 90] state that concomitant vortices are distributed throughout the vocal tract and that interactions between the vortex flows are the true source of sound production. The Teager energy operator has been developed in order to reflect the instantaneous energy of these nonlinear interactions.

In [Zhou 01], three features based on the TEP are proposed for the classification of speech under stress. For the first feature, the TEP is computed for a bandpass filtered speech signal of a vowel. The bandpass filter is centered around the median fundamental frequency with the bandwidth of $F_0/2$. Then, the TEP is used to decompose the signal where both the frequency and the amplitude are modulated into its FM (frequency modulation) and its AM (amplitude modulation) components. The final feature is computed for segments of constant length as the variation of the FM component within the respective segment.

The second feature has been proposed to capture modulation variations across different frequency bands. It is also applied to vowels only. According to the nonlinear speech production model proposed by Maragos et al. [Mara 93], voiced speech can be modeled as the sum of AM-FM signals, each of them being centered at a formant frequency. To avoid tracking the formant frequencies and the difficulties involved, four fixed bandpass filters are used that cover the frequency bands of 0-1 kHz, 1-2 kHz, 2-3 kHz, and 3-4 kHz. Depending on the type of stress and the stress level, the formants can migrate from one frequency band to an adjacent one. Furthermore, additional harmonics can occur in a frequency band due to changes of the fundamental frequency. The TEP is estimated for each of the four bandpass filtered signals. Each of the four profiles is filtered with a bandpass filter centered around $F_0$ as the AM component for a single formant exhibits periodicity similar to the fundamental frequency. Each filtered TEO stream is then segmented into frames. The length of the frames is set to four times the median pitch period. For each frame of each TEP stream, the autocorrelation function is computed. If there is no pitch variation within a frame, the TEO output is constant and the values of the normalized autocorrelation function are 1 (if the signal is periodically continued). In the case of a varying pitch, the

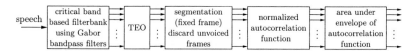

Figure 6.22:   Computational steps of the TEO-CB-Auto-Env features following [Zhou 01]

| band | critical band frequency information [Hz] | | | |
| number | lower | center | upper | bandwidth |
|---|---|---|---|---|
| 1 | 100 | 150 | 200 | 100 |
| 2 | 200 | 250 | 300 | 100 |
| 3 | 300 | 350 | 400 | 100 |
| 4 | 400 | 450 | 510 | 110 |
| 5 | 510 | 570 | 630 | 120 |
| 6 | 630 | 700 | 770 | 140 |
| 7 | 770 | 840 | 920 | 150 |
| 8 | 920 | 1000 | 1080 | 160 |
| 9 | 1080 | 1170 | 1270 | 190 |
| 10 | 1270 | 1370 | 1480 | 210 |
| 11 | 1480 | 1600 | 1720 | 240 |
| 12 | 1720 | 1850 | 2000 | 280 |
| 13 | 2000 | 2150 | 2320 | 320 |
| 14 | 2320 | 2500 | 2700 | 380 |
| 15 | 2700 | 2900 | 3150 | 450 |
| 16 | 3150 | 3400 | 3700 | 550 |

Table 6.1:   Critical frequency bands after [Zhou 01]

area under the envelope of the normalized autocorrelation function will decrease and reflects the degree of excitation variability within the respective band. In doing so, four features are obtained for each frame.

A third feature has been proposed with a higher frequency resolution compared to the only four frequency bands of the second feature. Applied to stress detection from speech, it has been proven to be the best feature in terms of both accuracy and consistency across different stress styles since it does not depend on the accuracy of the pitch estimation. For these reasons, the third feature, entitled *critical band based TEO autocorrelation envelope area* (TEO-CB-Auto-Env), has been reimplemented for this work. The sequence of the computational steps is depicted in Figure 6.22.

In a first step, a filterbank of 16 critical frequency bands is applied to the speech signal. The critical frequency bands, defined in Table 6.1, are based on empirical observations suggesting that the human auditory system performs a filtering operation which partitions the whole frequency range into many critical bands [Scha 70]. Gabor filters are used because of their excellent sidelobe cancellation [Mara 93]:

$$h_{\text{Gabor}}(n) = e^{-2\pi (b\,n/f_{\text{s}})^2} \cos(2\pi\,n\,f_{\text{c}}/f_{\text{s}}) \ . \tag{6.40}$$

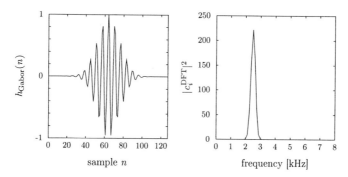

Figure 6.23: Gabor filter centered at 2,500 Hz with a bandwidth of 380 Hz (no. 14) in the time domain (left) and the spectral domain (right)

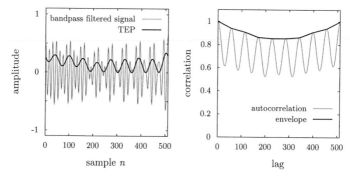

Figure 6.24: Bandpass filtered speech frame and Teager energy profile (left) and the autocorrelation function and its envelope of the periodically continued speech segment (right)

$f_s$ is the sampling frequency, $f_c$ the center frequency of the bandpass filter, and $b$ its bandwidth. Figure 6.23 shows the Gabor filter No. 14 in the time domain as well as its power spectrum. For each of the 16 bandpass filtered speech signals, the TEP is estimated. After segmentation into frames of fixed length (32 ms, time shift of 10 ms), the autocorrelation function and its envelope is computed. Unvoiced frames are discarded. Figure 6.24 shows the speech signal filtered by Gabor filter No. 14 and its Teager energy profile (left) and the autocorrelation function of the TEP and the envelope of the autocorrelation function (right). The area under the envelope of the autocorrelation function is used as a feature resulting in 16 features per frame. The TEO-CB-Auto-Env features are focused on representing the variations of pitch harmonics. Experiments in [Zhou 01] have shown that the fundamental frequency and consequently also the distribution pattern of pitch harmonics across critical frequency bands changes under stressful conditions compared to a neutral speaking style. The resulting TEO features are influenced both by the differences in the number of harmonic terms within each band as well as by differences in the regularity of each harmonic. The TEO-CB-Auto-Env features have been proposed for stress classification (stress subsuming the speaking styles angry, loud, and Lombard effect). In this thesis, they are evaluated for the classification of emotion-related user states. On the word, the turn, and the chunk level, the mean TEO-CB-Auto-Env features, averaged over all voiced frames, and the standard deviation are used as features. Furthermore, the feature vector is extended by the maximum and the minimum of the TEO-CB-Auto-Env values resulting in 64 features.

## 6.4   Linguistic Features

In contrast to many other emotional speech corpora, the FAU Aibo Emotion Corpus does not consist of a limited number of sentences that are portrayed in different emotions but of spontaneous speech of children interacting with the Aibo robot. Besides some 'well-formed' utterances, the speaking style of the children is dominated by a mixture of short sentences and one-word commands. Nevertheless, a linguistic analysis is possible and linguistic features can be used for the classification of the emotion-related states of the children.

### 6.4.1   Length of Words, Fragments, and Repetitions

**Length of Words**

In a first step, the impact of the length of a word on the emotion-related state is investigated. The length can be defined as the number of letters, the number of phonemes, or the number of syllables a word consists of. In contrast to the prosodic feature *duration*, the number of letters, phonemes, and syllables does not have to be measured from the speech signal, but can be looked up easily from a dictionary. Figure 6.25 shows the proportions of the four cover classes *Anger*, *Emphatic*, *Neutral*, and *Motherese* for words of different length. The evaluation is performed on the Aibo word set where the four cover classes are roughly balanced.

At the top of Figure 6.25, the length is defined as the number of letters a word consists of. Since single letters and words consisting of more than 9 letters make up less than 1.2 % of the words in the Aibo word set, the range of letters shown in the figure is limited to [2; 9] Significant differences of the proportions of the four classes can be observed for different numbers of letters. The proportion of *Emphatic*, for example, ranges from less than 10 % for words consisting of only two and three letters to almost 60 % for words consisting of five letters. Mainly, this maximum is due to the two words "links" (*left*) and "stopp" (*stop*) which are likely to be *Emphatic*. The proportion of *Motherese* tends to decrease for longer words whereas the one for *Anger* tends to increase with a higher number of letters. The high proportion of *Motherese* for words that are only two letters long is mainly caused by the words "ja" (*yes*) and "so" – like in the context of "so ist's fein" (*it's fine like that*) – and to some degree also by the word "du" (*you*).

There is a similar picture if the number of letters is substituted by the number of phonemes as illustrated in the middle of Figure 6.25. Diphthongs such as /aɪ/,

/aU/, /OY/, and combinations of a vowel followed by /6/, so-called r-diphthongs, are treated as one phoneme. Combinations of different consonants that are also modeled by separate HMMs in the speech recognizer such as /pf/, /br/, /ts/, /ks/, etc. are treated as two phonemes. The proportion of *Emphatic* is especially high for words consisting of four or five phonemes. This peak is caused by the same words as the peak for words consisting of five letters, namely the word "stopp" (*stop*), which consists of four phonemes, and the words "links" (*left*), "rechts" (*right*), and to some degree "stehen" (*stand*), which consist of five phonemes. The peak of *Anger* at seven phonemes is mainly due to the word "aufstehen" (*get up*).

Finally, the length of a word is defined as the number of syllables the word consists of as shown in Figure 6.25 (bottom). Only words consisting of up to four syllables occur in the FAU Aibo Emotion Corpus. Words with only one or two syllables occur most frequently. Significant differences can be observed between them. The proportion of *Anger* increases from about 15 % to about 44 % whereas the proportions of *Emphatic* and *Motherese* fall from 33 % to 17 % and from 24 % to 13 %, respectively. The proportion of *Neutral* remains nearly constant.

All three different ways to define the length of a word have shown that the proportions of the four cover classes change significantly with the length of the word. This effect is rather due to single words in the corpus than to general conclusions that the proportion of one class increases or decreases with the length of a word. It remains unclear whether these effects also occur in other scenarios with larger lexicons.

On the word level, the length of a word is used directly as a feature. On the turn and the chunk level, the word length is averaged over all words in the segment.

### Repetitions

If Aibo does not obey to the commands of the child, the child will use different strategies to make Aibo obey. Possible strategies are the reformulation of the command or the simple repetition of the utterance. Here, the number of repetitions of single words is used that can be determined without performing a semantic analysis. The proportion of *Emphatic* and *Anger* are expected to increase if a word is repeated whereas the proportion of *Neutral* is expected to decrease. The evaluation shown in Figure 6.26 confirms the expectations. Due to the small number of repetitions, the evaluation is performed on the whole German FAU Aibo Emotion Corpus for the six cover classes *Anger*, *Emphatic*, *Neutral*, *Motherese*, *Joyful*, and *Other*. Unfortunately, the six classes are highly unbalanced on this data set. The latter two as well as those cases where no majority vote exists are excluded for a higher clarity of the presented figure. In total, 5 % of the words in the whole corpus are repetitions: 2153 words are repeated once, 235 words are repeated twice, and 72 words are repeated three or more times (not shown in Figure 6.26 due to their low frequency). The proportion of *Anger* increases from 3 % if the word is not repeated to 10 % if the word is repeated once. For words that are repeated twice, the proportion of *Anger* is 9 % The proportion of *Emphatic* increases from 5 % over 15 % to 18 %. The proportion of *Neutral* falls from 83 % to 61 % and finally to 58 %, the one of *Motherese* from 3 % to 1 %. On the turn and the chunk level, the average number of repetitions is used as a feature.

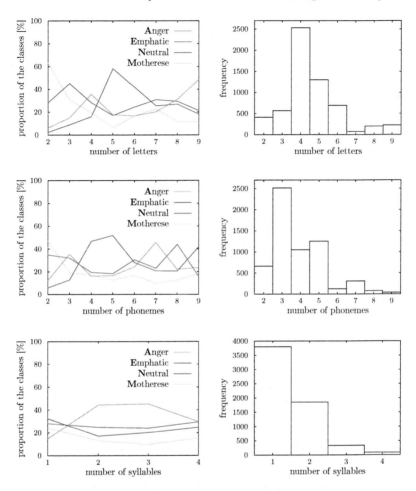

Figure 6.25: Distribution of the cover classes *Anger*, *Emphatic*, *Neutral*, and *Motherese* w.r.t. the length of a word defined as the number of letters (top), phonemes (middle), or syllables (bottom); evaluated on the Aibo word set

## Fragments

Disfluencies are expected to be a sign of emotional arousal. In a study on real dialogs between customers and agents in a web-based stock exchange customer service center [Devi 04], hesitations such as silent and filled pauses are reported to be cues especially for the negative emotions *anger* and *fear*. Word fragments are another type of disfluencies. These word fragments are marked in the transliteration of the FAU Aibo Emotion Corpus. Figure 6.27 shows the proportions of the four cover classes

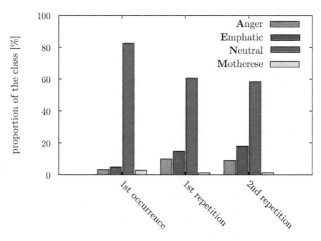

Figure 6.26: Distribution of the cover classes **A**nger, **E**mphatic, **N**eutral, and **M**otherese w.r.t. how often the word has been repeated; evaluated on the whole German FAU Aibo Emotion Corpus

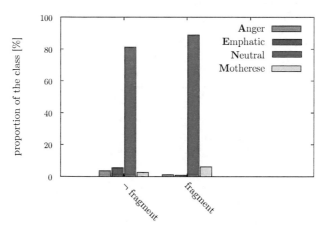

Figure 6.27: Distribution of the cover classes **A**nger, **E**mphatic, **N**eutral, and **M**otherese w.r.t. whether the word is a fragment or not; evaluated on the whole German FAU Aibo Emotion Corpus

**A**nger, **E**mphatic, **N**eutral, and **M**otherese for fragments and non-fragments. The whole German FAU Aibo Emotion Corpus is used for the evaluation. 29% of the lexicon entries (types) but only 3% of all words in the corpus (tokens) are fragments. The proportion of **A**nger and **E**mphatic decreases from 4% to 2% and from 6% to 1%, respectively, whereas the proportion of **N**eutral increases from 81% to 89%.

The proportion of **Motherese** increases as well from 3 % to 6 %. This observation is contradictory to the expectations and a peculiarity of the Aibo scenario. Due to Aibo's slow reaction time, the child has plenty of time to choose a strategy how to make Aibo obey. If the child produces an utterance in one of the emotion-related states **Emphatic** or **Anger**, the utterances are generally well thought out and shorter than in the other two states leading to less disfluencies. Word fragments are more likely to occur in off-talk, which is produced in the state **Neutral**.

### 6.4.2 Part-of-Speech Features

The FAU Aibo Emotion Corpus has been annotated with part-of-speech tags (s. Chapter 5.3.4). The set of POS tags consists of only six coarse lexical and morphological main word classes: NOUN, API, APN, VERB, AUX, and PAJ. They are defined in Table 5.4. Thus, the entries of the lexicon can be annotated without examining the context of the words in the utterance. Figure A.9 in Appendix A.2.6 and Figure 5.15 in Chapter 5.3.9 clearly show the impact of the different part-of-speech classes on the proportions of the six cover classes **Anger**, **Emphatic**, **Neutral**, **Motherese**, **Joyful**, and **Other**. The impact has been described in detail in Chapter 5.3.4.

Six features are used, one for each part-of-speech class. The feature of the POS class the word belongs to is set to one whereas the other features are set to zero. Along the same lines as for the prosodic features, the context of two words to the left and two word to the right of the current word is incorporated into the feature vector resulting in 30 POS features per word. On the turn and the chunk level, again, six features are used, one for each POS class. Each feature contains the relative frequency how often words of the respective POS class occured within the segment. This approach is very similar to the bag-of-words approach, which is described in the following section, if word categories are used instead of single words.

### 6.4.3 Bag-of-Words

The bag-of-words approach is used in text mining and information retrieval to classify a text into one of several categories. Each entry of the lexicon $w_i$ is assigned to one element $e_i$ of the feature vector. This element specifies the relative frequency of the corresponding word in the given text:

$$ e_i = \frac{\#(w_i)}{\sum_k \#(w_k)} \ . \tag{6.41} $$

Here, the bag-of-words approach is applied to single chunks or turns. In Figure 6.28, the principle is illustrated for the utterance "Aibo, geh nach links!" (*Aibo go to the left!*). The word order gets lost. The resulting feature vector is high-dimensional, but most of the entries are equal to zero. In order to reduce the dimension of the feature vector, the following steps are employed:

1. Word fragments and auxiliaries are clustered; each cluster is represented by only one entry. The lexicon consists of 1147 entries, 334 of them are word fragments, 42 entries are auxiliaries. Hence, the dimension of the feature vector is reduced from 1147 to only 773.

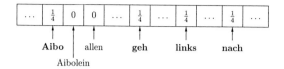

Figure 6.28: Bag-of-words feature vector of the utterance "Aibo, geh nach links!" (*Aibo walk to the left!*)

2. The following alternatives are investigated:

   (a) *Single words:* Words that occur five times or more are represented by separate entries. Less frequently used words are clustered and represented by only one common entry since their influence on the emotional state cannot be estimated robustly enough. Especially words that occur only once in the whole corpus can only be either in the training set or the test set. The number of entries is reduced to 254.

   (b) *Coarse semantic categories:* Words are clustered into the five semantic categories *vocatives* (2), *positive valence* (25), *negative valence* (30), *commands and directions* (76), and *interjections* (36). The number in brackets is the number of words subsumed under the respective category. The remaining 602 lexicon entries are put into the category *other*. By that, the dimension of the feature space is reduced to eight. If these categories are substituted by the POS classes, part-of-speech features can be obtained on the turn and the chunk level.

   (c) *Lemmatization:* This approach combines the previous two. Words that occur at least ten times are still represented by separate entries. Less frequently used words are lemmatized, i. e. words such as "böser", and "böses" are put into the same category as the lemma "böse" (*bad*). Terms with the same semantic meaning such as *feeding dish* and *feeding bowl* are put into one common category as well. The remaining words are categorized into *single characters, nouns with negative valence, nouns with neutral valence, nouns with positive valence, adjectives and adverbs with negative valence, adjectives and adverbs with neutral valence, adjectives and adverbs with positive valence, interjections, infinitives and imperatives of verbs with neutral valence, inflected verbs,* and *function words, articles, etc.* The number of features is reduced to 181.

3. The principal component analysis (PCA) is applied to decorrelate the features and to further reduce the dimension of the feature space.

## 6.4.4 Unigram Models

It is quite obvious that the emotional state influences the words the user chooses. If a person uses swear words, the person is highly likely to be angry. In general, this also holds for the FAU Aibo Emotion Corpus except that the emotion-related states that can be observed are weak and that the choice of words is not unique for a single emotion-related state. Swear words, for example, do not appear at all in the corpus. Nevertheless, utterances such as "Good dog, Aibo!", which are used to praise Aibo, are more likely to be produced in the state *Motherese* than in the states *Emphatic* and *Anger*.

The conditional probability $P(e|w)$ is the probability that the speaker is in the emotion-related state $e$ while he/she is producing the word $w$. Table A.13 shows the conditional probabilities of the six cover classes *Anger*, *Emphatic*, *Neutral*, *Motherese*, *Joyful*, and *Other*, and for those cases where no majority vote exists for the 40 most frequently used words of the German FAU Aibo Emotion Corpus. The high a priori probability $P(\mathbf{N})$ of the class *Neutral* leads to high conditional probabilities $P(\mathbf{N}|w)$ for almost all words. Nevertheless, significant differences can be observed: The word "stopp" (*stop*), for example, is more likely to be produced in the state *Emphatic* than the word "aufstehen" (*get up*), which is often produced in the state *Anger*. Yet, both words are most often observed in the state *Neutral*. For each of the four cover classes *Anger*, *Emphatic*, *Neutral*, and *Motherese*, Table 6.2 shows the 15 words with the highest conditional probabilities of their class. Only words that occur at least 50 times in the whole corpus are considered. Rare words can have higher but possibly less precise estimates of the conditional probability.

The conditional probability can be used directly as a feature on the word level. On the turn and the chunk level, the sequence of words $\boldsymbol{w} = w_1 w_2 \ldots w_{N_w}$ is classified as belonging to the emotion class $\hat{e}$ with the highest probability $P(e|\boldsymbol{w})$. It is computed using the Bayes formula:

$$\hat{e} = \operatorname*{argmax}_{e} P(e|\boldsymbol{w}) = \operatorname*{argmax}_{e} \frac{P(\boldsymbol{w}|e) \cdot P(e)}{P(\boldsymbol{w})} = \operatorname*{argmax}_{e} P(\boldsymbol{w}|e) \cdot P(e) \ . \qquad (6.42)$$

The most likely emotion $\hat{e}$ does not depend on the probability $P(\boldsymbol{w})$ of the word sequence $\boldsymbol{w}$. The probability $P(\boldsymbol{w}|e)$ is computed with the help of the probabilities $P(w_n|w_1 \ldots w_{n-1}, e)$, which can be approximated by trimming the context of the preceding words. Unigram models [Devi03, Schu05, Shaf05] omit the context completely:

$$
\begin{aligned}
P(\boldsymbol{w}|e) &= P(w_1|e) \cdot P(w_2|w_1, e) \cdot \ldots \cdot P(w_{N_w}|w_1 \ldots w_{N_w-1}, e) & (6.43) \\
&\approx P(w_1|e) \cdot P(w_2|e) \cdot \ldots \cdot P(w_{N_w}|e) & (6.44) \\
&= \frac{P(e|w_1)}{P(e)} \cdot \ldots \cdot \frac{P(e|w_{N_w})}{P(e)} \cdot P(w_1) \cdot \ldots \cdot P(w_{N_w}) \ . & (6.45)
\end{aligned}
$$

Due to the limited size of the FAU Aibo Emotion Corpus, the use of bigrams or trigrams is not promising since they cannot be estimated robustly. Again, the most probable emotion $\hat{e}$ does not depend on the product $P(w_1) \cdot \ldots \cdot P(w_{N_w})$. On the word level, four features are used, one for each emotion cover class:

$$u(w, e) = \log_{10} \left( \frac{P(e|w)}{P(e)} \right) \ . \qquad (6.46)$$

Furthermore, the feature vector is extended by the context of two words to the left and two words to the right resulting in 20 features. On the turn and the chunk level, the contour of the features on the word level (without the context) is described by

| Anger | $P(\mathbf{A}|w)$ |
|---|---|
| böser (*bad*) | 29.2 % |
| stehenbleiben (*stand still*) | 18.9 % |
| nein (*no*) | 17.0 % |
| aufstehen (*get up*) | 12.3 % |
| Aibo (*Aibo*) | 10.1 % |
| hinsetzen (*lay down*) | 10.0 % |
| umdrehen (*turn around*) | 9.3 % |
| nicht (*not*) | 7.4 % |
| Hund (*dog*) | 6.3 % |
| stehen (*stand*) | 5.6 % |
| bleiben (*stay*) | 5.3 % |
| auf (*up*) | 4.4 % |
| ganz (*very*) | 3.9 % |
| los (*go*) | 3.8 % |
| drehen (*turn*) | 3.8 % |

| Emphatic | $P(\mathbf{E}|w)$ |
|---|---|
| stopp (*stop*) | 30.5 % |
| halt (*halt*) | 29.3 % |
| links (*left*) | 20.5 % |
| rechts (*right*) | 18.9 % |
| nein (*no*) | 17.6 % |
| sitz (*sit*) | 16.9 % |
| hinsetzen (*sit down*) | 15.8 % |
| stehen (*stand*) | 15.2 % |
| bleiben (*stay*) | 14.7 % |
| tanz (*dance*) | 12.3 % |
| drehen (*turn*) | 12.3 % |
| vorwärts (*forwards*) | 11.5 % |
| stehenbleiben (*stand still*) | 11.3 % |
| zurück (*back*) | 8.6 % |
| g'rad'aus (*straight forward*) | 8.2 % |

| Neutral | $P(\mathbf{N}|w)$ |
|---|---|
| okay (*okay*) | 98.6 % |
| und (*and*) | 98.5 % |
| Stück (*bit*) | 98.5 % |
| in (*in*) | 98.2 % |
| noch (*still*) | 96.2 % |
| *n (*'n*) | 96.1 % |
| rum (*around*) | 95.8 % |
| der (*the*) | 95.6 % |
| wieder (*again*) | 95.4 % |
| ein (*a*) | 94.8 % |
| mal[1] | 94.5 % |
| jetzt (*now*) | 94.3 % |
| zum (*to*) | 94.0 % |
| geh (*go*) | 94.0 % |
| bisschen (*a little*) | 93.7 % |

| Motherese | $P(\mathbf{M}|w)$ |
|---|---|
| fein (*fine*) | 57.5 % |
| ganz (*very*) | 41.9 % |
| braver (*good*) | 36.0 % |
| sehr (*very*) | 23.5 % |
| brav (*good*) | 21.7 % |
| Hund (*dog*) | 18.9 % |
| gut (*good*) | 17.3 % |
| gemacht (*done*) | 17.1 % |
| ja (*yes*) | 14.7 % |
| das (*the, this*) | 14.6 % |
| schön (*nice*) | 12.8 % |
| her (*here*) | 12.0 % |
| so (*like that*) | 11.8 % |
| genau (*exactly*) | 11.7 % |
| hier (*here*) | 10.0 % |

[1] modal particle, typical for German, the equivalent in English is the use of specific intonation contours

Table 6.2: The 15 words with the highest conditional probability $P(e|w)$ for each of the four cover classes *Anger*, *Emphatic*, *Neutral*, and *Motherese*

the average, the standard deviation, the maximum, and the minimum resulting in 16 features. If a word $w_n$ produced in emotion $e$ does not appear in the training set because the size of the training set is too small, the estimate of $P(e|w_n)$ is equal to zero. Hence, the probability $P(e|\boldsymbol{w})$ is zero for the whole segment. To cope with this problem, an equal distribution of the conditional probabilities is assumed for words occurring less than ten times in the training set. Furthermore, each emotion class is assumed to be observed at least once for every word. The conditional probabilities are estimated in a leave-one-speaker-out procedure such that the data of the test speaker is excluded for the estimation of the statistics.

In [Schu 05], the unigram features are compared to several features based on the *emotional salience* [Lee 02] of a word $w$, which is defined as follows:

$$\text{sal}(w) = \sum_e P(e|w) \cdot i(w, e) \quad \text{with} \quad i(w, e) = \log \frac{P(e|w)}{P(e)} \ . \qquad (6.47)$$

A salient word w. r. t. the emotion class $e$ is a word that is produced more often in emotion $e$ than in other emotional states. The best results are reported for the feature $u(w, e)$ and the following feature, which are both summed up over all words in the utterance [Schu 05]:

$$t(w, e) = P(e|w) \cdot \log_{10} \left( \frac{P(e|w)}{P(e)} \right) \ . \qquad (6.48)$$

Both variants have been evaluated on the German FAU Aibo Emotion Corpus. As the differences are not significant [Maye 05], only the first variant is used in the experiments in Chapter 7.

## 6.5   Knowledge about Aibo's Behavior

During the recordings of the FAU Aibo Emotion Corpus, the children were led to believe that they can control Aibo by talking to the robot. They were told to reprimand Aibo if it does not obey or to praise Aibo if it takes orders. Instead, Aibo was remote-controlled and followed a pre-defined script of actions independently of the child's commands. Aibo's actions are categorized into non-verbal actions, co-operative actions, and non-cooperative actions. They are annotated for the parcours experiment as described in Chapter 5.3.1. The following binary function is used to describe Aibo's co-operation at a turn $t$:

$$\text{co-operation}(t) = \left\{ \begin{array}{ll} 1 & \text{Aibo is co-operative} \\ 0 & \text{Aibo does not obey} \end{array} \right. \ . \qquad (6.49)$$

Figure 6.29 shows this co-operation function for speaker Ohm_18 and a subset of the Aibo turn set (s. Chapter 5.4). Unfortunately, only a subset can be used for the evaluation since only 2046 of the 3996 turns of the Aibo turn set are actually part of the parcours experiment. In Figure 6.29, the emotion class of the turns (the turn label) is color-coded. For this speaker, a high correlation of 0.64 between Aibo's co-operation and the 2-class problems *Anger* vs. *no Anger* can be observed: the turns are mostly produced in the state *Anger* if and only if Aibo shows non-cooperative behavior. In order to compute the correlation, a binary emotion function is defined along the same lines as Aibo's co-operation function: the function is set to 1 if the turn is produced in the state *Anger* and to zero if the turn is produced in one of the three other states *Emphatic*, *Neutral*, and *Motherese*.

If all speakers are evaluated, the correlation for this 2-class problem is 0.37. Other 2-class problems can be correlated with Aibo's behavior as well. The results are given

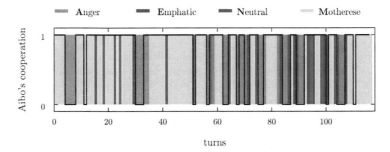

Figure 6.29: Influence of Aibo's co-operation on the turn labels for speaker Ohm_18: high correlation (0.64) between the 2-class problems *Anger* vs. no *Anger* and non-cooperative vs. co-operative behavior of Aibo

| 2-class problem | correlation |
|---|---|
| A vs. N | 0.47 |
| A vs. ¬A | 0.37 |
| E vs. N | 0.08 |
| E vs. ¬E | −0.09 |
| M vs. N | 0.04 |
| M vs. ¬M | −0.08 |
| ¬N vs. N | 0.18 |
| A,E vs. N | 0.23 |
| A,E vs. N,M | 0.22 |

Table 6.3: Correlation of Aibo's behavior and the cover classes *Anger*, *Emphatic*, *Neutral*, and *Motherese*, evaluated on the Parcours subset of the Aibo turn set

in Table 6.3. The highest correlation is obtained for the 2-class problem *Anger* vs. *Neutral* excluding the turns that are produced in one of the other two states. The correlation values vary strongly from one speaker to another. Some speakers show only little emotional behavior and deviate only seldom from the neutral speaking style. Hence, their correlation values are rather low. For other speakers, the correlation values are above 0.75.

The occurrence of the state *Emphatic* seems to be barely influenced by Aibo's behavior as the low correlation values for the 2-class problems *Emphatic* vs. the other three states and *Emphatic* vs. *Neutral* indicate. This also holds for *Motherese*.

In summary, if Aibo's behavior is known, a simple binary feature indicating Aibo's co-operation can be helpful to discriminate *Anger* and *Neutral*. It will not be able to distinguish *Neutral* from *Emphatic* and *Motherese*. For our 4-class problem, this feature will only be useful in combination with others. Experimental results on the subset of the Aibo turn set are reported in [Maye 05]. The class-wise averaged recognition rate (CL) could be improved from 44.7 % to 49.2 % if 55 linguistic features (mainly part-of-speech features (30) and unigram features (20) on the turn level) were used. Especially the low recognition rate for *Anger* could be improved. If bag-of-word features were added, the improvement was not significant (54.0 % to 55.6 %). Yet, the recognition rates of the four classes were more balanced.

**Summary**   The presented features for emotion recognition from speech cover the four main categories of features, namely prosodic, spectral, voice quality, and linguistic features. The features of the Erlangen Prosody Module differ from those of other research groups as a compact set of selected features is used to model energy, $F_0$, and temporal aspects for single words instead of whole utterances. This approach is especially suited for the classification on the word level, but can be used for larger segments as well by computing statistics of the word level features.

The presented spectral features model short-term spectral characteristics. The standard MFCC features for speech recognition and features of less compressed prestages of their computation, namely DFT and log-Mel frequency features, are described as well as features based on formants. The spectral features can be classified directly on the frame level. The a posteriori probabilities of the frames are then multiplied to obtain probabilities on the word level or for larger segments. Alternatively, the features can be averaged over the whole segment before classification.

The group of voice quality features is represented by jitter and shimmer, the harmonics-to-noise ratio, and features based on the Teager energy profile.

A special characteristic of the FAU Aibo Emotion Corpus is the spontaneous speech of the children which can be analyzed linguistically. The evaluation of simple features such as the length of a word, the number how often a word is repeated, and the information whether a word is a fragment or not have been shown to influence the emotion-related state of the child. Furthermore, part-of-speech features using six coarse lexical and morphological main word classes and bag-of-words features are presented. Three approaches to reduce the high dimensionality of the bag-of-words vector are suggested. Unigram models based on the conditional probabilities $P(e|w)$ are another type of linguistic features.

In the Aibo scenario, where Aibo follows strictly pre-defined plot of actions, it is known whether Aibo behaves co-operatively or not. The evaluation has shown that the emotion-related state *Anger* is produced mainly if Aibo does not obey. In contrast, there is almost no correlation with the states *Emphatic* and *Motherese*.

# Chapter 7

# Experimental Results on Emotion Recognition

In this chapter, the features described in Chapter 6 are evaluated on the German FAU Aibo Emotion Corpus for the 4-class problem consisting of the four cover classes *Anger, Emphatic, Neutral,* and *Motherese.* As the emotion-related state of the speaker changes even within utterances, each single word of the corpus is labeled as belonging to one of these cover classes (s. Chapter 5.3.7). Hence, the main focus is set on the classification on the word level. The different types of features are evaluated separately as well as in combination with the other feature types. In Chapter 5.3.8, procedures are described how emotion labels for turns (s. Chapter 5.2) and chunks, which are defined in Chapter 5.3.5, are obtained from the labels on the word level. By comparing the experimental results on the word level with those on the turn and the chunk level, conclusions can be drawn which unit of analysis is the most appropriate one for emotion recognition. If the whole German FAU Aibo Emotion Corpus is used for classification, the four cover classes are highly unbalanced. *Neutral* is the most dominating emotional state by far. The performance of some classifiers, especially the artificial neural networks, which are mainly used in our experiments, decreases if the classes are unbalanced. To avoid the upsampling of rare classes on a large scale and the disadvantages involved, subsets of the corpus (s. Chapter 5.4) are defined where the four cover classes are more balanced. Smaller differences between the frequencies of the four classes that still exist are compensated by upsampling prior to the classification. In the following section, the classification experiments on the word level are described, followed by the experiments on the turn and the chunk level. The chapter ends with a comparison of our classification results with the ones of the CEICES partners.

## 7.1 Word Level

On the word level, the experiments are conducted on the Aibo word set consisting of 6,070 words (tokens, s. Chapter 5.4). The word level features are classified using artificial neural networks (s. Chapter 4.1.4). In general, the choice of the classifier affects clearly the classification results. More elaborated classifiers such as a artificial neural networks (ANN) and support vector machines (SVM) perform generally

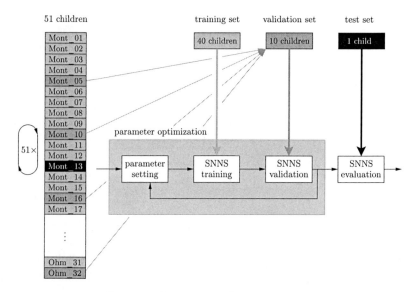

Figure 7.1: Leave-one-speaker-out procedure

clearly better than rather simple classifiers such as $k$ nearest neighbor classifiers. In [Schu 07a], various classifiers for emotion recognition as well as different bagging and boosting strategies are compared on two databases of emotion portrayals – the Berlin Emotional Speech Database and the Danish Emotional Speech Corpus – and the German FAU Aibo Emotion Corpus albeit a different subset with a higher inter-labeler agreement has been chosen. The two classifiers with the highest performance are artificial neutral networks and support vector machines, which yielded even better results than the bagging and boosting strategies. If the whole feature set is used, no significant differences between ANNs and SVMs could be observed for all three databases. If a reduced set of selected features is used, slightly better results are reported for SVMs than for ANNs mainly due to the feature selection procedure. In both cases, the features have been selected using the *sequential forward floating search* (SFFS) algorithm in combination with the SVM classifier.

Own experiments on the FAU Aibo Emotion Corpus using linear discriminant analysis (LDA, s. Chapter 4.1.3) have shown that equivalent results are achieved using the simple classifier LDA compared to ANNs. One reason may be overlapping class areas of the four cover classes such that more elaborated classifiers cannot profit by more complex separation functions compared to simple hyperplanes. Nevertheless, the results reported here are based on ANNs.

To get the most out of the small data set, a leave-one-speaker-out (LOSO) procedure is applied as depicted in Figure 7.1. The data of one of the 51 speakers is used for testing, the data of the other 50 speakers is split into a training and a validation set. The training set consists of the data of 40 speakers, the validation set of the data

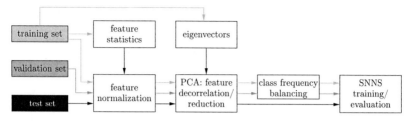

Figure 7.2: Feature processing before classification with SNNS

of the remaining 10 speakers. The procedure is repeated 51 times such that each speaker is used once for testing and the classifier can be evaluated on the complete Aibo word set. The data used for testing and the one for training and validation are disjoint not only w. r. t. the utterances but also w. r. t. the speakers. Within CEICES, a speaker-independent three-fold cross-validation is proposed using the splits defined in Appendix A.2.10. The splits are balanced as far as possible w. r. t. to the gender of the speakers, the two schools Mont and Ohm, and the frequencies of the four cover classes on the chunk level (chunk labels). Only slight improvements can be achieved using the 51-fold cross-validation compared to the 3-fold cross-validation. For those experiments where the PCA is used to reduce the number of features, only the 3-fold cross-validation is used to optimize the dimension of the feature vector in order to reduce the computational effort.

The experiments are conducted using the *Stuttgart neural network simulator*[1] (SNNS). The backpropagation algorithm is applied to estimate the weights $w_{ij}^{(l)}$ on the training set that are assigned to the edges of the artificial neural network (s. Chapter 4.1.4). For each node, the same activation function is applied, namely the hyperbolic tangent. Besides the weights $w_{ij}^{(l)}$, the topology of the ANN as well as the initialization of the weights and the weight decay $\eta$ controlling the step size of the gradient descent (s. Equation 4.44) has to be optimized. Topologies with one hidden layer and a varying number of hidden nodes and one topology without hidden layer are evaluated on the validation set for each of the 51 splits. Furthermore, five different random seeds providing different but fixed initializations of the weights with random numbers and five different values of the weight decay $\eta$ (0.1, 0.3, 1.0, 3.0, and 5.0) are tested. The experiments have shown that these three parameters greatly influence the performance of the ANN. Only the combination of the three parameters yields good results. To keep the effort within reasonable limits, the number of topologies is reduced after the first ten splits to only those topologies that occurred so far.

Before classification, the data is pre-processed as shown in Figure 7.2. The maximum and the minimum of each feature is determined on the training set and used to map the data of the training, the validation, and the test set onto the interval $[-1; +1]$. This is necessary as the values of the activation function change only little outside this interval. After this normalization, the features are decorrelated using the principal component analysis (PCA). The PCA is based on the eigenvalues and eigenvectors, which are calculated only on the training set. Furthermore, the PCA

---

[1]http://www.ra.cs.uni-tuebingen.de/SNNS/, last visited 01/12/2009

can be used to reduce the dimension of the feature vector. Finally, the class frequencies on the training and on the validation set are balanced by upsampling. Samples of less frequent classes are copied unless the frequency of the most frequent class is reached.

## 7.1.1   Acoustic Features

In this section, the acoustic features, i. e. the prosodic features of the Erlangen Prosody Module, the spectral features, and the voice quality features, are evaluated on the Aibo word set.

### Prosodic Features

First of all, the prosodic features are evaluated. The feature vector of the prosodic features is extended by the context of two words to the left and two words to the right of the word under consideration (s. Chapter 6.1). Since the Aibo word set is a subset of the Aibo corpus created by downsampling, the words of the context are not included in the Aibo word set in general. In order to use still the correct context, the features are calculated for the complete FAU Aibo Emotion Corpus and after that, only the features of the words that are part of the Aibo word set are selected for classification.

The experimental results for the prosodic features of the Erlangen Prosody Module are reported in Figure 7.1. The classification performance is given in terms of the classwise averaged recognition rate (CL) defined in Chapter 4.2.1. As the frequencies of the four cover classes are almost balanced in the Aibo word set, the classwise averaged recognition rate and the absolute recognition rate (RR) are almost identical. Results are reported for the case where all prosodic features are used in combination as well as for those cases where only features of one single type are evaluated.

The calculation of the features on the word level requires that the correct segmentation of the word, i. e. the information when a word begins and when it ends, has to be known. The segmentation has been obtained by a forced alignment of the actually spoken word sequence as described in Chapter 5.2. This automatic segmentation is error-prone and has been manually corrected. The segmentation errors are categorized and quantified in Chapter 5.3.2. Furthermore, the $F_0$ based features as well as those duration based features that model the position of the $F_0$ extrema are influenced by errors of the automatic $F_0$ extraction algorithm. Two automatic $F_0$ algorithms, a modified version of an algorithm by Medan and Bagshaw and the RAPT algorithm implemented in the *Entropic Signal Processing System* (ESPS) toolkit, are compared to a manually corrected version of the ESPS $F_0$ values. The types of $F_0$ errors and their quantification is given in Chapter 5.3.3. The following combinations of different segmentation and $F_0$ extraction variants are evaluated:

S1:  automatic segmentation obtained by a forced alignment of the actually spoken word sequence and $F_0$ values obtained by a modified version of an algorithm by Medan and Bagshaw (mbn)

S2:  manually corrected word segmentation but automatically extracted $F_0$ values using the mbn algorithm

| feature set | S1[1] | S2[2] | S3[3] | S4[4] |
|---|---|---|---|---|
| pause based features (8) | 36.1 | 35.5 | | |
| $F_0$ based features (26) | 46.3 | 45.7 | 47.1 | 48.1 |
| energy/$F_0$ position features (16) | 49.3 | 50.3 | 50.9 | 50.5 |
| duration based features (17) | 54.0 | 54.0 | | |
| duration and position features (33) | 55.1 | 53.4 | 53.9 | 55.4 |
| energy based features (33) | 55.4 | 56.6 | | |
| all prosodic features (100) | 59.4 | 59.2 | 59.7 | 58.7 |

[1] automatic word segmentation and $F_0$ values (mbn algorithm)

[2] manually corrected word segmentation and automatic $F_0$ values (mbn algorithm)

[3] manually corrected word segmentation and automatic $F_0$ values (ESPS algorithm)

[4] manually corrected word segmentation and $F_0$ values

Table 7.1: Classification results of the word based features of the Erlangen Prosody Module on the word level. Results are reported in terms of the classwise averaged recognition rate (CL)

S3: manually corrected word segmentation but automatically extracted $F_0$ values using the RAPT algorithm implemented in ESPS

S4: manually corrected word segmentation and manually corrected $F_0$ values based on the automatically extracted ESPS values

First, the results for different feature types are evaluated for the combination of automatic segmentation and automatic $F_0$ extraction using the mbn algorithm (S1). The eight features based on pauses perform worse than the other feature types. Only a classwise averaged recognition rate (CL) of 36 % is achieved. One reason may be the low number of features. Certainly, the meaning of pauses in the Aibo scenario plays an important role: The pauses before or after words are much more due to the fact that the child is waiting for Aibo's reactions than to hesitations that may characterize the emotion-related state of the child. Still, the result is clearly above chance level, which is only 25 % for four classes. The set of 26 $F_0$ based features performs clearly better than the features based on pauses: a CL of 46.3 % is achieved. Features modeling the position of the energy and $F_0$ extrema belong to the group of duration based features. If these 16 features are evaluated on their own, a CL of 49.3 % is achieved. This result is slightly better than the one for $F_0$ based features. The 'original' 17 duration features yield a CL of 54.0 %. This result can be improved by adding the other temporal features modeling the positions of the energy and $F_0$ extrema. Then, a CL of 55.1 % is achieved. Hence, the 33 duration based features clearly outperform the 26 $F_0$ based features. Energy based features perform slightly but not significantly better than the duration based features. With 33 energy based features, a CL of 55.4 % is achieved. Hence, energy and duration based features are the most important types of prosodic features for emotion recognition in this scenario. This is true even though the emotional-related states in the Aibo scenario are weak and no full-blown emotions can be observed, for which a high importance

hypothesis

|  |  | A | E | N | M | $\sum$ |
|---|---|---|---|---|---|---|
| r e f e r e n c e | **A** | 59.4 % | 15.9 % | 16.1 % | 8.5 % | 1557 |
|  | **E** | 19.8 % | 61.3 % | 13.6 % | 5.3 % | 1645 |
|  | **N** | 13.5 % | 14.4 % | 55.4 % | 16.7 % | 1645 |
|  | **M** | 10.5 % | 7.3 % | 20.6 % | 61.7 % | 1223 |

Table 7.2: Confusion matrix for the classification with all prosodic features (S1) on the word level

of the energy based features could be expected. The best classification result (59.4 % CL) is obtained if all 100 prosodic features are used. The results are summarized in Table 7.1.

The comparison of the results for the automatic and the manually corrected word segmentation (S1 vs. S2) show that the segmentation errors do not influence the emotion recognition. Only slight, not significant changes of the classwise averaged recognition rates can be observed.

The same holds for the comparison of the two automatic $F_0$ extraction algorithms mbn and ESPS (S2 vs. S3). The performance of the prosodic features cannot be improved if coarse $F_0$ errors are manually corrected (S3 vs. S2). Our $F_0$ based features model the course of the fundamental frequency within words. Some features, especially the extrema, are influenced by octave or other coarse errors. 4.5 % of all frames within words (s. Figure 5.3) are coarse errors. Nevertheless, the emotion recognition is not influenced significantly by these errors. From a current perspective, the quality of automatic $F_0$ extraction algorithms is sufficient for emotion recognition.

Table 7.2 shows the confusion matrix for the classification with all prosodic features based on the automatic word segmentation and the mbn algorithm to extract the fundamental frequency. Due to their low emotional intensity, the non-neutral states *Anger*, *Emphatic*, and *Motherese* are likely to be confused with *Neutral*. Furthermore, *Anger* and *Emphatic* are confused to some degree. They are confused only seldom with *Motherese*. Hence, the confusion pattern of the machine classifier is similar to the one obtained by human labelers. The lowest recognition rate for a single class is obtained for *Neutral*. This does not mean that the machine classifier generally recognizes this state with a lower performance than the other states. By a higher weighting of the a posteriori scores of the classifier for one state, the performance of this class can be increased – however, only at the cost of the performance for the other three classes.

**Spectral Features**

Next, the spectral features are evaluated. Theses features are computed for single frames and can be classified directly on the frame level. For this purpose, Gaussian mixture models (GMMs, s. Chapter 4.1.2) are used. The pre-processing of the features is depicted in Figure 7.3 and slightly differs from the one for ANNs: As no parameters have to be optimized on the validation set, the validation set is used to extend the training set. Furthermore, GMMs are less vulnerable to an unbalanced distribution of the classes. An initial codebook is estimated on the complete training set using

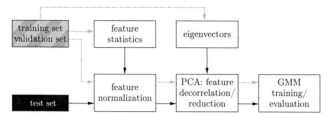

Figure 7.3: Feature processing before classification with GMMs

the samples of all four classes. This initial codebook is then adapted separately to each class using only the samples of the respective class. The parameters of these adapted codebooks cannot be estimated more robustly if the data is upsampled since no new information is added. For most experiments, 25 Gaussian probability density functions per class are used. Up to this number, the recognition rates increase and then remain at a high level for higher numbers. Hence, the number of Gaussians is not optimized on the validation set.

On the basis of the logarithmic DFT features (s. Chapter 6.2.1), the four cover classes can be classified on the frame level with an accuracy of 40.2 % CL and 39.7 % RR, respectively. Since only segments of 16 ms duration are classified, these results are impressive. Again, chance level is 25 % CL. The logarithmic DFT coefficients are the least compressed form in the chain of computational steps towards the final MFCCs. Nevertheless, experiments using PCA to decorrelate the features and to reduce the dimension of the feature space have shown that the best performance is achieved if the dimension is reduced from originally 129 to only 10. For higher numbers of features, the accuracy decreases slightly. This confirms the assumption that the DFT coefficients of adjacent frequency bands highly correlate. Furthermore, if the number of coefficients is not reduced, the number of GMM parameters that have to be estimated in the training phase increases quadratically with the dimension of the feature vector. For a robust estimation of all parameters, a large amount of data is required. Otherwise, the recognition rates drop as it is obviously the case on the Aibo word set. A posteriori probabilities on the word level can be obtained by multiplying the a posteriori probabilities on the frame level for all frames within one word. The classwise averaged recognition rate on the word level (53.4 %) is clearly above the value on the frame level (40.2 %). The absolute recognition rates for the spectral features are very close to the classwise averaged ones such that only the latter ones are reported here. Details are given in Table 7.3.

The next stage in the computation of the MFCCs are the logarithmic Mel frequency coefficients (s. Chapter 6.2.2). By applying a Mel filterbank of 22 triangular filters, the dimension of the feature space is reduced from 129 to 22. The first coefficient is the short-term energy. To evaluate the improvement due to the short-term energy, the feature vector is once classified with (41.4 % CL) and once without (39.0 % CL) the short-term energy. The contribution of the short-term energy to the performance of the log-Mel features is rather low. In both cases, the classwise averaged recognition rates on the word level are below the rates obtained by the log-DFT fea-

| feature set | frame level CL | frame level RR | word level CL | word level RR |
|---|---|---|---|---|
| log-DFT | | | | |
|   128 log-DFT coefficients (PCA: 128 → 10) | 40.2 | 39.7 | 53.4 | 53.3 |
| log-MEL | | | | |
|   static features without energy (22) | 39.0 | 39.2 | 50.5 | 51.3 |
|   static features (23) | 41.4 | 41.5 | 51.7 | 52.1 |
|   static and dynamic features (46) | 44.1 | 44.3 | 55.5 | 56.1 |
| MFCC | | | | |
|   static features without energy (11) | 39.8 | 40.0 | 51.9 | 52.5 |
|   static features (12) | 43.2 | 43.1 | 54.9 | 55.1 |
|   static and dynamic features (24) | 45.2 | 45.5 | 57.5 | 57.9 |
| formant based features | | | | |
|   formants 1-4: center frequencies and bandwidths (8) | 34.3 | 34.7 | 46.3 | 46.9 |
| voice quality features | | | | |
|   HNR (1) | 29.9 | 30.7 | 31.9 | 33.6 |
|   TEO-CB-Auto-Env (16) | 36.3 | 35.0 | 47.3 | 47.4 |

Table 7.3: Classification results of the frame based spectral and voice quality features on the frame and the word level. Results are reported in terms of the classwise averaged recognition rate (CL) and the absolute recognition rate (RR)

tures. If the first derivative is added to the feature vector, 55.5 % CL are achieved on the word level.

Surprisingly, the best results are achieved with the MFCC features (s. Chapter 6.2.3), which are the most compact set of features: 54.9 % CL on the word level. Although they have been designed to discard as much of the information how something is uttered and to keep only the information needed to discriminate phonemes, the compact form is obviously superior to the less compressed log-DFT and log-Mel representations of the signal. The contribution of the short-term energy is higher than for the log-Mel features. Without the short-term energy, only 51.9 % CL are achieved. Again, the performance can be improved by adding the first derivative to the feature vector resulting in 57.5 % CL. Astonishingly, this result is very close to the one obtained with the 100 prosodic features (59.4 % CL, S1). Yet, no information about the actually spoken words is required to compute the MFCC features.

Instead of the prior classification of the MFCC features on the frame level, MFCC features can be computed directly on the word level by averaging the 24 framewise MFCC features for all frames within the respective word. On the one hand, valuable information may get lost by averaging over all frames, on the other hand, linguistic information about the appearing phonemes within the respective word and thereby information about the word itself is gained to some degree. All in all, these long-term MFCC features proved to be very successful as well. A classwise averaged recognition rate of 55.2 % on the word level is achieved (s. Table 7.4).

Just like the other spectral features, the formant based features (s. Chapter 6.2.4) can be classified directly on the frame level. Compared to the other spectral features,

| feature set | CL | RR |
|---|---|---|
| spectral features | | |
| long-term MFCC (24) | 55.2 | 55.0 |
| long-term formant features (16) | 46.2 | 46.3 |
| voice quality features | | |
| long-term jitter and shimmer features (4) | 39.8 | 38.8 |
| long-term HNR features (2) | 37.3 | 37.8 |
| long-term HNR, long-term jitter and shimmer (6) | 39.9 | 39.7 |
| long-term TEO-CB-Auto-Env (64) | 51.6 | 51.1 |

Table 7.4: Classification results of the word based spectral and voice quality features on the word level. Results are reported in terms of the classwise averaged recognition rate (CL) and the absolute recognition rate (RR)

the formant based features perform worse. On the word level, only a CL of 46.3 % is achieved (s. Table 7.3). Nearly identical results are obtained with the long-term formant features, calculated by averaging the framewise features over all frames within one word prior to the classification with SNNS on the word level. Additionally, the standard deviation of the center frequencies and the bandwidths within one word is added to the feature vector for each of the first four formants. This approach results in a CL of 46.2 % (s. Table 7.4).

**Voice Quality Features**

In this section, features based on jitter and shimmer, on the harmonics-to-noise ratio (HNR), and on the TEO-CB-Auto-Env features are evaluated. Only the latter two are classified directly on the frame level. The harmonics-to-noise ratio (s. Chapter 6.3.2) is a single value calculated for each voiced frame. On the frame level, a classwise averaged recognition rate of only 29.9 % is achieved (s. Table 7.3). This result is only little above the chance level and obviously too low to get acceptable results on the word level (31.9 %) by multiplying the a posteriori probabilities of the frame level. The two long-term HNR features on the word level are superior to the prior classification on the frame level. With them, a CL of at least 37.3 % can be realized (s. Table 7.4).

Regarding their performance, the TEO-CB-Auto-Env features (s. Chapter 6.3.3) are comparable to the formant based features. If classified on the frame level first, a CL of 47.3 % on the word level (s. Table 7.3) is achieved compared to 46.3 % CL for the formant based features. The long-term TEO-CB-Auto-Env features yield even 51.6 % on the word level (s. Table 7.4). This result is close to the one of the long-term MFCC features (55.2 % CL).

The four long-term jitter and shimmer features are only slightly better than the two long-term HNR features and produce a CL of 39.8 % on the word level. The result cannot be improved significantly (39.9 %) if the long-term HNR and the long-term jitter and shimmer features are classified together.

| feature set | CL | RR |
|---|---|---|
| long-term MFCC, HNR, and jitter and shimmer features (30) | 55.4 | 55.1 |
| prosodic features (S1), MFCC (8) | 62.4 | 62.0 |
| prosodic features (S1), MFCC, formants, TEO-CB-Auto-Env (16) | 61.9 | 61.4 |

Table 7.5: Classification results for the combination of the acoustic features on the word level. Results are reported in terms of the classwise averaged recognition rate (CL) and the absolute recognition rate (RR)

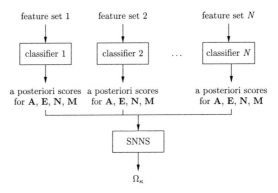

Figure 7.4: Combination of various types of features by combining classifier outputs (late fusion)

### Combination of Acoustic Features

The last section has shown that the presented voice quality features are suited to model to some extent the emotion-related states *Anger*, *Emphatic*, *Neutral*, and *Motherese*. Nevertheless, they perform worse than other types of acoustic features, namely prosodic features and spectral features, especially framewise MFCC features. This seems to be especially true for weak emotion-related states such as those states that can be observed in the FAU Aibo Emotion Corpus. In this section, prosodic, spectral and voice quality features are combined.

In the first experiment, long-term MFCC, long-term HNR, and long-term jitter and shimmer features are combined to one feature vector comprising 30 features. The approach to combine different feature sets to one big set prior to the classification is called *early fusion* and is best suited for smaller sets of features. Almost no improvement is achieved compared to the classification of the long-term MFCC features alone: 55.4 % CL (s. Table 7.5) vs. 55.2 %. Obviously, the voice quality features based on the HNR and the jitter and the shimmer do not contain more information about the emotion-related states in the Aibo scenario than the MFCC features alone.

In a second experiment, the prosodic features on the word level are combined with the framewise MFCC features by *late fusion*. As depicted in Figure 7.4, the two different types of features are first classified separately. The prosodic features are classified with SNNS on the word level and the MFCC features are classified with

| feature set | CL | RR |
|---|---|---|
| number of letters/syllables/phonemes, fragment, repetitions (LFR, 5) | 48.5 | 48.9 |
| part-of-speech features (POS, 30) | 52.1 | 52.2 |
| unigram models (UM, 20) | 61.5 | 60.8 |
| LFR, UM (25) | 61.3 | 60.7 |
| LFR, UM, POS (55) | 60.8 | 60.2 |

Table 7.6: Classification results of the linguistic features on the word level. Results are reported in terms of the classwise averaged recognition rate (CL) and the absolute recognition rate (RR)

GMMs on the frame level. Then, the a posteriori scores on the word level for the four classes obtained by each classifier are classified in a second step with a third classifier. Here, SNNS and the leave-one-speaker-out procedure is applied again. Through the combination of prosodic and MFCC features, the classwise averaged recognition rate can be further improved up to 62.4 % (s. Table 7.5) compared to the 59.4 % CL if the prosodic features (S1) are used alone and compared to the 57.5 % if the framewise MFCC features are used alone.

No further improvement can be achieved by combining the prosodic features, the MFCC features, the formant based features, and the TEO-CB-Auto-Env features by late fusion. The results (61.9 % CL, s. Table 7.5) are even slightly worse compared to the combination of prosodic and MFCC features.

## 7.1.2 Linguistic Features

In this section, the linguistic features are classified on the word level. First, the following five features are classified separately: the three features defining the length of a word as the number of letters, the number of phonemes, and the number of syllables, the feature characterizing whether the word is a fragment or not, and the feature counting how often a word is repeated. With these rather simple features, which are defined in Chapter 6.4.1, a classwise averaged recognition rate of 48.5 % can be achieved.

The 30 part-of-speech features (s. Chapter 6.4.2) modeling six coarse lexical and morphological main word classes and a context of five words can be obtained by a simple dictionary look-up, too. They perform slightly better (52.2 % CL) than the first group of linguistic features.

The unigram models (s. Chapter 6.4.4), based on the conditional probabilities $P(e|w)$ that the speaker is in one of the four cover classes *Anger*, *Emphatic*, *Neutral*, and *Motherese* while he/she is producing the word $w$, are the best linguistic features on the word level. The CL of 61.5 % is almost 10 %-points above the results obtained by the part-of-speech features. Again, a context of five words is used for classification resulting in 20 features. This result cannot be improved by adding the other linguistic features as the results in Table 7.6 show.

| feature set | CL | RR |
|---|---|---|
| late fusion (SNNS, GMMs) | | |
| prosodic features (S1), MFCC, POS (12) | 63.6 | 63.1 |
| prosodic features (S1), MFCC, UM (12) | 65.6 | 65.0 |
| prosodic features (S1), MFCC, POS, UM (16) | 65.0 | 64.3 |
| early fusion (LDA) | | |
| all features (265) | 67.2 | 66.9 |

Table 7.7: Combination of the acoustic and linguistic features on the word level. Results are reported in terms of the classwise averaged recognition rate (CL) and the absolute recognition rate (RR)

### 7.1.3   Combination

In the following, the best acoustic and linguistic features are combined in order to use the knowledge of both information sources. The best results using only acoustic features has been reached by combining word based prosodic and framewise MFCC features by late fusion (62.4 % CL). This combination is extended once by the part-of-speech feature, once by the unigram models, and once by a combination of both. The results are given in Table 7.7. The best result by late fusion on the word level – 65.5 % CL – is achieved if only the unigram models are added to the prosodic and MFCC features. If all 265 word level features are merged to one feature vector (early fusion), a CL of 67.2 % are reached. In this case, the data is classified with linear discriminant analysis (LDA, s. Chapter 4.1.3). For these high-dimensional feature vectors, LDA outperforms the artificial neural networks used so far due to the lower number of parameters that have to be estimated. Furthermore, no validation set is required. By that, the data of 50 speakers can be used for the training.

The entropy based measure to evaluate decoders, which has been introduced in Chapter 4.2.2, allows to compare the decisions of this machine classifier to the decisions of the five human labelers. In doing so, the performance of the machine classifier on this special type of data containing naturalistic emotion-related states can be better judged. Figure 7.5 shows a histogram of the entropy values if the machine classifier and if the average human labeler is compared to the group of reference labelers. In both cases, the distributions of the entropy values are very similar. This is expressed also in the average entropy values $H_{dec}$ for the Aibo word set: the average entropy is 0.712 for the machine classifier and 0.721 for the average of the five human labelers. If naïve classifiers are used, the histograms differ as Figure 4.8 in Chapter 4.2.2 shows. Figure 4.8 also shows the histogram of a perfect classifier that always decides for the majority vote of the human labelers. It marks the upper limit that can be reached by a decoder. The histogram in Figure 7.5 suggests that the machine classifier based on the acoustic and linguistic features makes about the same number of mistakes and has very similar confusion patterns if compared to the average human labeler.

The machine classifier is trained with hard labels. If soft labels are used for training, the machine classifier is able to learn the confusion patterns of the human labelers. Its confusion patterns are then even more similar to those of the human

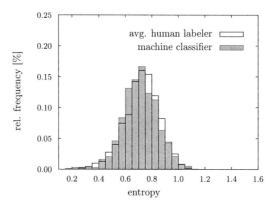

Figure 7.5: Entropy histograms: comparison of the average human labeler with the machine classifier that is based on the acoustic and linguistic features (265 features, LDA)

| agreement | CL | RR | F | # words |
|-----------|------|------|------|---------|
| ≥ 0.6 | 67.2 | 66.9 | 67.0 | 6,070 |
| ≥ 0.8 | 79.0 | 75.7 | 77.4 | 2,799 |
| = 1.0 | 85.5 | 78.6 | 81.9 | 824 |

Table 7.8: Classification results on the word level in dependency of the agreement of the five labelers. Results are reported in terms of the classwise averaged recognition rate (CL), the absolute recognition rate (RR), and the harmonic mean of both (F)

labelers resulting in even lower entropy values [Stei 05]. However, the recognition rate of the classifier slightly suffers if trained with soft labels.

Low entropy values prove that the machine classifier confuses not only the same states as human labelers in general but confuses the states only for those words where the agreement of the five labelers is low. This means, if the human labelers are sure in which state the word is produced, the classifier is highly likely to decide for the correct state as well. This fact is substantiated by evaluating the machine classifier only on those cases of the Aibo word set where the agreement of the five labelers is at least 0.8, i. e. at least four of the five labelers vote for the same cover class. In this case, a classwise averaged recognition rate of 79.0 % is reached (s. Table 7.8). If only those words are evaluated where all labelers agree on one common class (perfect agreement of 1.0), a CL of up to 85.5 % is reached. However, these cases are rather rare – only 824 of those words exist in the Aibo word set – and *Neutral* is the dominating state of these cases. As the recognition rate for *Neutral* is lower than for the other three states, the absolute and the classwise averaged recognition rate diverge such that the high CL value has to be taken with care. The truth will be somewhere between the two numbers CL and RR. For this reason, the F measure defined as the harmonic mean of CL and RR is given. As to be expected, the accuracy of the machine classifier highly correlates with the agreement of the labelers. Similar results based on a re-training of the classifier on the reduced data sets are reported in [Batl 05b].

## 7.2   Turn Level

It is rather exceptional that the emotional state of the speaker is annotated on the word level. The recordings of the children are characterized by many long pauses where the child is waiting for Aibo's reaction. Pauses that are at least 1 s long were used to automatically split the recordings into smaller units, the so-called turns (s. Chapter 5.2). The algorithm defined in Chapter 5.3.8 is applied to define the emotion-related state for the whole turn on the basis of the decisions of the labelers on the word level. Again, the four cover classes *Anger*, *Emphatic*, *Neutral*, and *Motherese* are classified. The selected subset of the German FAU Aibo Emotion Corpus is the Aibo turn set, defined in Chapter 5.4. It consists of 3,996 turns in total and is a superset of the Aibo word set. Each turn contains at least one word of the Aibo word set. The 'confidence' of the turn labels, defined in Chapter 5.4 as the proportion of raw labels of the five labelers on the word level matching the turn label, reflects the agreement of the labelers on the whole turn and the homogeneity of the child's emotion-related state within one turn. The 'confidence' has already been depicted in Figure 5.18. For the whole turn, the average agreement is clearly lower than for single words – a fact that already indicates that the optimal unit of emotion analysis might not be the turn but maybe some smaller unit. Acoustic and linguistic features are classified separately before the best features of each type are combined.

### 7.2.1   Acoustic Features

In the group of the acoustic features, the prosodic features of the Erlangen Prosody Module are evaluated. The prosodic features on the turn level are obtained by characterizing the course of the prosodic features on the word level within one turn. As it has been described in Chapter 6.1.5, the characteristics are the mean, the standard deviation, the minimum, and the maximum of the word level features. The 16 features based on pauses yield a classwise averaged recognition rate of 36.4 %. This is in the same range as the features based on pauses on the word level (36.1 %). The performance stays clearly behind the 29 $F_0$ based features. With them, a CL of 45.1 % on the turn level can be reached. This result differs only slightly from the one on the word level (46.3 %). Both the group of temporal features modeling the position of the $F_0$ and energy extrema and the group of duration based features achieve a CL of 46.5 % on the turn level. The combination of both yields 48.7 % CL. Hence, the performance of features modeling temporal aspects of words on the turn level is lower than on the word level (55.1 %). Nevertheless, the duration based features are the second most important type of prosodic features in this scenario. Only the energy based features perform slightly better. Here, a CL of 51.2 % can be reached on the turn level. This result also stays behind the performance of the energy based features on the word level (55.4 % CL). The ranking of the different types of prosodic features on the turn level is identical to the one on the word level. The experimental results obtained with different types of prosodic features are summarized in Table 7.9. The

| feature set | CL | RR |
|---|---|---|
| **prosodic features** | | |
| pause based features (16) | 36.4 | 36.2 |
| $F_0$ based features (29) | 45.1 | 44.7 |
| energy/$F_0$ position features (24) | 46.5 | 47.7 |
| duration based features (13) | 46.5 | 49.1 |
| duration and position features (37) | 48.7 | 50.0 |
| energy based features (25) | 51.2 | 50.7 |
| **spectral features** | | |
| long-term MFCC (24) | 51.5 | 50.7 |
| long-term formant based features (16) | 45.8 | 43.7 |
| **voice quality features** | | |
| long-term jitter and shimmer features (16) | 39.9 | 37.3 |
| long-term HNR features (2) | 30.9 | 28.5 |
| long-term TEO-CB-Auto-Env (64) | 46.2 | 43.9 |

Table 7.9: Classification results of the turn based acoustic features on the turn level. Results are reported in terms of the classwise averaged recognition rate (CL) and the absolute recognition rate (RR)

table also includes the results obtained with the long-term spectral and voice quality features. These results are described in the following sections.

On the word level, the MFCC features clearly outperformed the less compressed spectral representations of the signal. Hence, only the MFCC features and the formant based features are evaluated on the turn level in the group of the spectral features. The performance of the long-term MFCC features (51.5 % CL) is comparable to the one of the energy based features. However, the performance stays behind the one on the word level (55.2 % CL). The long-term formant based features yield a CL of 45.8 %, which is very close to the performance on the word level where a CL of 46.2 % has been reached.

In the group of the voice quality features, the jitter and shimmer features, the HNR features, and the TEO-CB-Auto-Env features are evaluated on the turn level. The result of the long-term jitter and shimmer features (39.9 %) is almost identical to the one obtained on the word level (39.8 % CL). The result of the long-term HNR features is barely above chance level (30.9 % CL) and does not reach the result on the word level (37.3 % CL). The TEO-CB-Auto-Env features also perform worse on the turn level (46.2 % CL) compared to the word level (51.6 % CL). On the turn level, their result is comparable to the one of the formant based features.

The results of the MFCC features can be improved if they are classified on the frame level first. A posteriori scores on the turn level are then obtained by multiplying the a posteriori scores of the GMM classifier on the frame level for all frames within one turn. By that, a CL of 56.2 % (s. Table 7.10) is reached compared to the 51.5 % CL of the turn based MFCC features. This result is close to the result of the framewise MFCC features on the word level (57.5 %). Also, the formant based features profit slightly by the classification on the frame level (47.1 % CL compared to 45.8 % CL).

| feature set | frame level CL | frame level RR | turn level CL | turn level RR |
|---|---|---|---|---|
| MFCC | | | | |
|   static and dynamic features (24) | 37.5 | 36.5 | 56.2 | 57.0 |
| formant based features | | | | |
|   formants 1-4: center frequencies and bandwidths (8) | 31.3 | 30.7 | 47.1 | 48.0 |
| voice quality features | | | | |
|   HNR (1) | 27.6 | 27.2 | 31.5 | 31.8 |
|   TEO-CB-Auto-Env features (16) | 31.8 | 30.2 | 45.2 | 44.7 |

Table 7.10: Classification results of the frame based acoustic features on the frame and the turn level. Results are reported in terms of the classwise averaged recognition rate (CL) and the absolute recognition rate (RR)

| feature set | CL | RR |
|---|---|---|
| Erlangen Prosody Module: acoustic features (PCA: 123 → 100) | 52.9 | 52.9 |
| prosodic features (S1), MFCC (8) | 57.6 | 55.9 |
| prosodic features (S1), MFCC, formants (12) | 58.6 | 57.0 |
| prosodic features (S1), MFCC, TEO-CB-Auto-Env (12) | 56.8 | 55.0 |
| prosodic features (S1), MFCC, formants, TEO-CB-Auto-Env (16) | 57.8 | 56.3 |

Table 7.11: Combination of acoustic features on the turn level. Results are reported in terms of the classwise averaged recognition rate (CL) and the absolute recognition rate (RR)

The result of the HNR features remains bad if they are classified on the frame level (31.5 % CL). In this case, the improvement of the prior classification on the frame level that can be observed for words cannot be observed for turns. The results w. r. t. the classwise averaged recognition rate of the TEO-CB-Auto-Env features is slightly worse if they are classified on the frame level first. In return, the absolute recognition rate is slightly increased.

In the following, the most promising types of acoustic features are combined. Table 7.11 shows the results on the Aibo turn set. The acoustic features of the Erlangen Prosody Module (including the jitter and shimmer features) yield a classwise averaged recognition rate of 52.9 %. The number of features is reduced by PCA from originally 123 to 100. If these features are combined by late fusion with the framewise MFCC features, the CL increases up to 57.6 %. The maximum of 58.6 % CL is reached if the classification results of the framewise formant based features are added. Other combinations with the framewise TEO-CB-Auto-Env features do not lead to a higher performance as the results in Table 7.11 show. In comparison, the best result obtained with acoustic features on the word level is 62.4 % CL.

## 7.2.2   Linguistic Features

Four groups of linguistic features for turns are evaluated. The first one comprises six features characterizing the length of the turn, the average length of the words defined as the number of letters, the number of phonemes, and the number of syllables, the proportion of fragments, and the average number of repetitions within one turn (s. Chapter 6.4.1). On the turn level, these features perform worse than the features for the word level: 44.6 % CL compared to 48.5 % CL.

With the second group of linguistic features, the six part-of-speech features for turns (s. Chapter 6.4.2), a CL of 48.8 % is achieved.

Better results are obtained with the unigram models for turns: 54.3 % CL. As on the word level, the unigram models are the best one of these three groups. Nevertheless, the unigram models performed clearly better on the word level: the CL is more than 7 %-points higher there (61.5 %).

The classification of units that are longer than one word allow for the evaluation of the bag-of-words approaches presented in Chapter 6.4.3. In general, bag-of-words approaches are characterized by their high dimension of the feature vector. The presented approaches differ in the way the dimension of the feature vector is reduced. The approach with the highest reduction uses only five coarse semantic categories, one category for fragments, one for auxiliaries, and one for the remaining words that are not covered by the other seven categories. The classification result on the turn level is 51.4 % CL. Although the number of categories is approximately the same as for the part-of-speech approach, the recognition rate is slightly higher compared to the POS features for turns. In the second bag-of-words approach, words of the same lemma and words with the same semantic meaning are clustered while keeping separate entries for words that occur at least ten times in the corpus. The dimension is reduced to 181 entries in the feature vector resulting in a higher classification performance (53.8 % CL). The third bag-of-words approach keeps separate entries for all words that appear at least five times in the whole German FAU Aibo Emotion Corpus. The resulting feature vector consists of 254 entries. In spite of this high dimension, this approach slightly outperforms the other two bag-of-words approaches (54.2 % CL) and is comparable to the unigram models for turns.

The unigram models, the length, fragments, and repetitions (LFR) features, and the part-of-speech features are combined by early fusion. The best result is obtained if only the part-of-speech features are added to the unigram models (55.1 % CL). Almost no improvement results from the late fusion of the bag-of-words features based on single words with the unigram and POS features: the CL increases slightly to 55.4 %.

## 7.2.3   Combination

The best result using only acoustic features – 58.6 % CL – results from a late fusion of the acoustic features of the Erlangen Prosody Module, the framewise MFCC features, and the framewise formant based features. If only linguistic features are used, the best result is 55.4 % CL, obtained by combining unigram models, part-of-speech features, and bag-of-words features.

| feature set | CL | RR |
|---|---|---|
| number of words, avg. number of letters/syllables/phonemes, proportion of fragments and repetitions (LFR, 6) | 44.6 | 44.2 |
| part-of-speech features (POS, 6) | 48.8 | 47.0 |
| unigram models (UM, 16) | 54.3 | 51.9 |
| bag-of-words features | | |
|   coarse semantic categories (BOW1, 8) | 51.4 | 49.3 |
|   lemmatization (BOW2, PCA: 181 → 60) | 53.8 | 52.5 |
|   single words (BOW3, PCA: 254 → 50) | 54.2 | 52.6 |
| UM, LFR (22) | 53.5 | 51.5 |
| UM, POS (22) | 55.1 | 52.9 |
| UM, LFR, POS (28) | 54.6 | 52.6 |
| UM+POS, BOW3 (8) | 55.4 | 52.5 |

Table 7.12: Classification results of the linguistic features on the turn level. Results are reported in terms of the classwise averaged recognition rate (CL) and the absolute recognition rate (RR)

| feature set | CL | RR |
|---|---|---|
| late fusion (SNNS, GMMs) | | |
|   prosodic features, MFCC, formants, UM+POS (16) | 59.7 | 58.7 |
|   prosodic features, MFCC, formants, UM+POS, BOW3 (20) | 61.1 | 58.7 |
| early fusion (LDA) | | |
|   all features (700) | 63.2 | 62.8 |

Table 7.13: Combination of the acoustic and linguistic features on the turn level. Results are reported in terms of the classwise averaged recognition rate (CL) and the absolute recognition rate (RR)

In order to combine both information sources, the acoustic features of the Erlangen Prosody Module, the framewise MFCC features, the framewise formant based features, and the unigram models and part-of-speech features are combined by late fusion resulting in 59.7 % CL. If also the bag-of-words features are added, the classwise averaged recognition rate increases above 60 % (61.1 % CL). The best result (63.2 % CL) is achieved by early fusion of all 700 turn level features using LDA as classifier. However, the best result on the turn level remains below the best result that could be achieved on the word level (67.2 %). As the 'confidence' values of the turn labels are significantly lower than for the word labels, this situation was to be expected. Along the same lines as for the evaluation on the word level, the machine classifier is evaluated only on those turns where the 'confidence' of the turn labels is above a certain threshold. The results are given in Table 7.14. The higher the agreement of the labelers and the more homogeneous the emotion-related state within one turn is, the higher the accuracy of the classifier gets. Again, the absolute and the classwise averaged recognition rate diverge for higher 'confidence' values due to the more and more dominating influence of the state *Neutral* and the lower recognition rate of the

| confidence | CL | RR | F | # words |
|---|---|---|---|---|
| ≥ 0.1 | 63.2 | 62.8 | 63.0 | 3,996 |
| ≥ 0.2 | 63.4 | 63.0 | 63.2 | 3,971 |
| ≥ 0.3 | 65.6 | 64.8 | 65.2 | 3,702 |
| ≥ 0.4 | 67.6 | 66.4 | 67.0 | 3,286 |
| ≥ 0.5 | 71.5 | 69.0 | 70.2 | 2,690 |
| ≥ 0.6 | 74.1 | 69.8 | 71.9 | 2,312 |
| ≥ 0.7 | 77.7 | 68.5 | 72.8 | 1,728 |
| ≥ 0.8 | 80.4 | 73.1 | 76.5 | 1,263 |
| ≥ 0.9 | 85.8 | 75.7 | 80.4 | 527 |
| = 1.0 | 87.9 | 75.9 | 81.5 | 316 |

Table 7.14: Classification results on the turn level in dependency of the 'confidence' of the turn label. Results are reported in terms of the classwise averaged recognition rate (CL), the absolute recognition rate (RR), and the harmonic mean of both (F)

classifier for this state. Because of that, additionally, the performance is given in terms of the F measure (harmonic mean of CL and RR).

# 7.3 Chunk Level

The combination of the acoustic and the linguistic features yielded the best results on both the turn and the word level. Nevertheless, the results on the turn level (61.1 % CL, 58.7 % RR) stayed behind the results obtained on the word level (65.6 % CL, 65.0 % RR). Two opposing phenomena can be observed for longer units: On the one hand, longer units provide a larger context helping to recognize the correct emotion-related state. Some features such as the bag-of-words features even only make sense for units that are longer than a single word. On the other hand, the average 'confidence' of the turn labels (s. Chapter 5.4) is smaller than for the labels on the word level. The reason is founded in the Aibo scenario where the children change the emotion-related state, in which they produce an utterance or only a single command, very quickly depending on Aibo's behavior, which changes just as quickly. Long utterances produced in one emotion, as they are typical for corpora of emotion portrayals, are rare in the Aibo scenario. This also seems to hold for other scenarios such as appointment scheduling dialogs [Batl03a]. The optimal unit for emotion analysis might be some intermediate chunk, which is longer than one word, but shorter than the turns in the Aibo scenario, and has some syntactic and semantic meaning. For this reason, chunks are defined for the German FAU Aibo Emotion Corpus (s. Chapter 5.3.5). In Chapter 5.3.8, the algorithm is described how to obtain emotion labels for these units from the decisions of the labelers on the word level. Figure 5.18 shows that the average 'confidence' of the chunk labels is higher than the one of the turn labels, but lower than for the word labels. In the following experiments, the four cover classes *Anger*, *Emphatic*, *Neutral*, and *Motherese* are classified on the Aibo chunk set, which is defined in Chapter 5.4. This subset of the Aibo corpus consists of 4,543 chunks and is a superset of the Aibo word set. Each chunk is part of one turn of the Aibo turn set and contains at least one word of the

Aibo word set. The experiments are along the same lines as for the turn level. First, acoustic and linguistic features are classified separately before they are combined.

## 7.3.1   Acoustic Features

Within the group of prosodic features of the Erlangen Prosody Module, different types of features are distinguished. Throughout all types of prosodic features, significantly higher recognition rates are achieved on the chunk level compared to the results obtained on the turn level. The ranking of the different types is the same as for the turn and the word level. The energy based features are again the best group of features in this scenario yielding a CL of 58.5 %. The results are very close to the results obtained on the word level (59.4 % CL) and about 8 %-points better than the results on the turn level (51.2 % CL). The features modeling temporal aspects of words are the second best group of prosodic features. With the duration based features, a CL of 51.9 % can be achieved. The features modeling the positions of the energy and $F_0$ extrema yield 53.3 % CL. If both groups of temporal features are combined, a CL of 54.4 % is reached being very close to the result on the word level (55.1 % CL) and significantly better than the results on the turn level (48.7 % CL). The $F_0$ based features can profit clearly by the definition of the chunks (50.6 % CL). Their result even exceeds the result on the word level (46.3 %) reducing the gap between the $F_0$ based features and the features modeling temporal aspects. The group of features based on pauses profits as well clearly by the definition of the chunks. Compared to the word level (36.1 % CL), the classification rates are significantly higher (42.0 % CL and 48.2 % RR). The results are summarized in Table 7.15 together with the results of the long-term spectral and voice quality features.

In the group of the spectral features, the long-term MFCC features and the long-term formant based features are evaluated on the Aibo chunk set. The performance of both feature types corresponds to the one on the word level: 55.5 % CL for the MFCC features (55.2 % CL on the word level) and 46.2 % CL for the formant based features (46.2 % CL on the word level).

In the group of the voice quality features, the long-term jitter and shimmer features, the long-term HNR features and the long-term TEO-CB-Auto-Env features are evaluated. The result of the TEO-CB-Auto-Env features (52.3 % CL) is comparable to the one on the word level (51.6 % CL). On the turn level, only 46.2 % CL are reached. The performance of the HNR features (33.4 % CL) stays behind the performance on the word level (37.8 % CL), but is still above the chance level and slightly better than on the turn level (30.9 %). In contrast, the long-term jitter and shimmer features perform very well on the chunk level (47.0 % CL). On the turn and even on the word level, only a CL of 39.9 % and 39.8 %, respectively, is reached. The results are summarized in Table 7.15.

Instead of calculating long-term features by averaging the features on the frame level for all frames within one chunk, the framewise features can be classified directly on the chunk level. In Table 7.16, the results are given for the framewise spectral and voice quality features on both the frame and the chunk level. As on the turn level, MFCC and formant based features can profit by the prior classification on the frame level. If the a posteriori scores are multiplied for all frames within one chunk,

| feature set | CL | RR |
|---|---|---|
| prosodic features | | |
| pause based features (16) | 42.0 | 48.2 |
| $F_0$ based features (29) | 50.6 | 52.2 |
| energy/$F_0$ position features (24) | 51.9 | 54.0 |
| duration based features (13) | 53.3 | 56.4 |
| duration and position features (37) | 54.4 | 56.5 |
| energy based features (25) | 58.5 | 58.6 |
| spectral features | | |
| long-term MFCC (24) | 55.0 | 53.6 |
| long-term formant based features (16) | 46.4 | 45.8 |
| voice quality features | | |
| long-term jitter and shimmer features (16) | 47.0 | 49.4 |
| long-term HNR features (2) | 32.5 | 33.4 |
| long-term TEO-CB-Auto-Env features (64) | 52.3 | 52.0 |

Table 7.15: Classification results of the acoustic features on the chunk level. Results are reported in terms of the classwise averaged recognition rate (CL) and the absolute recognition rate (RR)

| feature set | frame level CL | RR | chunk level CL | RR |
|---|---|---|---|---|
| MFCC | | | | |
| static and dynamic features (24) | 41.4 | 40.5 | 58.9 | 63.4 |
| formant based features | | | | |
| formants 1-4: center frequencies and bandwidths (8) | 31.6 | 31.6 | 48.2 | 52.7 |
| voice quality features | | | | |
| HNR (1) | 26.9 | 35.6 | 31.6 | 37.7 |
| TEO-CB-Auto-Env features (16) | 34.9 | 33.2 | 48.6 | 51.5 |

Table 7.16: Classification results of the frame based acoustic features on the frame and the chunk level. Results are reported in terms of the classwise averaged recognition rate (CL) and the absolute recognition rate (RR)

a CL of 58.9 % is reached on the chunk level with MFCC features. The absolute recognition rate is even higher: 63.4 %. The corresponding long-term features yield only 55.0 % CL and 53.6 % RR. The prior classification of the formant based features on the frame level yields a recognition rate of 47.0 % CL and 49.4 % RR, respectively compared to 46.4 % CL and 45.8 % RR for the long-term version of the features. In contrast, the classification of the HNR feature and the TEO-CB-Auto-Env features on the frame level is not beneficial.

Next, acoustic features of different types are combined. If the acoustic features of the Erlangen Prosody Module (including the jitter and shimmer features) are merged, a classwise averaged recognition rate of 59.0 % is achieved. The number of

| feature set | CL | RR |
|---|---|---|
| Erlangen Prosody Module: acoustic features (PCA: 123 → 100) | 59.0 | 60.7 |
| prosodic features (S1), MFCC (8) | 65.4 | 64.6 |
| prosodic features (S1), MFCC, formants (12) | 64.4 | 63.8 |
| prosodic features (S1), MFCC, TEO-CB-Auto-Env (12) | 64.9 | 64.2 |
| prosodic features (S1), MFCC, formants, TEO-CB-Auto-Env (16) | 63.9 | 63.6 |

Table 7.17: Combination of acoustic features on the chunk level. Results are reported in terms of the classwise averaged recognition rate (CL) and the absolute recognition rate (RR)

features is reduced by PCA to 100, which is the optimal dimension of the feature vector evaluated on a 3-fold cross-validation of the Aibo chunk set. Hence, prosodic and framewise MFCC features are the two most promising groups of features for emotion recognition in the Aibo scenario. If both types are combined by late fusion, a CL of 65.4 % is reached. This result is above the performance of both groups on the word level (62.4 % CL) and significantly better than the corresponding result on the turn level (57.6 % CL). The performance can neither be improved by adding the a posteriori scores of the framewise formant based classification nor by the scores of the framewise TEO-CB-Auto-Env feature based classification. The results are summarized in Table 7.17.

## 7.3.2   Linguistic Features

The linguistic features on the chunk level are evaluated along the same lines as on the turn level. Throughout the different types of linguistic features that are evaluated, the results on the chunk level are clearly better than on the turn level. The first group of features consists of the number of words per chunk, the average length of the words defined as the number of letters, phonemes, and syllables, the proportion of fragments, and the average number of repetitions. With a CL of 54.3 %, the result is even better than on the word level where 48.5 % CL is reached. On the turn level, the CL is 44.6 %.

The same holds for the part-of-speech features: The result on the chunk level (56.1 % CL) is even better than the one on the word level (52.1 % CL) and clearly better than the one on the turn level (48.8 % CL).

On the chunk and the word level, the unigram models yield similar results: 61.9 % CL on chunks compared to 61.5 % CL on words. On the turn level, they reach only a CL of 54.3 %.

Next, the three bag-of-words approaches are evaluated. Consistently with the evaluation on the turn level, the approach using eight coarse semantic categories (57.9 % CL) performs better than the part-of-speech approach (56.1 % CL), which uses six coarse lexical and morphological main word classes. The bag-of-words approach where words of the same lemma and the same meaning are clustered yields 61.4 % CL. The best result (61.9 % CL) is achieved if separate entries in the feature vector are kept for every word that occurs at least five times in the corpus.

| feature set | CL | RR |
|---|---|---|
| number of words, avg. number of letters/syllables/phonemes, proportion of fragments and repetitions (LFR, 6) | 54.3 | 54.9 |
| part-of-speech features (POS, 6) | 56.1 | 56.7 |
| unigram models (UM, 16) | 61.9 | 59.8 |
| bag-of-words features | | |
| coarse semantic categories (BOW1, 8) | 57.9 | 59.4 |
| lemmatization (BOW2, PCA: 181 → 120) | 61.4 | 60.5 |
| single words (BOW3, PCA: 254 → 100) | 61.9 | 60.8 |
| UM, LFR (22) | 61.1 | 60.1 |
| UM, POS (22) | 61.7 | 61.4 |
| UM, LFR, POS (28) | 61.6 | 60.7 |
| UM+POS, BOW3 (8) | 62.2 | 60.6 |

Table 7.18: Classification results of the linguistic features on the chunk level. Results are reported in terms of the classwise averaged recognition rate (CL) and the absolute recognition rate (RR)

The unigram models are merged with the length, fragments, and repetitions (LFR) features, and the part-of-speech features prior to the classification (early fusion). The differences in terms of the classwise averaged recognition rate are neglectable. However, the highest RR value is obtained for the combination of the unigram models and the POS features. The result of this classification is then combined by late fusion with the result of the single words bag-of-words approach. The resulting CL is 62.2 %, which is the best result obtained with linguistic features on the chunk level.

### 7.3.3  Combination

Using only acoustic features, the best result – 65.4 % – is obtained if the acoustic features of the Erlangen Prosody Module are combined by late-fusion with the framewise MFCC features. The best result using only linguistic features – 62.2 % – is obtained by combining unigram models, part-of-speech features, and bag-of-words features. Now, both acoustic and linguistic features are fused. The late fusion of all four classifier outputs results in a further little improvement: 67.1 % CL on the chunk level. As the figures in Table 7.19 show, the result is almost identical even if the bag-of-words features are omitted. If all chunk level features are merged (early fusion) and classified with LDA, up to 68.9 % CL is reached. If the three different levels of analysis – the word, the turn, and the chunk level – are compared, the best results are obtained on the chunk level (68.9 % CL, 68.9 % RR). Yet, they are very close to the best results obtained on the word level (67.2 % CL, 66.9 % RR). Obviously, the disadvantages of the lower 'confidence' values of the chunk labels are compensated to a large extent by the increase in information about the emotion-related state that the longer units imply. On the turn level, the even lower 'confidence' values of the turn labels prevail over the advantages of the longer turns resulting in lower recognition rates: 63.2 % CL and 62.8 % RR. Finally, these classification results prove that the emotion-related

| feature set | CL | RR |
|---|---|---|
| late fusion (SNNS, GMMs) | | |
| prosodic features, MFCC, UM+POS (12) | 67.0 | 65.3 |
| prosodic features, MFCC, UM+POS, BOW3 (16) | 67.1 | 65.5 |
| early fusion (LDA) | | |
| all features (700) | 68.9 | 68.9 |

Table 7.19: Combination of the acoustic and linguistic features on the chunk level. Results are reported in terms of the classwise averaged recognition rate (CL) and the absolute recognition rate (RR)

| confidence | CL | RR | F | # words |
|---|---|---|---|---|
| $\geq 0.2$ | 68.9 | 68.9 | 68.9 | 4,543 |
| $\geq 0.3$ | 69.0 | 69.0 | 69.0 | 4,538 |
| $\geq 0.4$ | 69.7 | 69.5 | 69.6 | 4,469 |
| $\geq 0.5$ | 72.1 | 71.3 | 71.7 | 4,147 |
| $\geq 0.6$ | 75.5 | 73.4 | 74.4 | 3,472 |
| $\geq 0.7$ | 81.4 | 77.7 | 79.5 | 2,012 |
| $\geq 0.8$ | 83.4 | 78.8 | 81.0 | 1,597 |
| $\geq 0.9$ | 84.4 | 79.7 | 82.0 | 630 |
| $= 1.0$ | 88.3 | 77.7 | 82.7 | 430 |

Table 7.20: Classification results on the chunk level in dependency of the 'confidence' of the chunk label. Results are reported in terms of the classwise averaged recognition rate (CL), the absolute recognition rate (RR), and the harmonic mean of both (F)

state of the children actually changes rather quickly even within turns justifying the rather exceptional approach to label the emotion-related state on the word level.

As for words and for turns, the best classifier combining acoustic and linguistic features is now evaluated only on those chunks whose 'confidence' is above a certain threshold. The results are given in Table 7.20. Due to the dominating influence of the state *Neutral* and the lower recognition rate of the classifier for this state, the absolute and the classwise averaged recognition rate diverge. Nevertheless, the (harmonic) mean of both measures clearly increases for higher 'confidence' values. Consequently, if the agreement of the labelers is high and the emotion-related state is homogeneous within one chunk, the accuracy of the classifier is high on average as well. Within CEICES, similar results are obtained based on the large feature set of the CEICES partners and a re-training of the classifier on the reduced data sets [Sepp 08a].

# 7.4   Comparison with Results within CEICES

The goal of the initiative CEICES is to bring together the heterogeneous expertise of various sites in order to cover the diversity of state-of-the-art emotion recognition feature. The participating sites all work in the area of emotion recognition from speech, but come from different backgrounds. The features of six CEICES partners (s. Chapter A.3.1) have been gathered forming a set of 4,265 features. Three different basic feature extraction approaches can be identified:

**selective, two-layered:** In this two-layered approach, features are calculated on the word level first before functionals such as the mean, the standard deviation, the extrema, etc. are applied in order to obtain features for the whole unit, i. e. the turn or the chunk. The features that are computed are selected based on phonetic and linguistic knowledge. The acoustic features of the Erlangen Prosody Module and the very similar features of the FBK are typical representatives of this approach. FAU contributes 92 acoustic and 24 linguistic features, FBK 26 acoustic and 6 linguistic features.

**selective, single-layered:** In the single-layered approach, features for the whole unit of analysis are calculated directly without the prior calculation of features on the word level. Again, features are selected based on phonetic and linguistic knowledge. LIMSI and TAU/AFEKA follow this approach. LIMSI contributes 90 acoustic and 12 linguistic features, TAU/AFEKA 222 acoustic features.

**brute-force, single-layered:** In this single-layered approach, features are calculated directly for the whole unit by systematically applying a fixed and large set of functions to time series of various base functions such as the $F_0$ or energy contour. By that, a very large number of features, generally more than 1,000 features, is computed. Feature selection mechanisms to reduce the number of features, which are partly highly correlated, are mandatory prior to the classification. This approach is followed by UA and TUM. UA provides 1,586 acoustic features, TUM 1,718 acoustic and 489 linguistic features.

A description of the features of each site is given in [Batl 09]. Along the same lines as for this thesis, the prosodic features are categorized into duration based, energy based, and $F_0$ based features. The spectral features are divided into the sub-categories *cepstrum* (MFCC features), *wavelets*, and *spectrum* (formants, band-energies, etc.). There is one category of voice quality features (jitter, shimmer, HNR, etc.). For the linguistic features, bag-of-words features, part-of-speech features, higher semantics (bag-of-words approach with six coarse semantic categories as described in Chapter 6.4.3), and one category subsuming disfluencies and non-verbals such as breathing or laughter are distinguished. 21 features of the whole feature set could not be attributed to one of these types resulting in 4,244 features.

The purpose of CEICES is to force co-operation in order to get insights which feature types are most important for emotion recognition. The primary goal is not to encourage competition which site has the best set of features. In [Batl 06b], each site reports their classification results for turns. The same cases, the same labels, and the same training and test sets are used, but the features and the classifiers that are used differ. Yet, all the recent classification experiments, which are referred to here, are conducted on chunks. In this thesis, the relevance of features types is evaluated by classifying features of the same type separately. Within CEICES, the same approach is followed in [Schu 07b]. The results of the evaluation using the features of all CEICES partners match the results obtained in this thesis using only our features. In the group of the acoustic features, the least performance is achieved with voice quality features. Most relevant are energy and duration based features. All other types of acoustic features ($F_0$ based features, spectral, cepstral, and wavelet based features) are of medium relevance. In the group of the linguistic features, the bag-of-words features are most relevant followed by features modeling higher semantics, and part-of-speech features.

In [Batl 09], a different approach is chosen: all features are pooled and feature selection is used to determine the set of features that are most relevant for the classification. The feature type is assigned to the 'surviving' features of this selection and the more frequently a type appears, the more important this type is for the classification of the emotion-related states in the Aibo scenario. The focus is set on interpretation and not on optimizing the classification performance. For each split of the 3-fold cross-validation (s. Appendix A.2.10), 50 features are selected using the *sequential forward floating search* (SFFS) algorithm and support-vector machines (linear kernel, one-against-one multi-class discrimination, sequential minimal optimization) as classifier. The final set of selected features consists of the union of the features selected for each split, i.e. 150 features allowing the appearance of the very same feature more than once. Table 7.21 shows the results of this feature selection if the features are selected from both acoustic and linguistic features (top) and if they are selected either from the set of acoustic features only or from the set of linguistic features only (bottom). Classification results are reported for single feature types in terms of the F measure defined as the harmonic mean of the absolute recognition rate and the classwise averaged recognition rate. If only acoustic features are used, the F measure is 63.4 %. With linguistic features only, 62.6 % F are reached. If features are selected from both feature sets, 65.5 % F are reported.

These results are very close to those presented in Chapter 7.3 where 65.0 % F for acoustic features only and 61.4 % F for linguistic features only are obtained. The early fusion of both types yields 68.9 % F. This demonstrates that our compact feature set is a very competitive, state-of-the-art set of features for emotion recognition. However, the following differences should be kept in mind if the results presented in this thesis and those reported in [Batl 09] are compared: The CEICES approach to select features requires to reduce the computational effort. The size of the reduced set of 150 features is chosen for a better interpretation of the different feature types, not for optimizing the classification performance. Only a 3-fold cross-validation is used in contrast to the 51-fold cross-validation used in the experiments of this work. Only features on the chunk level are evaluated discarding features on the frame level; a posteriori scores based on the prior classification on the frame level are not included. For some of the features presented in this thesis, the context of a word, which may be outside the chunk the word belongs to, is used. For the normalization of the energy and the duration of words, information of the whole turn is used. Furthermore, our word based prosodic features rely on the actually spoken word chain. Results on the turn and the chunk level based on automatic speech recognition (ASR) are given in [Schu 07c] for different ASR degrees of difficulty: audio data of the close-talk microphone (78.9 % word accuracy, WA), artificially reverberated audio data (68.2 % WA), and noisy and reverberated audio data of the video camera (47.5 % WA). Compared to a system based on the manual transcription and the manually corrected word segmentation, the accuracy of the prosodic features based on ASR is reduced only slightly by less than 4 %-points on the chunk level.

In Table 7.21, the F measure, the number of selected features ($\#$), and the SHARE and the PORTION values are given for each feature type. The SHARE value denotes the proportion of the 150 selected features that belong to the respective feature type. The PORTION value is the proportion of all features of the respective type that have been selected. As one and the same feature can be selected more than once in the three splits of the 3-fold cross-validation, the PORTION values can be higher than 100 %. If acoustic and linguistic features are pooled, two-thirds (67.3 % SHARE) of the 150 selected features are acoustic features and the remaining one third (32.7 % SHARE) are linguistic features. Although the approach to determine the most relevant feature types is different, comparable results are obtained: If the features are selected from the set of acoustic features only (bottom of Table 7.21), the SHARE values state that the energy based features (22.0 % SHARE) are the most relevant feature type, followed by the duration based features (18.7 % SHARE). The SHARE of the $F_0$ based features and the cepstral features (MFCC) is 15.3 % each. Wavelets and voice quality features make up only 10.0 % and 7.3 %, respectively, of the selected features. If the feature selection is based on the linguistic features only, the bag-of-words features have the highest SHARE value (62.7 %), followed by features modeling higher semantics (18.0 %) and part-of-speech features (18.0 %). If the features are selected from both feature sets (top of Table 7.21), two-thirds of the selected features are acoustic features. Hence, the SHARE values of the acoustic feature types should be roughly two-thirds of the respective SHARE values if the features are selected using only acoustic features. The SHARE values of the linguistic feature types are expected to be one-third. A strong deviation from the expected SHARE value can be observed for the duration based features which loose some of their impact. The gap is mainly filled with energy based and spectral features. The bag-of-words features loose some of their relevance as well. This is compensated by a higher contribution of the features modeling higher semantics. The reason for these deviations is that duration based features implicitly encode linguistic information: longer words are content words that are more likely to carry information about the emotion-related state, shorter words are function words. Shorter chunks in terms of the number of words are more likely to be produced in a non-neutral state than longer chunks.

**Summary**    In this chapter, experimental results for the 4-class problem *Anger*, *Emphatic*, *Neutral*, and *Motherese* are presented. The experiments are conducted on three different levels of analysis: the word, the turn, and the chunk level. These levels differ w. r. t. the length of the unit and the homogeneity of the emotion-related state within this unit. The turn is the longest unit characterized by the highest inhomogeneity of the emotion-related state. The shortest unit is the word for which the emotion-related state is assumed to be constant. The chunk is an intermediate unit w. r. t. both the length and the homogeneity. For each level, the different types of features are evaluated separately in order to find those types that are most relevant for emotion recognition. Then, promising feature types are combined by late fusion. However, the best results are obtained if all features are merged and classified with LDA. The highest recognition rates (68.9 % CL) are obtained for the chunk level, which obviously is a good compromise between the length of the unit of analysis and the homogeneity of the emotion-related state within this unit. Comparable results (67.2 % CL) are obtained on the word level. Significantly lower results are obtained on the turn level where only 63.2 % CL are reached. These results are summarized once again in Table 7.22.

The four emotion-related states in the Aibo scenario can be classified both with acoustic features and with linguistic features only. The performance of the linguistic features is slightly worse than the one of the acoustic features. The largest difference (3.2 %-points CL, 4.5 %-points RR) can be observed on the turn level. On all three levels, the classification performance can be improved by combining acoustic and linguistic features. The highest performance gain is observed on the word level: 3.2 %-points CL and 3.0 %-points RR. The most relevant acoustic features are prosodic features – especially energy and duration based features – and MFCC features. The latter are classified on the frame level first before their a posteriori scores on the word, turn, or chunk level are combined with the prosodic features by late fusion. On the turn level, framewise formant based features help to improve the classification result additionally. The most relevant linguistic features are unigram models. On the turn and the chunk level, their performance can be improved slightly if they are fused with part-of-speech and bag-of-words features (single words approach).

The confusion patterns show that the machine classifiers confuse the non-neutral states often with the state *Neutral*. Furthermore, *Emphatic* and *Anger* are often confused. Yet, *Motherese* is mixed up only seldom with *Emphatic* and *Anger*. These confusion patterns match the behavior of the human labelers. The higher the homogeneity of the emotion-related state and the higher the agreement of the human labelers is, the higher is the performance of the machine classifier. This holds for all three levels of analysis. These observations are substantiated by the evaluation of the entropy based measure on the word level showing that the machine classifier performs even slightly better than the average of the five human labelers employed for labeling the Aibo corpus.

The comparison with the results obtained within CEICES shows that the relatively small feature set presented in this work is highly competitive. Concerning the relevance of feature types, similar results are obtained although a different approach to determine the most relevant feature types and a much larger feature set comprising more than 4,000 features of six CEICES partners is used.

| | duration | energy | $F_0$ | spectrum | cepstrum | voice quality | wavelets | all acoustic | BOW | POS | higher semantics | varia | all linguistic | all |
|---|---|---|---|---|---|---|---|---|---|---|---|---|---|---|
| # total | 391 | 265 | 333 | 656 | 1699 | 153 | 216 | **3713** | 476 | 31 | 12 | 12 | **531** | **4244** |
| # (SPFS) | 10 | 32 | 16 | 15 | 16 | 7 | 5 | 101 | 25 | 7 | 17 | 0 | 49 | **150** |
| F MEASURE | 49.6 | 56.3 | 46.8 | 46.2 | 46.4 | 38.7 | 35.3 | – | 37.4 | 48.1 | 56.0 | – | – | **65.5** |
| SHARE | 6.7 | 21.3 | 10.7 | 10.0 | 10.7 | 4.7 | 3.4 | 67.3 | 16.7 | 4.7 | 11.3 | 0.0 | 32.7 | **100.0** |
| PORTION | 2.6 | 12.1 | 4.8 | 2.3 | 1.0 | 4.6 | 2.3 | 2.7 | 5.3 | 22.6 | 141.7 | 0.0 | 9.6 | **3.5** |
| # (SPFS) | 28 | 33 | 23 | 17 | 23 | 11 | 15 | **150** | 94 | 27 | 27 | 2 | 150 | |
| F MEASURE | 54.9 | 56.9 | 46.7 | 49.9 | 50.4 | 41.5 | 44.9 | **63.4** | 53.2 | 54.9 | 57.9 | – | 62.6 | |
| SHARE | 18.7 | 22.0 | 15.3 | 11.3 | 15.3 | 7.3 | 10.0 | **100.0** | 62.7 | 18.0 | 18.0 | 0.1 | 100.0 | |
| PORTION | 7.2 | 12.5 | 6.9 | 2.6 | 1.4 | 7.2 | 6.9 | **4.0** | 19.7 | 87.1 | 225.0 | 16.7 | 28.2 | |

Table 7.21: Summary of the CEICES results on the relevance of feature types for emotion recognition [Batl09]. Top: exploitation of both acoustic and linguistic features. Bottom: exploitation of acoustic and linguistic features separately. Definition of F-MEASURE, SHARE, and PORTION is given in the text

| feature set | CL | RR | Table |
|---|---|---|---|
| **word level** | | | |
| acoustic features: prosodic features, framewise MFCC (8)[1] | 62.4 | 62.0 | 7.5 |
| linguistic features: unigram models (20) | 61.5 | 60.8 | 7.6 |
| acoustic and linguistic features: prosodic features, framewise MFCC, unigram models (12)[1] | 65.6 | 65.0 | 7.7 |
| all features[2] (265) | 67.2 | 66.9 | 7.7 |
| **turn level** | | | |
| acoustic features: prosodic features, framewise MFCC, framewise formants (12)[1] | 58.6 | 57.0 | 7.11 |
| linguistic features: unigram models, POS, BOW3 (8)[1] | 55.4 | 52.5 | 7.12 |
| acoustic and linguistic features: prosodic features, framewise MFCC, formants, unigram models, POS, BOW3 (20)[1] | 61.1 | 58.7 | 7.13 |
| all features[2] (700) | 63.2 | 62.8 | 7.13 |
| **chunk level** | | | |
| acoustic features: prosodic features, framewise MFCC (8)[1] | 65.4 | 64.6 | 7.17 |
| linguistic features: unigram models, POS, BOW3 (8)[1] | 62.2 | 60.6 | 7.18 |
| acoustic and linguistic features: prosodic features, framewise MFCC, unigram models, POS, BOW3 (16)[1] | 67.1 | 65.5 | 7.19 |
| all features[2] (700) | 68.9 | 68.9 | 7.19 |

[1] a posteriori scores, features combined by late fusion
[2] classified with linear discriminant analysis (LDA)

Table 7.22: Summary of the best results using a selection of the best acoustic features only, a selection of the best linguistic features only, a combination of both types, and the full feature set on the word, the turn, and the chunk level

# Chapter 8

# Outlook

The focus in the area of emotion recognition has to shift from emotion portrayals to naturally occurring emotions and states that are related to emotions in a broader sense. However, corpora of naturally occurring emotions that are freely available for scientific research are rare. The FAU Aibo Emotion Corpus is a major contribution in this area. It is a corpus of various emotion-related states that occur in a speech based, application-oriented scenario where children interact with the Sony robot Aibo. The goal of this work is to be as application-oriented as possible regarding the emotional states that are investigated. Nevertheless, the experiments differ from a real application in some aspects.

The sparse data problem leads to a very high proportion of neutral utterances. To train statistical models, similar but different states are mapped onto cover classes. In the classification experiments, the four cover classes *Anger*, *Emphatic*, *Neutral*, and *Motherese* are to be discriminated. To reduce the computational effort, subsets of the Aibo corpus are defined with a more balanced distribution of these cover classes. Cases where no majority vote of the labelers exists are discarded as well as cases that are not subsumed under one of these cover classes. Yet, it has not been investigated what happens to these rare states such as *joyful* for which no statistical models can be trained. On which classes are they mapped if they are classified with the existing classifiers for the 4-class problem? Which confusion patterns appear? For the experiments in this thesis, all four classes should be recognized equally well. In a real application, the high frequency of the state *Neutral* has to be taken care of by defining an appropriate cost function for the various types of misclassifications.

Another aspect is the assumption of a perfect speech recognition system providing the actually spoken word sequence. Experiments in [Schu 07c] have shown that the performance of the prosodic features on the chunk level decreases only slightly ($\leq 4\,\%$-points). Other feature types such as MFCC features are not affected since they are not based on the word information. The impact on the linguistic features has not been investigated so far. It is expected that the performance of the more fine grained bag-of-words approaches decreases to a larger extent than the part-of-speech features based on only six coarse lexical and morphological word main classes and the features based on higher semantics, which also use only eight coarse classes.

In the Aibo scenario, the experimental results suggest that the chunk level is the best of the three levels of analysis that have been investigated. The chunks are not defined by concatenating words of the same emotion-related state although this approach would result in long units with a high homogeneity of the emotion-related state. Yet, this approach would require that the emotion-related state is labeled manually on the word level before the chunks can be defined rendering an automatic chunking impossible. Instead, the chunks are defined by syntactic and prosodic criteria. The syntactic boundaries are also labeled manually but experiments within the German VERBMOBIL project showed that these boundaries can be detected automatically with prosodic features [Batl 98]. Initial experiments on emotion recognition using different chunking procedures are reported in [Schu 07c]. The research on emotion could be continued in this direction by searching for the optimal unit of analysis taking into account the requirements of an application that eventually has to work on these units.

This work only comprises the part of an application that recognizes the emotional state of the user. The part how to use this information is not addressed. Nevertheless, it is an important aspect of a real application. In a call-center scenario, the emotional state can be used to find those dialogs where something went 'wrong' to monitor the behavior of the human agents in these situations [Gupt 07]. In an automatic dialog system, the information can be used to direct those users to a human agent who got angry because their needs could not be satisfied by the machine. In the Aibo scenario, the behavior of the toy can be adapted to the behavior of the child. Aibo could move its paws, for example, if the child addresses Aibo in the state *Motherese*. By that, the impression can be evoked that Aibo really reacts to the child letting the toy appear more like a real dog. In a human-machine conversation, the long-term goal has certainly to be that the machine produces emotionally colored speech output that is adapted to the behavior of the human user to generate a more natural dialog.

The experiments are conducted in an offline procedure. The emotion recognition module is not integrated in an online demonstrator. In an online scenario, the problem of automatic speech recognition is aggravated by the out-of-vocabulary problem. So far, every online demonstrator is very specific w. r. t. the problem which emotion-related states can be discriminated. These states highly depend on the actually chosen scenario. Some of the states present in the FAU Aibo Emotion Corpus such as *Neutral* and *Emphatic* are likely to be found in other scenarios as well. In contrast, *Motherese* is a typical state in our scenario but unlikely to occur in an automatic dialog system used by adults to retrieve information. Anger can be found in many other scenarios but the type of anger that appears is different. In the Aibo scenario, *Anger* is a cover class for *angry, reprimanding,* and *touchy*. These states are different from hot and cold anger. The classification experiments are rather discrimination experiments where the classifier decides for the most likely state given a set of pre-defined possible states. Even if new states appear, the classifier decides for one of the pre-defined states. Experiments where the classifier is allowed to reject a class have not been conducted so far. One major research topic is the problem of how the results can be transferred to other scenarios with different states. So far, the problem is bypassed by collecting new data and retraining the classifier. Fortunately, the existing set of emotion features seem to work for a large variety of emotional states albeit the relevance of the different feature types may change. The collection of emotional data is not only time-consuming and expensive but it is a major problem how to obtain naturally occurring emotional data at all. Hence, it would be favorable if the collection of new data could be avoided. One solution might be the prediction of the degree of arousal and the the degree of valence by regression techniques instead of the classification of emotion categories. As the emotional intensity of the observed states is rather low, it might be interesting to predict also the degree of emotional intensity. However, the FAU Aibo Emotion Corpus has to be re-labeled for this purpose.

Within the CEICES initiative, a large set of state-of-the-art features could be collected from various sites. Nevertheless, the research on new and better features is still going on. Based on studies on emotion portrayals and on human perception experiments with synthesized speech, voice quality features are often regarded as potential candidates (cf. [Gobl 03]). Unfortunately, these features have fallen short of the high expectations put upon them so far in emotion recognition. The reasons might be that they are multi-functional and more susceptible to speaker-idiosyncrasies [Batl 09, Batl 07a]. Another reason is certainly the difficulty in the separation of the vocal source, especially for non-modal voice qualities. Further research on the relevance of voice quality features in spontaneous speech is suggested.

The experimental results show that the performance of the machine classifier is comparable to the average of the five human labelers who labeled the FAU Aibo Emotion Corpus. The human abilities to interpret the emotional state of another person are clearly higher if the human labeler is familiar with the other person. In the Aibo scenario, this is neither the case for the human labelers nor are the automatically extracted features normalized w. r. t. the current speaker. In many application-oriented scenarios, the data available for speaker normalization is very limited or not available at all. Nevertheless, the research on emotion could be continued in this direction.

The FAU Aibo Emotion Corpus exists in a German and an English version. So far, mainly the German version has been investigated. Classification experiments on the English corpus have not been conducted so far due to the smaller size of the English version and the very low number of non-neutral words. Nevertheless, the same set of emotion-related states are annotated. An interesting research topic is the question whether these states can be classified with a system based on acoustic features that is trained on the German data. If this is possible, the different states are expressed in the same way in both the German and the British culture.

# Chapter 9

# Summary

This work is motivated by the long-term goal to make human-machine communication more natural. The focus is set on mono-modal systems where speech is the only input channel being available. Current research in this area focuses mainly on emotion portrayals for which high recognition rates are reported. A large number of features has been proposed so far. They can be categorized into prosodic features modeling suprasegmental speech phenomena such as pitch, loudness, speaking rate, duration, pauses, and rhythm, spectral features modeling spectral characteristics of the signal such as formants and the standard MFCC features in speech recognition, voice quality features modeling characteristics of the vocal source, and linguistic features modeling the linguistic content of the utterances. The FAU Aibo Emotion Corpus providing spontaneous children's speech of naturally occurring emotion-related states is a major contribution in this area of research. Features covering all four groups are evaluated w. r. t. their relevance for emotion recognition on this type of data.

Most of the states in the FAU Aibo Emotion Corpus such as *motherese, reprimand-ing*, etc. are not emotions proper but *emotion-related*. This term is delimited from Scherer's definition of *emotion* and other affective states such as *mood, interpersonal stance, attitudes*, and *personal traits*. Different modern emotion theories exist trying to explain at least parts of the complex phenomenon *emotion*: What are emotions? How many different emotions exist? Why and when do emotions occur? Modern emotion theories are rooted in the theories of Plato, Descartes, Darwin, and James. Dimensional theories claim that emotions can be distinguished according to a small number of dimensions. The most popular ones are *arousal* and *valence*. Discrete emotion models suggest that only a few discrete emotions exist determined by evolutionarily developed neural circuits or by their specific elicitation conditions and their physiological, expressive, and behavioral reaction patterns. Many corpora of emotion portrayals are based on Ekman's basic six emotions. Componential models assume that emotions are elicited by the cognitive appraisal of antecedent events. Five types of studies can be derived from Scherer's modified version of Brunswik's functional lens model of perception: encoding studies searching for acoustic patterns that are characteristic for certain emotions, decoding studies examining to what extent human lay judges are able to infer emotions from speech samples, inference studies investigating the underlying voice–emotion inference mechanism, transmission studies examining the role of the transmission channel, and representation studies focusing on mental algorithms. The research on relevant features in computer science, the comparison of the performance of a machine classifier with the one of human labelers, and the classification of emotions under noisy and reverberated conditions nicely fit into this framework. The most common way to collect emotional data is to simulate vocal expressions of emotion (emotion portrayals). Various ways to induce emotions and their drawbacks (weak emotions, mixtures of multiple affective states) are reviewed. The highest ecological validity is obtained for natural vocal expressions. Nevertheless, many problems (weak emotional states, mixtures of states, sparse data problem, ethical and legal issues, Observer's Paradox) arise if such data is collected.

If the person's emotional state is unknown, human judges are employed to label the utterances. In some situations, another possibility is to ask the subjects about their emotions (self report). The use of category labels is the most common way. Different lists of key emotions have been proposed. Yet, the emotional states that actually appear in a given application-oriented scenario are very specific for the chosen scenario. States that are related to emotion such as *emphatic, helpless,* or *tired* are more likely to appear than emotions proper. The sparse data problem necessitates the mapping of similar but different states onto broader cover classes. An alternative based on dimensional emotion theories is dimensional labeling. Two existing tools, *FeelTrace* and the *Geneva Emotion Wheel*, are reviewed allowing to label the emotional state in the activation-evaluation and the control-valence space, respectively. Category labels can be assigned to positions in these spaces and vice versa. Time dependent labeling tools do not require pre-defined segments of constant emotion. Cohen's kappa and its variants (weighted kappa, multi-rater kappa) are introduced as measures to evaluate the agreement amongst the human labelers on category data.

In order to classify emotion-related states automatically, the structure of a classification system and the principle of the optimal classifier minimizing the expected costs is revisited. The optimal classifier requires that the probability density functions $p(c|\Omega_\lambda)$ are known. In the case of Gaussian mixture models (GMMs), these density functions are modeled with a mixture of $M$ multivariate Gaussians whose parameters can be estimated with the expectation maximization (EM) algorithm. This classifier is suited for the classification of the spectral features on the frame level. On higher levels, linear discriminant analysis (LDA) and artificial neural networks (ANN) are used. The Fisher linear discriminant maximizes the ratio between the between-class and the within-class scatter resulting in a linear decision boundary. Complex decision boundaries are realized with ANNs. Multilayer perceptrons and the backpropagation algorithm to estimate the parameters are introduced. The performance of a machine classifier is often evaluated in terms of the absolute recognition rate which is not suited for unbalanced data. Hence, the classwise averaged recognition rate in introduced as a single performance figure in contrast to recall and precision for each class. Our entropy based measure allows to compare the decision of a machine classifier with the decision of the average human labeler. Confusions similar to those of the human labelers are weighted less in cases where the labelers are unsure themselves. The Sammon transformation and the NMDS are presented to visualize emotion clusters of MFCC features and to derive data-driven dimensions of emotion from the confusion matrices of the human labelers, respectively.

Speech corpora of naturally occurring emotions are rare and in general not freely available for scientific research. The FAU Aibo Emotion Corpus is a major contribution in this area of research. It consists of emotionally colored, spontaneous speech of children at the age of 10 to 13 years interacting with the Sony robot Aibo. The data (8.9 h of speech) is transliterated and automatically segmented into smaller turns at pauses $\geq 1$ s. The outstanding qualities of the corpus are its various annotations. For the parcours experiment, the turns of the children are aligned to Aibo's pre-defined plot of actions. Aibo's non-cooperative behavior correlates clearly with *Anger* (0.47 for **A** vs. **N**). Word based features in general and duration based prosodic features in particular rely on a correct word segmentation. According to a manual correction of the forced alignment, the segmentation of 39 % of all words is wrong even if deviations of up to three frames are tolerated at both word boundaries. 1 % of words are totally misplaced. $F_0$ based features rely on the correct $F_0$ extraction. The ESPS contour has been manually corrected in terms of 'smoothed and adjusted to human perception'. 4.5 % of all frames within words are octave errors or other gross errors. However, no significant impact on the performance of the prosodic features could be found. Syntactic boundaries are annotated in order to split the turns into shorter, syntactically and semantically meaningful chunks. 11 emotion-related states are labeled on the word level. Besides *neutral*, the most frequent states are *emphatic, motherese, reprimanding, touchy, angry*, and *joyful*. To reduce the sparse data problem, the classes are mapped onto the cover classes *Anger*, *Emphatic*, *Neutral*, *Motherese*, *Joyful*, and *Other*. Algorithms are proposed to obtain emotion labels for chunks and turns from the word level labels. As only six coarse POS classes are used, the corpus is annotated with part-of-speech tags by annotating only the lexicon entries. The relative frequency of the POS classes changes for different emotion-related states. Furthermore, prosodic peculiarities such as *clear articulation, laughter*, etc. are annotated. The distribution of the prosodic labels is also characteristic for certain emotion-related states. Based on a two-dimensional NMDS solution of the confusion matrices of the human labelers, two dimensions of emotion are derived. The first one can be clearly interpreted as the well-known dimension *valence*. The second one is not *arousal* but describes the degree of *interaction* between the child and the Aibo. Three more balanced subsets of the German FAU Aibo Emotion Corpus are defined for the classification on the word, the chunk, and the turn level. The corpus is the common data basis of the initiative CEICES.

Classification experiments are conducted for the the 4-class problem *Anger*, *Emphatic*, *Neutral*, and *Motherese* on three different levels of analysis: the word, the turn, and the chunk level. The presented features cover all four main types of features: prosodic, spectral, voice quality, and linguistic features. The evaluation of different feature types w. r. t. their relevance for emotion recognition yields a similar ranking on all three levels of analysis. The features of the existing Erlangen Prosody Module are a compact set of selected features which model energy, $F_0$, and temporal aspects for single words instead of whole utterances. This approach is especially suited for the classification on the word level, but can be used for larger segments as well by computing statistics of the word level features. The most important prosodic features in the Aibo scenario are energy and duration based features. $F_0$ based features perform clearly worse. Pause based features are of minor relevance since the pauses are mainly due to Aibo's long reaction times. MFCC features are highly relevant as well. This compact set of spectral features outperforms the less compressed DFT and log-Mel frequency features. Features based on the first four formants are clearly inferior compared to the MFCC features. The best classification results are obtained by directly classifying the spectral features on the frame level. Long-term spectral features perform slightly worse. Jitter and shimmer features, the HNR, and the TEO-CB-Auto-Env features represent the group of voice quality features. The performance of the latter is in the same range as the one of the formant based features. Jitter, shimmer, and HNR features are clearly inferior. The best combination of acoustic features is the late fusion of prosodic features and the framewise MFCC features. On the turn level, the formant based features are added, too. As the children's speech in the FAU Aibo Emotion Corpus is spontaneous, the utterances can be analyzed linguistically. A good performance can already be achieved with simple features such as the word length, the number how often a word is repeated, and the information whether a word is a fragment or not. Better results are obtained with POS features using six coarse lexical and morphological main word classes. Bag-of-words approaches yield even better results. Three approaches to reduce the high dimensionality of the BOW vector are evaluated. The one with the lowest reduction (one entry for each word) outperforms the other two. The best results in the group of linguistic features are obtained with unigram models based on the conditional probabilities $P(e|w)$. Only slight improvements can be achieved by combining the different types of linguistic features. In total, the performance of the linguistic features is slightly worse than the one of the acoustic features. Yet, the differences are small (3.2 %-points CL, 4.5 %-points RR on the turn level). On all three levels of analysis, the combination of both acoustic and linguistic features helps to improve the classification performance. The highest performance gain is achieved on the word level (3.2 %-points CL and 3.0 %-points RR). MFCC features and duration based features model to some extent linguistic information. Classification results up to 68.9 % CL are obtained by early fusion of all features and classification with LDA. Regarding the type of data – weak, naturally occurring emotion-related states – this is an excellent result. The comparison with the results obtained within CEICES shows that the relatively small feature set presented in this work is highly competitive. Concerning the relevance of feature types, similar results are obtained although a different approach to determine the most relevant feature types and a much larger feature set comprising more than 4,000 features of six CEICES partners is used. The confusion patterns of the machine classifiers are similar to those of the human labelers. The recognition rates highly correlate with the 'confidence' of the labels, which is a measure for the homogeneity of the emotion-related states and the agreement of the labelers. The evaluation of the entropy based measure on the word level shows that the machine classifier performs even slightly better than the average of the five human labelers employed for labeling the Aibo corpus. Chunks are the best compromise between the length of the unit of analysis and the homogeneity of the emotion-related state within this unit (68.9 % CL). The best results on the word level (67.2 % CL) are comparable, those on the turn level (63.2 % CL) are significantly lower.

# Appendix A

# FAU Aibo Emotion Corpus Addenda

## A.1 Design of the Experiments

### A.1.1 Parcours Experiment

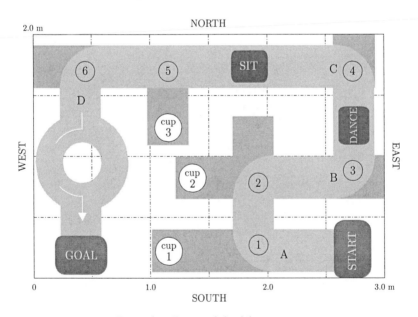

Figure A.1: Design of the Aibo parcours

| | |
|---|---|
| POS: | START |
| NV: | gesture 'Hi' |
| CH: | tells Aibo what to do |
| +C: | gets up |
| +C: | goes forward |
| POS: | A |
| -C: | stops |
| -C: | goes backwards |
| +C: | goes forward |
| -C: | stops |
| -C: | begs (gesture 'please') |
| +C: | goes forward |
| POS: | 1st crossing |
| NV: | turns head towards child |
| +C: | goes forward |
| POS: | 1st cup |
| +C: | sits down |
| +C: | gets up |
| +C: | turns round |
| +C: | goes forward |
| POS: | 1st crossing |
| +C: | goes left |
| POS: | 2nd crossing |
| -C: | goes straight on |
| POS: | cul-de-sac |
| +C: | stops |
| +C: | turns round |
| +C: | goes forward |
| POS: | 2nd crossing |
| +C: | turns right |
| POS: | 2nd cup |
| +C: | sits down |
| +C: | gets up |
| +C: | turns round |
| +C: | goes forward |
| POS: | 2nd crossing |
| -C: | stops |
| NV: | turns head towards child |
| +C: | goes forward |
| POS: | B, 3rd crossing |
| -C: | lays down |
| +C: | gets up |
| NV: | turns head towards child |
| +C: | turns left |
| +C: | goes forward |

POS: DANCE
+C: stops
CH: Aibo, dance!
-C: stands still
+C: dances
+C: goes forward
-C: stops
-C: lays down
+C: stands up

---

POS: C, 4th crossing
-C: lays down
+C: stands up
-C: lays down
+C: stands up
+C: turns left
NV: turns head towards child
+C: goes forward

---

POS: SIT
+C: stops
CH: Aibo, sit down!
-C: goes backwards
+C: stops
+C: goes forward

---

POS: SIT
+C: sits down
+C: gets up
+C: goes forward

---

POS: 5th crossing
-C: goes straight on
+C: stops
+C: turns round
+C: goes forward
POS: 5th crossing
-C: goes straight on
POS: SIT
+C: stops
+C: turns round
+C: goes forward
POS: 5th crossing
+C: turns left

---

POS: 3rd cup
+C: sits down
NV: looks to child
+C: gets up
+C: turns round
+C: goes forward

---

| POS: | 5th crossing |
| --- | --- |
| +C: | turns left |
| +C: | goes forward |
| POS: | 6th crossing |
| -C: | stops |
| NV: | turns head towards child |
| +C: | turns left |
| +C: | goes forward |
| POS: | D |
| -C: | sits down |
| -C: | 'blows a kiss' |
| +C: | gets up |
| +C: | goes forward |
| POS: | roundabout (now: follows arrow) |
| +C: | goes right |
| +C: | turns left |
| +C: | goes forward |
| -C: | stops |
| -C: | waits |
| +C: | turns left |
| +C: | goes forward |
| +C: | turns right |
| +C: | goes forward |
| POS: | GOAL |
| +C: | stops |
| +C: | sits down |
| NV: | gesture 'bye' |

Table A.1: Plot of the parcours experiment; POS: Aibo's position within the parcours, +C: cooperative action of Aibo, -C: non-cooperative action of Aibo, NV: non-verbal action of Aibo, CH: communicative action of the child

## A.1.2  Object Localisation Tasks

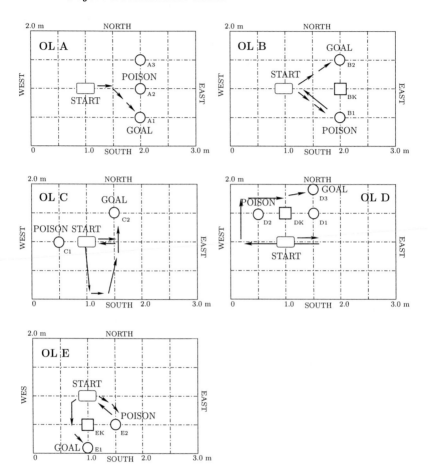

Figure A.2: Design of the five object localization tasks

| cups: A1 (goal), A2 (poison), A3; box: – |
| :-- |
| description: Aibo obeys |

| POS: Aibo lying on PILLOW, looking eastwards |
| :-- |
| NV: gesture 'Hello' |
| CH: tells Aibo what to do |
| +C: gets up |
| -C: goes E |
| +C: stops |
| +C: goes SE |
| -C: stops |
| -C: sits down |
| NV: turns head towards child |
| +C: gets up |
| +C: goes to cup A1 |
| +C: stops at cup A1 |
| +C: sits down |

Table A.2: Plot of the object localization task **OL A**; POS: Aibo's position within the object localization task,  +C: cooperative action of Aibo, -C: non-cooperative action of Aibo,  NV: non-verbal action of Aibo,  CH: communicative action of the child

| cups: B1 (poison), B2 (goal); box: BK |
| description: Aibo goes first to the poisoned cup |

| POS: Aibo lying on PILLOW, looking eastwards |
| NV: gesture 'Hello' |
| CH: tells Aibo what to do |

| +C: gets up |
| -C: goes SE |
| +C: stops |
| -C: sits down |
| +C: gets up |
| -C: goes SE to cup B1 |
| +C: stops |
| NV: turns head towards child |
| +C: goes backwards NW |
| POS: PILLOW |
| +C: turns around NE |
| +C: goes towards cup B2 |
| -C: stops |
| -C: lays down |
| +C: gets up |
| NV: gesture 'Hello' |
| +C: goes towards cup B2 |
| +C: stops at cup B2 |
| +C: sits down |

Table A.3: Plot of the object localization task **OL B**; POS: Aibo's position within the object localization task, +C: cooperative action of Aibo, -C: non-cooperative action of Aibo, NV: non-verbal action of Aibo, CH: communicative action of the child

cups: C1 (poison), C2 (goal); box: −
description: Aibo goes back to pillow, then in
opposite direction, then in a curve to cup C2.

| | |
|---|---|
| POS: | Aibo lying on PILLOW, looking eastwards |
| NV: | gesture 'Hello' |
| CH: | tells Aibo what to do |
| +C: | gets up |
| +C: | goes E |
| -C: | stops |
| -C: | lays down |
| +C: | gets up |
| NV: | turns head towards child |
| -C: | goes backwards to pillow |
| POS: | PILLOW |
| -C: | turns towards S |
| -C: | sits down |
| NV: | looks towards child |
| +C: | gets up |
| -C: | goes S towards child |
| +C: | turns around E |
| +C: | turns around N |
| +C: | goes N |
| -C: | stops, waits |
| +C: | goes towards cup C2 |
| +C: | stops at cup C2 |
| +C: | sits down |

Table A.4: Plot of the object localization task **OL C**; POS: Aibo's position within the object localization task,  +C: cooperative action of Aibo, -C: non-cooperative action of Aibo,  NV: non-verbal action of Aibo,  CH: communicative action of the child

cups: D1, D2 (poison), D3 (goal); box: DK
description: Aibo goes backwards, passes pillow and goes into
the wrong, opposite direction, passes poisoned cup D2, i.e., the
other, longer way to the goal, sits down, hidden behind box; the
same 'sitting down and getting up' - sequence as in the parcours

POS: Aibo lying on PILLOW
NV: gesture 'Hello'
CH: tells Aibo what to do

+C: gets up
-C: goes E
+C: stops
NV: turns head towards child
-C: turns around 180°
-C: goes W, straight on, passes pillow
+C: stops at border of carpet
-C: lays down
+C: gets up
-C: lays down
+C: gets up
-C: lays down
+C: gets up
+C: turns right
NV: turns head towards child
-C: goes north
+C: passes cup D2 westside
+C: turns right 90°
+C: goes E, towards cup D3
-C: stops behind box
-C: sits down
+C: gets up
+C: goes towards cup D3
+C: stops at cup D3
+C: sits down

Table A.5: Plot of the object localization task **OL D**; POS: Aibo's position within the object localization task, +C: cooperative action of Aibo, -C: non-cooperative action of Aibo, NV: non-verbal action of Aibo, CH: communicative action of the child

cups: E1 (goal), E2 (poison); box: EK
description: parallel to OL B: Aibo goes to poisoned cup first

POS: Aibo lying on PILLOW, looking southwards
NV: gesture 'Hello'
CH: tells Aibo what to do

+C: gets up
-C: goes SE
+C: stops
-C: sits down
-C: goes SE towards cup E2
+C: stops
NV: turns head towards child
+C: goes backward to pillow
POS: PILLOW
+C: turns SW
+C: goes S
+C: passes box westside
-C: stops
-C: lays down
+C: gets up
NV: gesture 'Hello'
+C: goes towards cup 1
+C: stops at cup E1
+C: sits down

Table A.6: Plot of the object localization task **OL E**; POS: Aibo's position within the object localization task,  +C: cooperative action of Aibo,  -C: non-cooperative action of Aibo,  NV: non-verbal action of Aibo,  CH: communicative action of the child

# A.2    Statistics of the FAU Aibo Emotion Corpus

## A.2.1    Information about the Speakers

| speaker ID | gender | age | speaker ID | gender | age |
|---|---|---|---|---|---|
| Mont_01 | f | 11 | Ohm_01 | f | 10 |
| Mont_02 | f | 10 | Ohm_02 | m | 10 |
| Mont_03 | f | 11 | Ohm_03 | f | 10 |
| Mont_04 | m | 10 | Ohm_04 | f | 11 |
| Mont_05 | f | 11 | Ohm_05 | m | 11 |
| Mont_06 | f | 11 | Ohm_06 | f | 11 |
| Mont_07 | f | 11 | Ohm_07 | m | 11 |
| Mont_08 | f | 11 | Ohm_08 | m | 10 |
| Mont_09 | f | 11 | Ohm_10 | f | 11 |
| Mont_10 | m | 12 | Ohm_11 | m | 11 |
| Mont_11 | m | 12 | Ohm_13 | m | 10 |
| Mont_12 | f | 12 | Ohm_14 | f | 11 |
| Mont_13 | f | 12 | Ohm_16 | f | 11 |
| Mont_14 | f | 12 | Ohm_18 | f | 11 |
| Mont_15 | f | 11 | Ohm_19 | m | 10 |
| Mont_16 | f | 12 | Ohm_20 | f | 10 |
| Mont_17 | m | 11 | Ohm_21 | m | 11 |
| Mont_18 | m | 11 | Ohm_22 | f | 11 |
| Mont_19 | m | 11 | Ohm_23 | m | 10 |
| Mont_20 | m | 12 | Ohm_24 | f | 10 |
| Mont_21 | m | 12 | Ohm_25 | m | 10 |
| Mont_22 | f | 12 | Ohm_27 | m | 10 |
| Mont_23 | f | 13 | Ohm_28 | f | 10 |
| Mont_24 | f | 12 | Ohm_29 | m | 11 |
| Mont_25 | f | 12 | Ohm_31 | m | 11 |
|  |  |  | Ohm_32 | f | 10 |

Table A.7: Information about gender and age of the German speakers

## A.2.2    General Characteristics of the FAU Aibo Emotion Corpus

| | FAU Aibo Emotion Corpus | |
| --- | --- | --- |
| | German | English |
| number of speakers | 51 | 30 |
| female | 30 | |
| male | 21 | |
| size (hours of speech) | 8.9 | 1.3 |
| number of words | 48,401 | 8,474 |
| number of chunks | 18,216 | – |
| number of turns | 13,642 | 5,302 |
| average chunk length [words] | | |
| - Aibo corpus | 2.66 | – |
| - Aibo turn set | 2.75 | – |
| - Aibo chunk set | 2.91 | – |
| average turn length [words] | | |
| - Aibo corpus | 3.5 | 1.6 |
| - Aibo turn set | 4.4 | – |
| lexicon entries | 1,147 | 236 |

Table A.8: Statistics of the German and the British FAU Aibo Emotion Corpus

## A.2.3  Distribution of the Turn Length

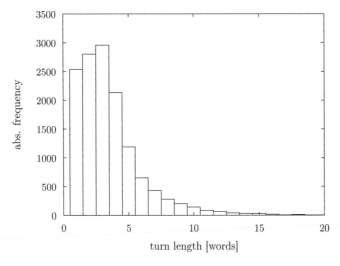

Figure A.3: Distribution of the turn length (number of words) on the German FAU Aibo Emotion Corpus

## A.2.4   Distribution of the Word Duration

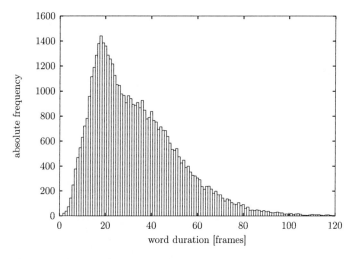

Figure A.4: Distribution of the word duration on the German FAU Aibo Emotion Corpus; every 10 ms overlapping frames à 16 ms

## A.2.5 Distribution of $F_0$ Values

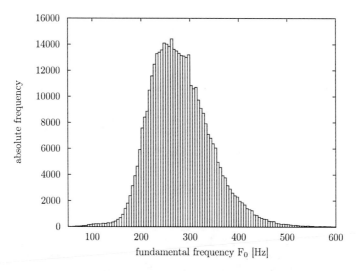

Figure A.5: Distribution of the manually corrected $F_0$ values on the Aibo turn set

## A.2.6    Cross-tabulation of POS Labels and Emotion Categories

| POS label | emotion label (cover classes) | | | | | | | $\sum$ |
|---|---|---|---|---|---|---|---|---|
| | **A** | **E** | **N** | **M** | **J** | **O** | – | |
| NOUN | 788 | 272 | 6,071 | 146 | 11 | 5 | 982 | 8,275 |
| AUX | 10 | 1 | 427 | 18 | 2 | 0 | 16 | 474 |
| VERB | 401 | 1,066 | 10,608 | 204 | 28 | 14 | 876 | 13,197 |
| PAJ | 475 | 1,238 | 20,969 | 544 | 54 | 25 | 1,212 | 24,517 |
| APN | 14 | 16 | 1,106 | 324 | 9 | 1 | 114 | 1,584 |
| API | 30 | 12 | 227 | 64 | 3 | 0 | 18 | 354 |
| total | 1,718 | 2,605 | 39,408 | 1,300 | 107 | 45 | 3,218 | 48,401 |

Table A.9: Cross-tabulation of emotion categories (cover classes) and part-of-speech tags

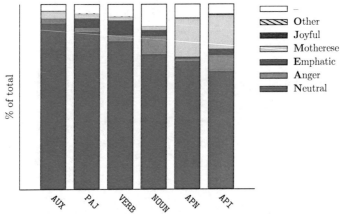

Figure A.6: Distribution of the emotion categories for different part-of-speech tags

## A.2.7 Cross-tabulation of Prosodic Peculiarities and Emotion Categories

| prosodic label | emotion label (cover classes) | | | | | | | $\sum$ |
| --- | --- | --- | --- | --- | --- | --- | --- | --- |
| | **A** | **E** | **N** | **M** | **J** | **O** | – | |
| no prosodic peculiarities | 456 | 742 | 34,233 | 792 | 56 | 29 | 1,752 | 38,060 |
| CLEAR_ART | 128 | 167 | 1,589 | 34 | 2 | 0 | 148 | 2,068 |
| EMPHASIS | 310 | 1,042 | 1,614 | 24 | 5 | 4 | 474 | 3,473 |
| SHOUTING | 50 | 21 | 22 | 0 | 0 | 0 | 37 | 130 |
| ACC_SHIFT | 1 | 2 | 2 | 0 | 0 | 0 | 3 | 8 |
| LENGTH_SYLL | 347 | 223 | 1,317 | 413 | 9 | 12 | 495 | 2,816 |
| INS_SYLL | 23 | 28 | 0 | 0 | 0 | 0 | 18 | 69 |
| PAUSE_LONG | 2 | 2 | 96 | 12 | 0 | 0 | 7 | 119 |
| PAUSE_WORD | 2 | 3 | 165 | 0 | 0 | 0 | 15 | 185 |
| PAUSE_SYLL | 1 | 2 | 2 | 0 | 0 | 0 | 0 | 5 |
| LAUGHTER | 0 | 2 | 26 | 0 | 29 | 0 | 6 | 63 |
| VOCATIVE | 89 | 3 | 41 | 12 | 0 | 0 | 70 | 215 |
| EMPHASIS + LENGTH_SYLL | 141 | 186 | 112 | 6 | 2 | 0 | 89 | 536 |
| CLEAR_ART + EMPHASIS | 42 | 88 | 62 | 0 | 0 | 0 | 28 | 220 |
| CLEAR_ART + LENGTH_SYLL | 22 | 17 | 44 | 6 | 0 | 0 | 21 | 110 |
| LENGTH_SYLL + VOCATIVE | 29 | 1 | 2 | 0 | 0 | 0 | 7 | 39 |
| EMPHASIS + PAUSE_WORD | 1 | 8 | 19 | 0 | 0 | 0 | 3 | 31 |
| LENGTH_SYLL + SHOUTING | 10 | 12 | 1 | 0 | 0 | 0 | 7 | 30 |
| CLEAR_ART + PAUSE_WORD | 5 | 3 | 16 | 0 | 0 | 0 | 4 | 28 |
| CLEAR_ART + EMPHASIS + LENGTH_SYLL | 12 | 7 | 5 | 0 | 0 | 0 | 3 | 27 |
| LENGTH_SYLL + PAUSE_LONG | 2 | 6 | 13 | 0 | 0 | 0 | 4 | 25 |
| other combinations | 45 | 40 | 27 | 1 | 4 | 0 | 27 | 144 |
| total | 1,718 | 2,605 | 39,408 | 1,300 | 107 | 45 | 3,218 | 48,401 |

Table A.10: Cross-tabulation of emotion categories (cover classes) and prosodic peculiarities

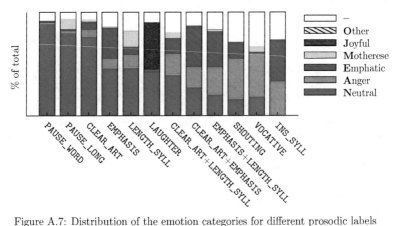

Figure A.7: Distribution of the emotion categories for different prosodic labels

## A.2.8 Most Frequently Used Words

| no. | word | translation | frequency | |
|---:|---|---|---:|---:|
| 1 | Aibo | Aibo | 7,469 | 15.43 % |
| 2 | nach | (go) to | 2,960 | 6.11 % |
| 3 | links | left | 2,560 | 5.28 % |
| 4 | stopp | stop | 1,807 | 3.73 % |
| 5 | geh | go | 1,756 | 3.62 % |
| 6 | lauf | walk | 1,586 | 3.27 % |
| 7 | rechts | to the right | 1,441 | 2.97 % |
| 8 | und | and | 1,333 | 2.75 % |
| 9 | jetzt | now | 1,231 | 2.54 % |
| 10 | dich | yourself | 1,139 | 2.35 % |
| 11 | steh | get (up) | 1,111 | 2.29 % |
| 12 | auf | (get) up | 1,088 | 2.24 % |
| 13 | komm | come | 1,011 | 2.08 % |
| 14 | g'radeaus | straight forward | 899 | 1.85 % |
| 15 | dreh | turn | 883 | 1.82 % |
| 16 | weiter | (go) on | 874 | 1.80 % |
| 17 | mal[1] | – | 839 | 1.73 % |
| 18 | sitz | sit | 722 | 1.49 % |
| 19 | ja | yes | 721 | 1.48 % |
| 20 | aufstehen | get up | 702 | 1.45 % |
| 21 | so | that way | 618 | 1.27 % |
| 22 | stehen | stand | 594 | 1.22 % |
| 23 | geradeaus | straight forward | 526 | 1.08 % |
| 24 | bleib | stay | 489 | 1.01 % |
| 25 | laufen | go, walk | 453 | 0.93 % |
| 26 | wieder | again | 388 | 0.80 % |
| 27 | um | around | 388 | 0.80 % |
| 28 | gut | well done | 335 | 0.69 % |
| 29 | nein | no | 330 | 0.68 % |
| 30 | du | you | 319 | 0.65 % |
| 31 | okay | okay | 291 | 0.60 % |
| 32 | hin | towards, there | 286 | 0.59 % |
| 33 | brav | good | 286 | 0.59 % |
| 34 | ein | a | 269 | 0.55 % |
| 35 | *is | is | 261 | 0.53 % |
| 36 | bisschen | a little | 253 | 0.52 % |
| 37 | da | there | 245 | 0.50 % |
| 38 | vorne | ahead | 222 | 0.45 % |
| 39 | gehen | go | 218 | 0.45 % |
| 40 | setz | sit | 200 | 0.41 % |
| 41 | nicht | not | 176 | 0.36 % |

[1]modal particle, typical for German, the equivalent in English is the use of specific intonation contours

| 42 | umdrehen | turn around | 172 | 0.35 % |
|----|----------|-------------|-----|--------|
| 43 | noch | still (further), (not) yet | 159 | 0.32 % |
| 44 | zu | to | 155 | 0.32 % |
| 45 | schön | nice | 149 | 0.30 % |
| 46 | bitte | please | 149 | 0.30 % |
| 47 | genau | exactly | 137 | 0.28 % |
| 48 | dem | the (feeding dish), this one | 133 | 0.27 % |
| 49 | mach | do | 132 | 0.27 % |
| 50 | tanz | dance | 130 | 0.26 % |
| 51 | ganz | very (nice) | 129 | 0.26 % |
| 52 | *n | 'n | 127 | 0.26 % |
| 53 | hinsetzen | sit down | 120 | 0.24 % |
| 54 | fein | nice | 120 | 0.24 % |
| 55 | weiterlaufen | go on | 116 | 0.23 % |
| 56 | vorwärts | forwards | 113 | 0.23 % |
| 57 | rückwärts | backwards | 110 | 0.22 % |
| 58 | hopp | chop | 107 | 0.22 % |
| 59 | drehen | turn | 106 | 0.21 % |
| 60 | zurück | back | 105 | 0.21 % |
| 61 | Futternapf | feeding dish | 102 | 0.21 % |
| 62 | na | well | 100 | 0.20 % |
| 63 | her | here | 100 | 0.20 % |
| 64 | braver | good | 100 | 0.20 % |

Table A.11: Most frequently used words in the German FAU Aibo Emotion Corpus which appeared at least 100 times

| no. | word | frequency | |
|---|---|---|---|
| 1 | stop | 1,456 | 17.18 % |
| 2 | forward | 816 | 9.63 % |
| 3 | turn | 732 | 8.64 % |
| 4 | left | 686 | 8.10 % |
| 5 | walk | 393 | 4.64 % |
| 6 | right | 330 | 3.89 % |
| 7 | forwards | 301 | 3.55 % |
| 8 | up | 265 | 3.13 % |
| 9 | stand | 206 | 2.43 % |
| 10 | go | 157 | 1.85 % |
| 11 | sit | 147 | 1.73 % |
| 12 | around | 146 | 1.72 % |
| 13 | the | 140 | 1.65 % |
| 14 | a | 136 | 1.60 % |
| 15 | dance | 133 | 1.57 % |
| 16 | backwards | 118 | 1.39 % |
| 17 | Aibo | 110 | 1.30 % |
| 18 | round | 108 | 1.27 % |
| 19 | ok | 108 | 1.27 % |
| 20 | and | 101 | 1.19 % |
| 21 | bit | 76 | 0.90 % |
| 22 | move | 72 | 0.85 % |
| 23 | back | 68 | 0.80 % |
| 24 | to | 66 | 0.78 % |
| 25 | degrees | 62 | 0.73 % |
| 26 | no | 55 | 0.65 % |
| 27 | get | 55 | 0.65 % |
| 28 | do | 49 | 0.56 % |
| 29 | yellow | 45 | 0.53 % |
| 30 | on | 45 | 0.53 % |
| 31 | chief | 42 | 0.50 % |
| 32 | way | 41 | 0.48 % |
| 33 | ninety | 38 | 0.45 % |
| 34 | little | 34 | 0.40 % |
| 35 | cup | 34 | 0.40 % |
| 36 | um | 33 | 0.39 % |
| 37 | line | 33 | 0.39 % |
| 38 | that | 32 | 0.38 % |
| 39 | follow | 32 | 0.38 % |
| 40 | look | 31 | 0.37 % |
| 41 | at | 28 | 0.33 % |
| 42 | your | 27 | 0.32 % |
| 43 | now | 27 | 0.32 % |
| 44 | steps | 26 | 0.31 % |

| 45 | keep | 24 | 0.28 % |
| 46 | paw | 23 | 0.27 % |
| 47 | oh | 23 | 0.27 % |
| 48 | good | 22 | 0.26 % |
| 49 | boy | 21 | 0.25 % |
| 50 | you | 20 | 0.24 % |

Table A.12: Most frequently used words in the British FAU Aibo Emotion Corpus which appeared at least 20 times

## A.2.9 Conditional Probabilities $P(e|w)$

| no. | word | $P(\mathbf{A}|w)$ | $P(\mathbf{E}|w)$ | $P(\mathbf{N}|w)$ | $P(\mathbf{M}|w)$ | $P(\mathbf{J}|w)$ | $P(\mathbf{O}|w)$ | $P(-|w)$ | # |
|---|---|---|---|---|---|---|---|---|---|
| 1 | Aibo | 10.1 | 3.5 | 72.2 | 1.4 | 0.0 | 0.0 | 12.7 | 7469 |
| 2 | nach | 0.6 | 2.2 | 93.5 | 0.4 | 0.1 | 0.0 | 3.2 | 2960 |
| 3 | links | 3.0 | 20.5 | 65.9 | 0.7 | 0.1 | 0.2 | 9.5 | 2560 |
| 4 | stopp | 3.7 | 30.5 | 57.4 | 0.1 | 0.4 | 0.0 | 8.0 | 1807 |
| 5 | geh | 0.6 | 0.8 | 94.0 | 1.2 | 0.0 | 0.0 | 3.4 | 1756 |
| 6 | lauf | 0.9 | 1.7 | 91.5 | 1.0 | 0.1 | 0.4 | 4.4 | 1586 |
| 7 | rechts | 2.5 | 18.9 | 69.3 | 1.0 | 0.2 | 0.1 | 7.9 | 1441 |
| 8 | und | 0.1 | 0.2 | 98.5 | 0.6 | 0.0 | 0.0 | 0.7 | 1333 |
| 9 | jetzt | 2.2 | 0.7 | 94.3 | 0.2 | 0.0 | 0.0 | 2.6 | 1231 |
| 10 | dich | 1.4 | 0.9 | 93.5 | 0.2 | 0.0 | 0.0 | 4.0 | 1139 |
| 11 | steh | 2.8 | 3.2 | 86.2 | 0.7 | 0.2 | 0.0 | 6.9 | 1111 |
| 12 | auf | 4.4 | 1.9 | 82.7 | 1.7 | 0.1 | 0.3 | 8.9 | 1088 |
| 13 | komm | 1.5 | 1.2 | 84.1 | 8.0 | 0.1 | 0.3 | 4.8 | 1011 |
| 14 | g'radeaus | 3.3 | 5.3 | 83.4 | 0.7 | 0.4 | 0.1 | 6.7 | 899 |
| 15 | dreh | 1.5 | 0.9 | 93.0 | 0.6 | 0.0 | 0.0 | 4.1 | 883 |
| 16 | weiter | 1.0 | 2.2 | 88.9 | 3.1 | 0.1 | 0.9 | 3.8 | 874 |
| 17 | mal | 1.1 | 0.6 | 94.5 | 1.7 | 0.1 | 0.0 | 2.0 | 839 |
| 18 | sitz | 2.6 | 16.9 | 75.6 | 0.7 | 0.0 | 0.0 | 4.2 | 722 |
| 19 | ja | 0.3 | 0.4 | 78.5 | 14.7 | 1.2 | 0.0 | 4.9 | 721 |
| 20 | aufstehen | 12.3 | 3.1 | 65.7 | 2.4 | 0.3 | 0.0 | 16.2 | 702 |
| 21 | so | 0.2 | 0.5 | 81.9 | 11.8 | 0.6 | 0.0 | 5.0 | 618 |
| 22 | stehen | 5.6 | 15.2 | 68.0 | 0.0 | 0.2 | 0.0 | 11.1 | 594 |
| 23 | geradeaus | 2.9 | 5.3 | 83.3 | 1.3 | 0.2 | 0.0 | 7.0 | 526 |
| 24 | bleib | 3.3 | 6.7 | 83.0 | 0.0 | 0.0 | 0.0 | 7.0 | 489 |
| 25 | laufen | 3.3 | 6.0 | 78.8 | 0.4 | 0.2 | 0.4 | 10.8 | 453 |
| 26 | wieder | 1.0 | 0.5 | 95.4 | 0.8 | 0.0 | 0.0 | 2.3 | 388 |
| 27 | um | 2.6 | 1.5 | 90.7 | 0.0 | 0.0 | 0.0 | 5.2 | 388 |
| 28 | gut | 0.0 | 1.2 | 74.9 | 17.3 | 0.0 | 0.0 | 6.6 | 335 |
| 29 | nein | 17.0 | 17.6 | 45.8 | 1.8 | 0.0 | 0.6 | 17.3 | 330 |
| 30 | du | 3.1 | 0.3 | 85.6 | 8.5 | 0.0 | 0.0 | 2.5 | 319 |
| 31 | okay | 0.3 | 0.0 | 98.6 | 0.7 | 0.0 | 0.0 | 0.3 | 291 |
| 32 | hin | 1.7 | 3.5 | 88.8 | 0.7 | 0.7 | 0.0 | 4.5 | 286 |
| 33 | brav | 0.0 | 0.0 | 62.2 | 21.7 | 0.3 | 0.0 | 15.7 | 286 |
| 34 | ein | 0.0 | 0.4 | 94.8 | 2.6 | 0.0 | 0.0 | 2.2 | 269 |
| 35 | *is | 0.0 | 0.0 | 87.0 | 8.4 | 0.4 | 0.0 | 4.2 | 261 |
| 36 | bisschen | 0.0 | 2.0 | 93.7 | 1.2 | 0.4 | 0.0 | 2.8 | 253 |
| 37 | da | 2.0 | 3.3 | 85.3 | 5.3 | 0.4 | 0.0 | 3.7 | 245 |
| 38 | vorne | 1.8 | 6.8 | 85.1 | 1.4 | 0.0 | 0.0 | 5.0 | 222 |
| 39 | gehen | 1.8 | 2.3 | 82.6 | 0.0 | 0.9 | 0.0 | 12.4 | 218 |
| 40 | setz | 0.0 | 2.5 | 92.5 | 0.5 | 0.0 | 0.0 | 4.5 | 200 |

Table A.13: Conditional probabilities $P(e|w)$ that the speaker is in the emotion-related state $e$ while he/she is producing the word $w$ for the 40 most frequently occurring words in the German FAU Aibo Emotion Corpus

## A.2.10   Splits for a 3-fold Cross-validation

| speaker | gender | | Aibo chunk set | | | | |
|---------|---|---|---|---|---|---|---|
|         | m | f | **A** | **E** | **N** | **M** | $\sum$ |
| Mont_03 | ☐ | ☑ | 0 | 0 | 3 | 0 | 3 |
| Mont_05 | ☐ | ☑ | 32 | 52 | 49 | 16 | 149 |
| Mont_06 | ☐ | ☑ | 12 | 5 | 29 | 2 | 48 |
| Mont_08 | ☐ | ☑ | 27 | 24 | 50 | 10 | 111 |
| Mont_10 | ☑ | ☐ | 16 | 6 | 65 | 15 | 102 |
| Mont_11 | ☑ | ☐ | 1 | 4 | 27 | 0 | 32 |
| Mont_23 | ☐ | ☑ | 2 | 14 | 58 | 12 | 86 |
| Mont_24 | ☐ | ☑ | 30 | 23 | 67 | 30 | 150 |
| Ohm_02 | ☑ | ☐ | 8 | 24 | 58 | 1 | 91 |
| Ohm_03 | ☐ | ☑ | 34 | 24 | 40 | 36 | 134 |
| Ohm_04 | ☐ | ☑ | 44 | 9 | 43 | 14 | 110 |
| Ohm_05 | ☑ | ☐ | 18 | 30 | 53 | 13 | 114 |
| Ohm_14 | ☐ | ☑ | 5 | 25 | 16 | 0 | 46 |
| Ohm_16 | ☐ | ☑ | 4 | 5 | 29 | 2 | 40 |
| Ohm_21 | ☑ | ☐ | 19 | 39 | 41 | 27 | 126 |
| Ohm_25 | ☑ | ☐ | 44 | 3 | 26 | 1 | 74 |
| Ohm_28 | ☐ | ☑ | 16 | 42 | 24 | 24 | 106 |
| $\sum$ | 6 | 11 | 312 | 329 | 678 | 203 | 1,522 |

Table A.14: Splits for a 3-fold cross-validation: first subset

| speaker | gender | | Aibo chunk set | | | | |
|---------|--------|---|---|---|---|---|---|
| | m | f | **A** | **E** | **N** | **M** | **Σ** |
| Mont_04 | ☑ | ☐ | 17 | 16 | 31 | 1 | 65 |
| Mont_07 | ☐ | ☑ | 25 | 6 | 83 | 7 | 121 |
| Mont_09 | ☐ | ☑ | 37 | 25 | 33 | 0 | 95 |
| Mont_12 | ☐ | ☑ | 3 | 29 | 35 | 0 | 67 |
| Mont_13 | ☐ | ☑ | 3 | 16 | 16 | 0 | 35 |
| Mont_14 | ☐ | ☑ | 12 | 10 | 21 | 0 | 43 |
| Mont_18 | ☑ | ☐ | 2 | 6 | 22 | 0 | 30 |
| Mont_21 | ☑ | ☐ | 13 | 25 | 17 | 13 | 68 |
| Mont_25 | ☐ | ☑ | 9 | 12 | 39 | 3 | 63 |
| Ohm_01 | ☐ | ☑ | 16 | 29 | 49 | 55 | 149 |
| Ohm_08 | ☑ | ☐ | 32 | 14 | 26 | 10 | 82 |
| Ohm_10 | ☐ | ☑ | 23 | 36 | 43 | 30 | 132 |
| Ohm_19 | ☑ | ☐ | 16 | 51 | 39 | 3 | 109 |
| Ohm_20 | ☐ | ☑ | 4 | 13 | 17 | 0 | 34 |
| Ohm_22 | ☐ | ☑ | 7 | 24 | 7 | 5 | 43 |
| Ohm_23 | ☑ | ☐ | 22 | 21 | 46 | 0 | 89 |
| Ohm_29 | ☑ | ☐ | 51 | 5 | 42 | 17 | 115 |
| Ohm_31 | ☑ | ☐ | 19 | 15 | 70 | 46 | 150 |
| **Σ** | 8 | 10 | 311 | 353 | 636 | 190 | 1,490 |

Table A.15: Splits for a 3-fold cross-validation: second subset

| speaker | gender | | Aibo chunk set | | | | |
|---------|--------|---|---|---|---|---|---|
| | m | f | **A** | **E** | **N** | **M** | **Σ** |
| Mont_01 | ☐ | ☑ | 10 | 40 | 42 | 0 | 92 |
| Mont_02 | ☐ | ☑ | 11 | 3 | 68 | 4 | 86 |
| Mont_15 | ☐ | ☑ | 15 | 0 | 48 | 7 | 70 |
| Mont_16 | ☐ | ☑ | 3 | 11 | 32 | 1 | 47 |
| Mont_17 | ☑ | ☐ | 36 | 27 | 49 | 0 | 112 |
| Mont_19 | ☑ | ☐ | 26 | 31 | 22 | 0 | 79 |
| Mont_20 | ☑ | ☐ | 20 | 25 | 53 | 3 | 101 |
| Mont_22 | ☐ | ☑ | 0 | 2 | 14 | 0 | 16 |
| Ohm_06 | ☐ | ☑ | 17 | 42 | 49 | 7 | 115 |
| Ohm_07 | ☑ | ☐ | 5 | 20 | 48 | 3 | 76 |
| Ohm_11 | ☑ | ☐ | 1 | 20 | 37 | 0 | 58 |
| Ohm_13 | ☑ | ☐ | 24 | 53 | 46 | 0 | 123 |
| Ohm_18 | ☐ | ☑ | 79 | 20 | 41 | 157 | 297 |
| Ohm_24 | ☐ | ☑ | 20 | 18 | 49 | 9 | 96 |
| Ohm_27 | ☑ | ☐ | 8 | 26 | 60 | 0 | 94 |
| Ohm_32 | ☐ | ☑ | 16 | 25 | 26 | 2 | 69 |
| **Σ** | 7 | 9 | 291 | 363 | 684 | 193 | 1,531 |

Table A.16: Splits for a 3-fold cross-validation: third subset

## A.3  Initiative CEICES

### A.3.1  Members

**FAU**       Lehrstuhl für Informatik 5 (Mustererkennung)
             Technische Fakultät
             Friedrich-Alexander-Universität Erlangen-Nürnberg (FAU), Germany
             *Anton Batliner, Stefan Steidl, Elmar Nöth*

**TUM**       Lehrstuhl für Mensch-Maschine-Kommunikation
             Fakultät für Elektrotechnik und Informationstechnik
             Technische Universität München (TUM), Germany
             *Björn Schuller*

**UA**        Lehrstuhl für Multimedia Konzepte und ihre Anwendungen
             Fakultät für Angewandte Informatik
             Universität Augsburg (UA), Germany
             *Thurid Vogt, Johannes Wagner*

**UKA**       Institut für Theoretische Informatik
             Fakultät für Informatik
             Universität Karlsruhe (UKA), Germany
             *Kornel Laskowski*

**FBK**       Centro per la ricerca scientifica e tecnologica (ITC-irst)
             Fondazione Bruno Kessler (FBK), Trento, Italy
             *Dino Seppi*

**LIMSI**     Laboratoire d'Informatique pour la Mécanique et
             les Sciences de l'Ingénieur (LIMSI)
             Centre National de la Recherche Scientifique (CNRS), France
             *Laurence Devillers, Laurence Vidrascu*

**TAU**       Department of Communication Disorders
             Sackler Faculty of Medicine
             Tel Aviv University, Israel
             *Loïc Kessous, Noam Amir*

**AFEKA**    Tel Aviv Academic College of Engineering, Israel
             *Vered Aharonson*

**GERG**      Geneva Emotion Research Group (GERG)
             Faculté de Psychologie et des Sciences de l'Éducation
             Université de Genève, Switzerland
             *Tanja Bänziger*

**QU**        School of Psychology
             Queen's University, Belfast, Great Britain
             *Roddie Cowie*

## A.3.2   Contract

# Agreement of use

### between

Lehrstuhl für Informatik 5 (Mustererkennung)
Friedrich-Alexander-Universität Erlangen-Nürnberg
Martensstr. 3, 91058 Erlangen, Germany

### and

.............................................................................
.............................................................................
.............................................................................

**Agreement of Use within CEICES: Combining Efforts for Improving automatic Classification of Emotional user States, a "forced co-operation" initiative under the guidance of HUMAINE (Network of Excellence "Human-Machine Interaction Network on Emotion, IST FP6, Contract Nr. 507422)**

The classification performance of emotional user states found in realistic, spontaneous speech is not very high, compared to the performance reported for acted speech in the literature. This might be partly due to the difficulty of providing reliable annotations, partly due to suboptimal feature vectors used for classification, and partly simply to the difficulty of the task. CEICES aims at improving this state of affairs by combining the competence found a different sites that deal with this topic within a "forced co-operation" initiative under the guidance of HUMAINE. The initiative is open for partners outside of HUMAINE.

The database to be used – at least in the beginning of the initiative – is the so-called AIBO-database, recorded, processed, and annotated by the Friedrich-Alexander-Universität Erlangen-Nürnberg (henceforth FAU), Martensstr. 3, 91058 Erlangen, Germany. At least for the time span of 2005-2006, this database will only be released under the conditions specified in the following for the sole scientific, non-commercial use:

The licensee pays a nominal fee of 100 Euros (excl. VAT) for handling etc. The corpus is handed over without guarantee. No legal claims of any kind can be derived from accepting and using the corpus. FAU is not liable for any damage resulting from receiving, installing or using the corpus or any other files provided by FAU in this context. Handing over the corpus or any other files which have been provided by FAU containing information derived from it (labelling files, etc.) by the licensee to any third party may not be done without the expressed written consent of FAU.

The licensee agrees to join the CEICES initiative as a partner whose conditions are described in the following; note that as for CEICES, FAU complies to the same conditions as any other partner in CEICES but will moreover take care of defining subsamples, definition of training, validation and test files, providing manually corrected label files, etc.; by that, FAU tries to make the processing at different sites as comparable as possible.

If a partner concentrates on additional labelling, he agrees to share with all the other partners additional analyses, esp. additional annotations. Basically, this will be done on a bilateral basis.

If a partner concentrates on features with subsequent automatic classification, using the label files provided by FAU, he commits himself to share with all the other partners extracted feature values together with the necessary information (which feature models which acoustic or linguistic phenomenon, format of feature values, classifier used, etc.). The files containing the feature values will be exchanged via email, via the HUMAINE portal, or via ftp up- and download accessible with a password. The format of these files will be ASCII and some agreed-upon standard, e.g., arff (each case = each word in one line, values delimited by comma, etc.).

By sharing features computed at different sites, CEICES aims at improving classification performance and gaining insight into the impact of different types of features. Even if a partner is not actively involved in writing a paper and might thus not appear as an author, he agrees that results obtained with his feature values can be published giving credit to each site for their specific contributions; however, common publications are the most preferred way. Of course, the partners are free to co-operate on a bilateral basis with other partners more closely by, e.g., sharing source code etc.
Apart from these conditions specific for CEICES, the following general conditions apply:

Any models, derived from data containing the corpus may – just as the speech data themselves – only be used for scientific, non-commercial applications. As special condition for the reduced fee for the corpus in combination with the appropriate annotation files, the licensee lets FAU know results obtained in due time. Common publications on the results obtained should be aimed at.

For publications and talks concerning directly or indirectly the use of the corpus the licensee has to cite FAU with a citation provided by FAU. Currently this is:

*A. Batliner, C. Hacker, S. Steidl, E. Nöth, S. D'Arcy, M. Russell, and M. Wong. "You stupid tin box" - children interacting with the AIBO robot: A cross-linguistic emotional speech corpus. In Proc. LREC 2004, Lisbon, pages 171-174.*

Contact person at FAU:
Dr.-Ing. E. Nöth

Contact person at licensee:
............................................

# Appendix B

# Software EDE

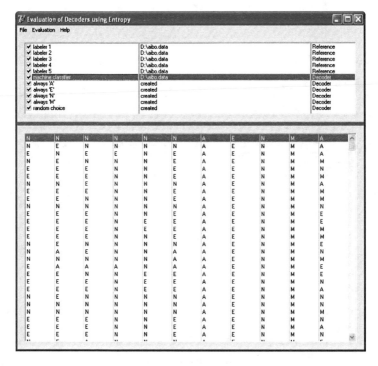

Figure B.1: EDE: Data of the five human labelers, the machine classifier, and five naïve classifiers

Figure B.2:  EDE: Average entropy values reported for the average human labeler, the machine classifier, and the five naïve classifiers

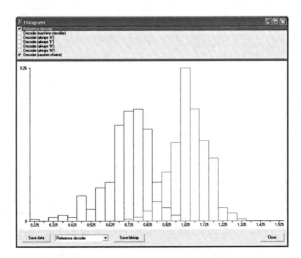

Figure B.3:  EDE: Entropy histograms for the chosen two decoders: the average human labeler vs. a naïve classifier picking randomly one of the four classes with equal a priori probabilities

# Appendix C

# Software eLabel

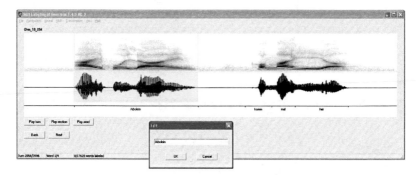

Figure C.1: eLabel is suited to easily correct the transliteration and the word segmentation

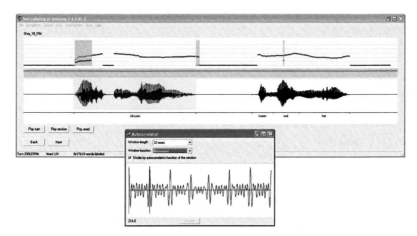

Figure C.2: eLabel: Manual correction of the fundamental frequency by selecting the maximum of the autocorrelation function

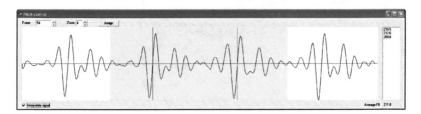

Figure C.3: eLabel: Correction of the fundamental frequency by manually defining periods

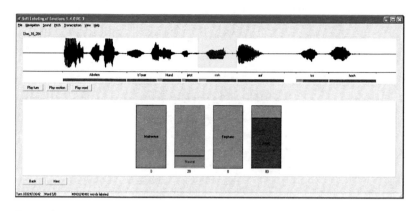

Figure C.4: eLabel: Labeling emotion-related states with category labels. eLabel allows the labeler to make soft decisions (s. Chapter 3.4). As it is used in this figure, eLabel can also be used to visualize the agreement of the labelers for each word. For the current word 'steh', four labelers decided for **A**nger and one for **N**eutral

# List of Figures

# List of Tables

# Bibliography

[Ahme 74]  N. Ahmed, T. Natarajan, and K. Rao. "Discrete Cosine Transform". *IEEE Transactions on Computers*, Vol. 23, pp. 90–93, 1974.

[Albr 05]  I. Albrecht, M. Schröder, J. Häber, and H.-P. Seidel. "Mixed feelings: Expression of non-basic emotions in a muscle-based talking head". *Virtual Reality*, Vol. 8, No. 4, pp. 201–212, 2005.

[Alku 97]  P. Alku, H. Strik, and E. Vilkman. "Parabolic spectral parameter – A new method for quantification of the glottal flow". *Speech Communication*, Vol. 22, pp. 67–79, 1997.

[Ang 02]  J. Ang, R. Dhillon, E. Shriberg, and A. Stolcke. "Prosody-based Automatic Detection of Annoyance and Frustration in Human-Computer Dialog". In: *Interspeech 2002 – ICSLP, 7th International Conference on Spoken Language Processing, September 16-20, 2002, Denver, U. S. A., Proceedings*, pp. 2037–2040, 2002.

[Arim 07]  Y. Arimoto, S. Ohno, and H. Iida. "Acoustic Features of Anger Utterances during Natural Dialog". In: *Interspeech 2007 – Eurospeech, 10th European Conference on Speech Communication and Technology, August 27-31, 2007, Antwerp, Belgium, Proceedings*, pp. 2217–2220, 2007.

[Arno 60]  M. B. Arnold. *Emotion and Personality. Vol. 1, Psychological Aspects.* Columbia University Press, New York, 1960.

[Aver 75]  J. R. Averill. "A semantic atlas of emotional concepts". *JSAS Catalog of Selected Documents in Psychology*, Vol. 5, p. 330, 1975.

[Bach 99]  J. Bachorowski. "Vocal Expression and Perception of Emotion". *Current Directions in Psychological Science*, Vol. 8, pp. 53–57, 1999.

[Bags 93]  P. C. Bagshaw, S. M. Hiller, and M. A. Jack. "Enhanced Pitch Tracking and the Processing of F0 Contours for Computer Aided Intonation Teaching". In: *Eurospeech, 3rd European Conference on Speech Communication and Technology, September 22-25, 1993, Berlin, Germany, Proceedings*, pp. 1003–1006, 1993.

[Bans 96]  R. Banse and K. R. Scherer. "Acoustic Profiles in Vocal Emotion Expression". *Journal of Personality and Social Psychology*, Vol. 70, No. 3, pp. 614–636, 1996.

[Banz 05]  T. Bänziger, V. Tran, and K. R. Scherer. "The Geneva Emotion Wheel: A tool for the verbal report of emotional reactions". In: *ISRE 2005, Conference of the International Society for Research on Emotions, July 11-15, 2005, Bari, Italy, Proceedings*, 2005.

[Batl 00a]  A. Batliner, J. Buckow, H. Niemann, E. Nöth, and V. Warnke. "The Prosody Module". In: W. Wahlster, Ed., *Verbmobil: Foundations of Speech-to-Speech Translations*, pp. 106–121, Springer, New York, Berlin, 2000.

[Batl 00b]  A. Batliner, K. Fischer, R. Huber, J. Spilker, and E. Nöth. "Desperately Seeking Emotions: Actors, Wizards, and Human Beings". In: *ISCA Tutorial and Research Workshop on Speech and Emotion, September 5-7, 2000, Newcastle, Northern Ireland, Proceedings*, pp. 195–200, 2000.

[Batl 00c]  A. Batliner, R. Huber, H. Niemann, E. Nöth, J. Spilker, and K. Fischer. "The Recognition of Emotion". In: W. Wahlster, Ed., *Verbmobil: Foundations of Speech-to-Speech Translations*, pp. 122–130, Springer, New York, Berlin, 2000.

[Batl 03a]  A. Batliner, K. Fischer, R. Huber, J. Spilker, and E. Nöth. "How to Find Trouble in Communication". *Speech Communication*, Vol. 40, pp. 117–143, 2003.

[Batl 03b]  A. Batliner, C. Hacker, S. Steidl, E. Nöth, and J. Haas. "User States, User Strategies, and System Performance: How to Match the One with the Other". In: *ISCA Tutorial and Research Workshop on Error Handling in Spoken Dialogue Systems, August 28-31, 2003, Chateau d'Oex, Switzerland, Proceedings*, pp. 5–10, 2003.

[Batl 03c]  A. Batliner, V. Zeissler, C. Frank, J. Adelhardt, R. Shi, and E. Nöth. "We are not amused - but how do you know? User states in a multimodal dialogue system". In: *Interspeech 2003 – Eurospeech, 8th European Conference on Speech Communication and Technology, September 1-4, 2003, Geneva, Switzerland, Proceedings*, pp. 733–736, 2003.

[Batl 04a]  A. Batliner, C. Hacker, S. Steidl, E. Nöth, S. D'Arcy, M. Russell, and M. Wong. "'You stupid tin box' - children interacting with the AIBO robot: A cross-linguistic emotional speech corpus". In: *LREC 2004, 4th International Conference of Language Resources and Evaluation, May 24-30, 2004, Lisbon, Portugal, Proceedings*, pp. 171–174, 2004.

[Batl 04b]  A. Batliner, C. Hacker, S. Steidl, E. Nöth, and J. Haas. "From Emotion to Interaction: Lessons from Real Human-Machine-Dialogues". In: E. André, L. Dybkiaer, W. Minker, and P. Heisterkamp, Eds., *Affective Dialogue Systems, Proceedings of a Tutorial and Research Workshop*, pp. 1–12, Springer, Berlin, 2004.

[Batl 05a]  A. Batliner, S. Steidl, C. Hacker, and E. Nöth. "Private Emotions vs. Social Interaction - towards New Dimensions in Research on Emotion". In: *Proceedings of a Workshop on Adapting the Interaction Style to Affective Factors, 10th International Conference on User Modelling*, 2005.

[Batl 05b]  A. Batliner, S. Steidl, C. Hacker, and E. Nöth. "Tales of Tuning - Prototyping for Automatic Classification of Emotional User States". In: *Interspeech 2005 – Eurospeech, 9th European Conference on Speech Communication and Technology, September 4-8, 2003, Lisbon, Portugal, Proceedings*, pp. 489–492, 2005.

[Batl 06a]  A. Batliner, S. Biersack, and S. Steidl. "The Prosody of Pet Robot Directed Speech: Evidence from Children". In: R. Hoffmann and H. Mixdorff, Eds., *Proc. Speech Prosody, 3rd International Conference*, pp. 1–4, TUDpress, Dresden, 2006.

[Batl 06b]  A. Batliner, S. Steidl, B. Schuller, D. Seppi, K. Laskowski, T. Vogt, L. Devillers, L. Vidrascu, N. Amir, L. Kessous, and V. Aharonson. "Combining Efforts for Improving Automatic Classification of Emotional User States". In: T. Erjavec and J. Gros, Eds., *Language Technologies, IS-LTC 2006*, pp. 240–245, Infornacijska Druzba (Information Society), Ljubljana, Slovenia, 2006.

[Batl 07a]  A. Batliner, S. Steidl, and E. Nöth. "Laryngealizations and Emotions: How Many Babushkas?". In: M. Schröder, A. Batliner, and C. d'Alessandro, Eds., *ParaLing 2007, International Workshop on Paralinguistic Speech - between Models and Data, August 3, 2007, Saarbrücken*, pp. 17–22, 2007.

[Batl 07b]  A. Batliner, S. Steidl, B. Schuller, D. Seppi, T. Vogt, L. Devillers, L. Vidrascu, N. Amir, L. Kessous, and V. Aharonson. "The Impact of F0 Extraction Errors on the Classification of Prominence and Emotion". In: *ICPhS 2007, International Congress of Phonetic Sciences, Saarbrücken, Germany, 6.8.-10.8.2007, Proceedings*, pp. 2201–2204, 2007.

[Batl 08a]  A. Batliner, B. Schuller, S. Schaeffler, and S. Steidl. "Mother, Adults, Children, Pets – Towards the Acoustics of Intimacy". In: *ICASSP 2008, International Conference on Acoustics, Speech, and Signal Processing, March 30 - April 04, 2008, Las Vegas, U. S. A., Proceedings*, pp. 4497–4500, 2008.

[Batl 08b]  A. Batliner, S. Steidl, C. Hacker, and E. Nöth. "Private Emotions vs. Social Interaction – a Data-driven Approach towards Analysing Emotion in Speech". *User Modeling and User-Adapted Interaction (umuai)*, Vol. 18, No. 1-2, pp. 175–206, 2008.

[Batl 09]  A. Batliner, S. Steidl, B. Schuller, D. Seppi, T. Vogt, J. Wagner, L. Devillers, L. Vidrascu, V. Aharonson, and N. Amir. "Whodunnit – Searching for the Most Important Feature Types Signalling Emotional User States in Speech". *Computer Speech and Language*, 2009. Manuscript, submitted.

[Batl 93]  A. Batliner, S. Burger, B. Johne, and A. Kießling. "MÜSLI: A Classification Scheme for Laryngealizations". In: *ESCA Workshop on Prosody, September 27-29, 1993, Lund, Sweden, Proceedings*, pp. 176–179, 1993.

[Batl 98]  A. Batliner, R. Kompe, A. Kießling, M. Mast, H. Niemann, and E. Nöth. "M = Syntax + Prosody: A syntactic-prosodic labelling scheme for large spontaneous speech databases". *Speech Communication*, Vol. 25, pp. 193–222, 1998.

[Bera 49]  L. L. Beranek. *Acoustic Measurements*. Wiley, New York, 1949.

[Bezo 84]  R. van Bezooijen. *The characteristics and recognizability of vocal expression of emotions*. Foris, Dordrecht, The Netherlands, 1984.

[Bilm 98]  J. A. Bilmes. "A Gentle Tutorial of the EM Algorithm and its Application to Parameter Estimation for Gaussian Mixture and Hidden Markov Models". Tech. Rep., International Computer Science Institute (ICSI), Berkeley, CA, U. S. A., 1998.

[Boer 93]  P. Boersma. "Accurate Short-term Analysis of the Fundamental Frequency and the Harmonics-to-Noise Ratio of a Sampled Sound". *Proceedings of the Institute of Phonetic Sciences (University of Amsterdam)*, Vol. 17, pp. 97–110, 1993.

[Brac 84]   R. N. Bracewell. "The Fast Hartley Transform". *Proceedings of the IEEE*, Vol. 72, No. 8, pp. 1010–1018, 1984.

[Brun 56]   E. Brunswik. *Perception and the Representative Design of Psychological Experiments*. University of California Press, Berkeley, 1956.

[Buck 99a]  R. Buck. "Biological affects: a typology". *Psychological Review*, Vol. 106, pp. 301–336, 1999.

[Buck 99b]  J. Buckow, V. Warnke, R. Huber, A. Batliner, E. Nöth, and H. Niemann. "Fast and Robust Features for Prosodic Classification". In: V. Matousek, P. Mautner, J. Ocelíková, and P. Sojka, Eds., *Text, Speech and Dialogue, 2nd International Workshop, September 13-17, 1999, Plzen, Czech Republic, Proceedings*, pp. 193–198, Springer, Berlin, 1999.

[Bulu 07]   M. Bulut, S. Lee, and S. S. Narayanan. "Analysis of emotional speech prosody in terms of part of speech tags". In: *Interspeech 2007 – Eurospeech, 10th European Conference on Speech Communication and Technology, August 27-31, 2007, Antwerp, Belgium, Proceedings*, pp. 626–629, 2007.

[Burk 05]   F. Burkhardt, A. Paeschke, M. Rolfes, W. Sendlmeier, and B. Weiss. "A Database of German Emotional Speech". In: *Interspeech 2005 – Eurospeech, 9th European Conference on Speech Communication and Technology, September 4-8, 2003, Lisbon, Portugal, Proceedings*, pp. 1517–1520, 2005.

[Buss 07]   C. Busso, S. Lee, and S. S. Narayanan. "Using Neutral Speech Models for Emotional Speech Analysis". In: *Interspeech 2007 – Eurospeech, 10th European Conference on Speech Communication and Technology, August 27-31, 2007, Antwerp, Belgium, Proceedings*, pp. 2225–2228, 2007.

[Camp 00]   N. Campbell. "Databases of Emotional Speech". In: *ISCA Tutorial and Research Workshop on Speech and Emotion, September 5-7, 2000, Newcastle, Northern Ireland, Proceedings*, pp. 114–121, 2000.

[Camp 03]   N. Campbell. "Databases of Expressive Speech". In: *Oriental COCOSDA Workshop 2003, October 1-3, 2003, Singapore, Proceedings*, 2003.

[Caul 00]   R. T. Cauldwell. "Where did the anger go? The role of context in interpreting emotion in speech". In: *ISCA Tutorial and Research Workshop on Speech and Emotion, September 5-7, 2000, Newcastle, Northern Ireland, Proceedings*, pp. 127–131, 2000.

[Chwa 88]   K. Chwalisz, E. Diener, and D. Gallagher. "Autonomic arousal feedback and emotional experience: Evidence from the spinal cord injured.". *Journal of Personality and Social Psychology*, Vol. 54, pp. 820–828, 1988.

[Cicc 72]   D. V. Cicchetti. "Assessing inter-rater reliability for rating scales: Resolving some basic issues". *British Journal of Psychiatry*, Vol. 129, pp. 452–456, 1972.

[Clav 06]   C. Clavel, I. Vasilescu, L. Devillers, T. Ehrette, and G. Richard. "Fear-type emotions of the SAFE Corpus: annotation issues". In: *LREC 2006, 5th International Conference of Language Resources and Evaluation, May 22-28, 2006, Genoa, Italy, Proceedings*, pp. 1099–1104, 2006.

[Cohe 60]   J. Cohen. "A Coefficient of Agreement for Nominal Scales". *Educational and Psychological Measurement*, Vol. 20, pp. 37–46, 1960.

Bibliography 235

[Cohe 68] J. Cohen. "Weighted Kappa: Nominal Scale Agreement with Provision for Scaled Disagreement or Partial Credit". *Psychological Bulletin*, Vol. 70, No. 4, pp. 213–220, 1968.

[Corn 00] R. R. Cornelius. "Theoretical Approaches to Emotion". In: *ISCA Tutorial and Research Workshop on Speech and Emotion, September 5-7, 2000, Newcastle, Northern Ireland, Proceedings*, pp. 3–10, 2000.

[Corn 96] R. R. Cornelius. *The science of emotion. Research and tradition in the psychology of emotion*. Prentice Hall, Upper Saddle River, NJ, 1996.

[Cowi 00] R. Cowie, E. Douglas-Cowie, S. Savvidou, E. McMahon, M. Sawey, and M. Schröder. "FEELTRACE: An instrument for recording perceived emotion in real time". In: *ISCA Tutorial and Research Workshop on Speech and Emotion, September 5-7, 2000, Newcastle, Northern Ireland, Proceedings*, pp. 19–24, 2000.

[Cowi 01] R. Cowie, E. Douglas-Cowie, N. Tsapatsoulis, G. Votsis, S. Kollias, W. Fellenz, and J. Taylor. "Emotion Recognition in Human-Computer Interaction". *IEEE Signal Processing Magazine*, Vol. 18, No. 1, pp. 32–80, 2001.

[Cowi 03] R. Cowie and R. R. Cornelius. "Describing the emotional states that are expressed in speech". *Speech Communication*, Vol. 40, No. 1-2, pp. 5–32, 2003.

[Cowi 99] R. Cowie, E. Douglas-Cowie, B. Apolloni, J. Taylor, A. Romano, and W. Fellenz. "What a neural net needs to know about emotion words". *Journal of Computational Intelligence and Applications*, pp. 109–114, 1999.

[dAll 95] C. d'Allesandro and P. Mertens. "Automatic Pitch Contour Stylization Using a Model of Tonal Perception". *Computer Speech and Language*, Vol. 9, pp. 257–288, 1995.

[Darw 72] C. Darwin. *The Expression of the Emotions in Man and Animals*. John Murray, London, 1872. (P. Ekman, Ed., Oxford University Press, Oxford, 3. Ed., 1998).

[Davi 80] S. B. Davis and P. Mermelstein. "Comparison of parametric representation for monosyllabic word recognition in continuously spoken sentences". *IEEE Transactions on Acoustics, Speech and Signal Processing*, Vol. 28, No. 4, pp. 357–366, 1980.

[Davi 82] M. Davies and J. L. Fleiss. "Measuring agreement for multinomial data". *Biometrics*, Vol. 38, pp. 1047–1051, 1982.

[Demp 77] A. P. Dempster, N. M. Laird, and D. B. Rubin. "Maximum Likelihood from Incomplete Data via the EM Algorith". *Journal of the Royal Statistic Society. Series B (Methodological)*, Vol. 39, No. 1, pp. 1–38, 1977.

[Devi 03] L. Devillers, L. Lamel, and I. Vasilescu. "Emotion Detection in Task-oriented Spoken Dialogs". In: *ICME 2003, 4th IEEE International Conference on Multimedia and Expo, July 6-9, 2003, Baltimore, U. S. A., Proceedings*, pp. 549–552, 2003.

[Devi 04]   L. Devillers, I. Vasilescu, and L. Vidrascu. "F0 and pause features anal-ysis for Anger and Fear detection in real-life spoken dialogs". In: *Speech Prododu 2004, March 23-26, 2004, Nara, Japan, Proceedings*, 2004. No pagination.

[Devi 06]   L. Devillers and L. Vidrascu. "Real-life Emotions Detection with Lexi-cal and Paralinguistic Cues on Human-Human Call Center Dialogs". In: *Interspeech 2006 – ICSLP, 9th International Conference on Spoken Lan-guage Processing, September 17-21, 2006, Pittsburgh, U. S. A., Proceed-ings*, pp. 801–803, 2006.

[Doug 00]   E. Douglas-Cowie, R. Cowie, and M. Schröder. "A New Emotion Database: Considerations, Sources and Scope". In: *ISCA Tutorial and Research Workshop on Speech and Emotion, September 5-7, 2000, New-castle, Northern Ireland, Proceedings*, pp. 39–44, 2000.

[Doug 03]   E. Douglas-Cowie, N. Campbell, R. Cowie, and P. Roach. "Emotional speech: Towards a new generation of databases". *Speech Communication*, Vol. 40, No. 1-2, pp. 33–60, 2003.

[Duda 00]   R. O. Duda, P. E. Hart, and D. G. Stork. *Pattern Classification*. John Wiley & Sons, New York, 2nd Ed., 2000.

[Duff 41]   E. Duffy. "An explanation of 'emotional' phenomena without the use of the concept 'emotion'". *Journal of General Psychology*, Vol. 25, pp. 283–293, 1941.

[Durb 60]   J. Durbin. "The Fitting of Time Series Models". *Review of the Interna-tional Statistical Institute*, Vol. 28, No. 3, pp. 233–244, 1960.

[Ekma 72]   P. Ekman. "Universals and cultural differences in facial expressions of emo-tion". In: J. R. Cole, Ed., *Nebraska Symposium on Motivation*, pp. 207–283, University of Nebraska Press, Lincoln, 1972.

[Ekma 73]   P. Ekman. "Darwin and cross-cultural studies of facial expression". In: P. Ekman, Ed., *Darwin and Facial Expression*, pp. 1–83, Academic Press, New York, 1973.

[Ekma 80]   P. Ekman. *The Face of Man: Universal Expression in a New Guinea Village*. Garland, New York, 1980.

[Ekma 92]   P. Ekman. "Facial expression of emotion: New findings, new questions". *Psychological Science*, Vol. 3, pp. 34–38, 1992.

[Ekma 94]   P. Ekman. "Strong Evidence for Universals in Facial expressions. A Reply to Russel's Mistaken Critique". *Psychological Bulletin*, Vol. 115, No. 2, pp. 268–287, 1994.

[Ekma 99]   P. Ekman. "Basic Emotions". In: T. Dalgleish and M. Power, Eds., *Handbook of Cognition and Emotion*, pp. 301–320, John Wiley, New York, 1999.

[Engb 96]   I. S. Engbert and A. V. Hansen. "Documentation of the Danish Emo-tional Speech Database DES". Tech. Rep., Center for PersonKommu-nikation, Aalborg University, Denmark, 1996. `http://cpk.auc.dk/~tb/speech/Emotions/`, last visited 01/12/2009.

[Enos 07]    F. Enos, E. Shriberg, M. Graciarena, J. Hirschberg, and A. Stolcke. "Detecting Deception Using Critical Segments". In: *Interspeech 2007 – Eurospeech, 10th European Conference on Speech Communication and Technology, August 27-31, 2007, Antwerp, Belgium, Proceedings*, pp. 2281–2284, 2007.

[Fant 60]    G. Fant. *The Acoustic Theory of Speech Production*. Mouton, The Hague, 1960.

[Fant 68]    G. Fant. "Analysis and synthesis of speech processes". In: B. Malmberg, Ed., *Manual of Phonetics*, Chap. 8, pp. 173–276, North-Holland Publ. Co, Amsterdam, 1968.

[Fant 85]    G. Fant, J. Liljencrants, and Q. Lin. "A four-parameter model of glottal flow". *STL-QPSR, Quarterly Progress and Status Report of the Dept. for Speech, Music and Hearing, KTH Stockholm, Sweden*, Vol. 26, No. 4, pp. 1–13, 1985.

[Fehr 84]    B. Fehr and J. A. Russel. "Concept of emotion viewed from a prototype perspective". *Journal of Experimental Psychology: General*, Vol. 113, pp. 464–486, 1984.

[Fern 03]    R. Fernandez and R. W. Picard. "Modeling drivers' speech under stress". *Speech Communication*, Vol. 40, pp. 145–159, 2003.

[Fern 05]    R. Fernandez and R. W. Picard. "Classical and Novel Discriminant Features for Affect Recognition from Speech". In: *Interspeech 2005 – Eurospeech, 9th European Conference on Speech Communication and Technology, September 4-8, 2003, Lisbon, Portugal, Proceedings*, pp. 473–476, 2005.

[Flei 69]    J. L. Fleiss, J. Cohen, and B. S. Everitt. "Large sample standard errors of kappa and weighted kappa". *Psychological Bulletin*, Vol. 72, pp. 323–327, 1969.

[Flei 71]    J. L. Fleiss. "Measuring nominal scale agreement among many raters". *Psychological Bulletin*, Vol. 76, No. 5, pp. 378–382, 1971.

[Frie 89]    J. H. Friedman. "Regularized Discriminant Analysis". *Journal of the American Statistical Association*, Vol. 84, No. 405, pp. 165–175, 1989.

[Frij 86]    N. H. Frijda. *The Emotions*. Cambridge University Press, Cambridge, 1986.

[Frij 93]    N. H. Frijda. "Moods, emotion episodes, and emotions". In: M. Lewis and J. M. Haviland, Eds., *Handbook of Emotions*, pp. 381–403, Guilford Press, New York, London, 1993.

[Froh 01]    M. Fröhlich, D. Michaelis, and H. W. Strube. "SIM – simultaneous inverse filtering and matching of a glottal flow model for acoustic speech signals". *Journal of the Acoustic Society of America*, Vol. 110, pp. 479–488, 2001.

[Furu 86]    S. Furui. "Speaker-Independent Isolated Word Recognition Using Dynamic Features of Speech Spectrum". *IEEE Transactions on Acoustics, Speech, and Signal Processing*, Vol. 34, No. 1, pp. 52–59, 1986.

[Gall 02]    F. Gallwitz, H. Niemann, E. Nöth, and V. Warnke. "Integrated Recognition of Words and Phrase Boundaries". *Speech Communication*, Vol. 36, No. 1-2, pp. 81–95, 2002.

[Gerh 03]   D. Gerhard. "Pitch Extraction and Fundamental Frequency: History and Current Techniques". Tech. Rep., Department of Computer Science, University of Regina, Regina, Canada, 2003.

[Gerr 94]   A. Gerrards-Hesse, K. Spies, and F. W. Hesse. "Experimental inductions of emotional states and their effectiveness: A review". *British Journal of Psychology*, Vol. 85, No. 1, pp. 55–78, 1994.

[Gobl 03]   C. Gobl and A. Ní Chasaide. "The role of voice quality in communicating emotion, mood and attitude". *Speech Communication*, Vol. 40, pp. 189–212, 2003.

[Gram 88]   P. Gramming and J. Sundberg. "Spectrum factors relevant to phonetogram measurement". *Journal of the Acoustical Society of America*, Vol. 83, pp. 2352–2360, 1988.

[Gupt 07]   P. Gupta and N. Rajput. "Two-Stream Emotion Recognition for Call Center Monitoring". In: *Interspeech 2007 – Eurospeech, 10th European Conference on Speech Communication and Technology, August 27-31, 2007, Antwerp, Belgium, Proceedings*, pp. 626–629, 2007.

[Hack 03]   C. Hacker, G. Stemmer, S. Steidl, E. Nöth, and H. Niemann. "Various Information Sources for HMM with Weighted Multiple Codebooks". In: A. Wendemuth, Ed., *Speech Processing Workshop, September 9, 2003, Magdeburg, Germany, Proceedings*, pp. 9–16, Magdeburg, 2003.

[Hade 06]   T. Haderlein, D. Zorn, S. Steidl, E. Nöth, M. Shozakai, and M. Schuster. "Visualization of Voice Disorders Using the Sammon Transform". In: P. Sojka, I. Kopecek, and K. Pala, Eds., *Text, Speech and Dialogue, 9th International Conference, September 11-15, 2006, Brno, Czech Republic, Proceedings*, pp. 589–596, Springer, Berlin, Heidelberg, 2006.

[Hade 07]   T. Haderlein. *Automatic Evaluation of Tracheoesophageal Substitute Voices*. Logos Verlag, Berlin, 2007.

[Helf 94]   H. Helfrich, R. Standke, and K. R. Scherer. "Vocal Indicators of Psychoactive Drug Effects". *Speech Communication*, Vol. 3, No. 3, pp. 245–252, 1994.

[Hohm 66]   G. W. Hohmann. "Some effects of spinal cord lesions on experiences emotional feelings". *Psychophysiology*, Vol. 3, pp. 143–156, 1966.

[Hu 07a]    H. Hu, M.-X. Xu, and W. Wu. "Fusion of Global Statistical and Segmental Spectral Features for Speech Emotion Recognition". In: *Interspeech 2007 – Eurospeech, 10th European Conference on Speech Communication and Technology, August 27-31, 2007, Antwerp, Belgium, Proceedings*, pp. 2269–2272, 2007.

[Hu 07b]    H. Hu, M.-X. Xu, and W. Wu. "GMM Supervector Based SVM with Spectral Features for Speech Emotion Recognition". In: *Interspeech 2007 – Eurospeech, 10th European Conference on Speech Communication and Technology, August 27-31, 2007, Antwerp, Belgium, Proceedings*, pp. 413–416, 2007.

[Huan 06]   R. Huang and C. Ma. "Toward a Speaker-independent Real-time Affect Detection System". In: *ICPR 2006, 8th International Conference on Pattern Recognition, August 20-24, 2006, Hong Kong*, pp. I:1204–1207, 2006.

[Hube 02] R. Huber. *Prosodisch-linguistische Klassifikation von Emotion. Studien zur Mustererkennung*, Logos Verlag, Berlin, 2002.

[Izar 72] C. E. Izard. *The Face of Emotion*. Appleton-Century-Crofts, New York, 1972.

[Izar 80] C. E. Izard, R. R. Huebner, D. Risser, G. C. McGinnes, and L. M. Dougherty. "The young infant's ability to produce discrete emotion expressions". *Developmental Psychology*, Vol. 16, No. 2, pp. 132–140, 1980.

[Izar 90] C. E. Izard. "Facial Expressions and the regulation of emotions". *Journal of Personality and Social Psychology*, Vol. 58, No. 3, pp. 487–498, 1990.

[Izar 94] C. E. Izard. "Innate and universal facial expressions: Evidence from developmental and cross-cultural research". *Psychological Bulletin*, Vol. 115, No. 2, pp. 288–299, 1994.

[Izar 95] C. E. Izard, C. A. Fantauzzo, J. M. Castle, and O. M. Haynes. "The ontogeny and significance of infants' facial expressions in the first 9 months of life". *Developmental Psychology*, Vol. 31, No. 6, pp. 997–1013, 1995.

[Jame 84] W. James. "What is an emotion?". *Mind*, Vol. 19, pp. 188–205, 1884.

[John 00] T. Johnstone and K. R. Scherer. "Vocal Communication of Emotion". In: M. Lewis and J. M. Haviland-Jones, Eds., *Handbook of Emotions*, Chap. 14, pp. 220–235, Guilford Press, New York, London, 2000.

[Kais 90] J. F. Kaiser. "On a simple algorithm to calculate the 'energy' of a signal". In: *ICASSP 1990, International Conference on Acoustics, Speech, and Signal Processing, April 3-6, 1990, Albuquerque, NM, U. S. A., Proceedings*, pp. 381–384, 1990.

[Kais 93] J. F. Kaiser. "Some Useful Properties of Teager's Energy Operators". In: *ICASSP 1993, International Conference on Acoustics, Speech, and Signal Processing, April 27-30, 1993, Minneapolis, MN, U. S. A., Proceedings*, pp. 149–152, 1993.

[Kapo 07] A. Kapoor, W. Burleson, and R. W. Picard. "Automatic prediction of frustration". *International Journal of Human-Computer Studies*, Vol. 65, pp. 724–736, 2007.

[Kawa 07] H. Kawatsu and S. Ohno. "An analysis of individual differences in the $F_0$ contour and the duration of anger utterances at several degrees". In: *Interspeech 2007 – Eurospeech, 10th European Conference on Speech Communication and Technology, August 27-31, 2007, Antwerp, Belgium, Proceedings*, pp. 2213–2216, 2007.

[Kenn 72] G. Kennedy. *The Art of Rhetoric in the Roman World. 300 BC–AD 300*. Princeton University Press, Princeton, NJ, 1972.

[Kies 97] A. Kießling. *Extraktion und Klassifikation prosodischer Merkmale in der automatischen Sprachverarbeitung. Berichte aus der Informatik*, Shaker, Aachen, 1997.

[Kim 06] C. Kim, K. Seo, and W. Sung. "A Robust Formant Extraction Algorithm Combining Spectral Peak Picking and Root Polishing". *EURASIP Journal on Applied Signal Processing*, Vol. 2006, 2006. Article ID 67960.

[Knox 07]   M. T. Knox and N. Mirghafori. "Automatic Laughter Detection Using Neural Networks". In: *Interspeech 2007 – Eurospeech, 10th European Conference on Speech Communication and Technology, August 27-31, 2007, Antwerp, Belgium, Proceedings*, pp. 2973–2976, 2007.

[Kohl 95]   K. J. Kohler. *Einführung in die Phonetik des Deutschen.* Erich Schmidt, Berlin, 2nd Ed., 1995.

[Komp 97]   R. Kompe. *Prosody in Speech Understanding Systems.* Vol. 1307 of *Lecture Notes in Artificial Intelligence*, Springer, Berlin, 1997.

[Kraj 07]   J. Krajewski and B. Kröger. "Using Prosodic and Spectral Characteristics for Sleepiness Detection". In: *Interspeech 2007 – Eurospeech, 10th European Conference on Speech Communication and Technology, August 27-31, 2007, Antwerp, Belgium, Proceedings*, pp. 1841–1844, 2007.

[Krip 04]   K. Krippendorff. *Content Analysis, an Introduction to Its Methodology.* Sage Publications, Thousand Oaks, CA, U. S. A., 2nd Ed., 2004.

[Krip 07]   K. Krippendorff. "Computing Krippendorff's Alpha-Reliability". Tech. Rep., Annenberg School of Communication, University of Pennsylvania, 2007. http://www.asc.upenn.edu/usr/krippendorff/webreliability.doc, last visited 01/12/2009.

[Krus 64a]  J. B. Kruskal. "Multidimensional Scaling by Optimizing Goodness of Fit to a Nonmetric Hypothesis". *Psychometrika*, Vol. 29, No. 1, pp. 1–27, 1964.

[Krus 64b]  J. B. Kruskal. "Nonmetric Multidimensional Scaling: A Numerical Method". *Psychometrika*, Vol. 29, No. 2, pp. 115–129, 1964.

[Lair 84]   J. D. Laird. "The real role of facial response in the experience of emotion: A reply to Tourangeau and Ellsworth and others". *Journal of Personality and Social Psychology*, Vol. 47, pp. 909–917, 1984.

[Lask 07]   K. Laskowski and S. Burger. "Analysis of the Occurence of Laughter in Meetings". In: *Interspeech 2007 – Eurospeech, 10th European Conference on Speech Communication and Technology, August 27-31, 2007, Antwerp, Belgium, Proceedings*, pp. 1258–1261, 2007.

[Lave 80]   J. Laver. *The Phonetic Description of Voice Quality.* Cambridge University Press, Cambridge, 1980.

[Lave 91]   J. Laver. *The Gift of Speech.* Edinburgh University Press, Edinburgh, 1991.

[Laza 66]   R. S. Lazarus. *Psychological Stress and the Coping Process.* McGraw Hill, New York, 1966.

[Laza 94]   R. S. Lazarus. "The stable and the unstable in emotion. Fundamental questions". In: P. Ekman and R. Davidson, Eds., *The Nature of Emotion: Fundamental Questions*, pp. 79–85, Oxford University Press, Oxford, 1994.

[Laza 99]   R. S. Lazarus. *Stress and Emotion: A New Synthesis.* Springer, New York, 1999.

[Lee 02]   C. M. Lee, S. S. Narayanan, and R. Pieraccini. "Combining Acoustic and Language Information for Emotion Recognition". In: *Interspeech 2002 – ICSLP, 7th International Conference on Spoken Language Processing, September 16-20, 2002, Denver, U. S. A., Proceedings*, pp. 873–376, 2002.

[Lee 04]   C. M. Lee, S. Yildirim, M. Bulut, A. Kazemzadeh, C. Busso, Z. Deng, S. Lee, and S. S. Narayanan. "Emotion Recognition based on Phoneme Classes". In: *Interspeech 2004 – ICSLP, 8th International Conference on Spoken Language Processing, October 4-8, 2004, Jeju Island, Korea, Proceedings*, 2004. No pagination.

[Lee 05]   C. M. Lee and S. S. Narayanan. "Toward Detecting Emotions in Spoken Dialogs". *IEEE Transactions on Speech and Audio Processing*, Vol. 13, No. 2, pp. 293–303, 2005.

[Leve 80]  H. Leventhal. "Toward a comprehensive theory of emotion". In: L. Berkowitz, Ed., *Advances in Social Psychology*, pp. 139–207, Academic Press, New York, 1980.

[Leve 90]  R. W. Levenson, P. Ekman, and W. V. Friesen. "Voluntary facial action generates emotion-specific autonomic nervous system activity". *Psychophysiology*, Vol. 27, pp. 363–384, 1990.

[Leve 92a] R. W. Levenson. "Autonomic nervous system differences among emotions". *Psychological Science*, Vol. 3, pp. 23–27, 1992.

[Leve 92b] R. W. Levenson, P. Ekman, K. Heider, and W. V. Friesen. "Emotion and automatic nervous system activity in the Minangkabau of West Sumatra". *Journal of Personality and Social Psychology*, Vol. 62, No. 6, pp. 972–988, 1992.

[Levi 47]  N. Levinson. "The Wiener RMS Error Criterion in Filter Design and Prediction". *Journal of Mathematics and Physics*, Vol. 25, pp. 261–278, 1947.

[Lewi 93]  M. Lewis and J. M. Haviland, Eds. *Handbook of Emotions*. Guilford Press, New York, London, 1993.

[Maie 08]  A. Maier, J. Exner, S. Steidl, A. Batliner, T. Haderlein, and E. Nöth. "An Extension to the Sammon Mapping for the Robust Visualization of Speaker Dependencies". In: P. Sojka, I. Kopecek, and K. Pala, Eds., *Text, Speech and Dialogue, 11th International Conference, September 08-12, 2008, Brno, Czech Republic, Proceedings*, pp. 381–388, Springer, Berlin, Heidelberg, 2008.

[Mara 93]  P. Maragos, J. F. Kaiser, and T. F. Quatieri. "Energy Separation in Signal Modulations with Application to Speech Analysis". *IEEE Transactions on Signal Processing*, Vol. 41, No. 10, pp. 1532–1550, 1993.

[Maye 05]  M. Mayer. *Emotionserkennung anhand linguistischer Merkmale*. Studienarbeit, Lehrstuhl für Mustererkennung, Friedrich-Alexander-Universität Erlangen-Nürnberg, 2005.

[Meda 91]  Y. Medan, E. Yair, and D. Chazan. "Super Resolution Pitch Determination of Speech Signals". *IEEE Transactions on Acoustics, Speech, and Signal Processing (ASSP)*, Vol. 39, No. 1, pp. 40–48, 1991.

[Mich 97]   D. Michaelis, T. Gramss, and H. W. Strube. "Glottal-to-Noise Excitation Ratio – a New Measure for Describing Pathological Voices". *Acustica*, Vol. 83, pp. 700–706, 1997.

[Mori 07]   H. Mori and H. Kasuya. "Voice Source and Vocal Tract Variations as Cues to Emotional States Perceived from Expressive Conversational Speech". In: *Interspeech 2007 – Eurospeech, 10th European Conference on Speech Communication and Technology, August 27-31, 2007, Antwerp, Belgium, Proceedings*, pp. 102–105, 2007.

[Niem 03]   H. Niemann. *Klassifikation von Mustern.* published online, 2nd, revised and extended Ed., 2003. http://www5.informatik.uni-erlangen.de/Personen/niemann/klassifikation-von-mustern/m00links.html, last visited 09/20/2007.

[Niem 90]   H. Niemann. *Pattern Analysis and Understanding.* Vol. 4 of *Springer Series in Information Sciences*, Springer, Berlin, 2nd Ed., 1990.

[Nogu 01]   A. Nogueiras, A. Moreno, A. Bonafonte, and J. B. Mariño. "Speech Emotion Recognition Using Hidden Markov Models". In: *Interspeech 2001 – Eurospeech, 7th European Conference on Speech Communication and Technology, September 3-47, 2001, Aalborg, Denmark, Proceedings*, pp. 2267–2270, 2001.

[Noth 00]   E. Nöth, A. Batliner, A. Kießling, R. Kompe, and H. Niemann. "Verbmobil: The Use of Prosody in the Linguistic Components of a Speech Understanding System". *IEEE Transactions on Speech and Audio Processing*, Vol. 8, No. 5, pp. 519–532, 2000.

[Noth 01]   E. Nöth, A. Batliner, H. Niemann, G. Stemmer, F. Gallwitz, and J. Spilker. "Language Models beyond Word Strings". In: *ASRU 2001, Automatic Speech Recognition and Understanding Workshop, December 9-13, 2001, Trento, Italy, Proceedings*, 2001. No pagination.

[Noth 02]   E. Nöth, A. Batliner, V. Warnke, J.-P. Haas, M. Boros, J. Buckow, R. Huber, F. Gallwitz, M. Nutt, and H. Niemann. "On the Use of Prosody in Automatic Dialogue Understanding". *Speech Communication*, Vol. 36, No. 1-2, pp. 45–62, 2002.

[Noth 88]   E. Nöth and R. Kompe. "Der Einsatz prosodischer Information im Spracherkennungssystem EVAR". In: H. Bunke, O. Kübler, and P. Stucki, Eds., *Mustererkennung 1988 (10. DAGM Symposium)*, pp. 2–9, Berlin, 1988.

[Noth 91]   E. Nöth. *Prosodische Information in der automatischen Spracherkennung – Berechnung und Anwendung.* Niemeyer, Tübingen, 1991.

[Noth 93]   E. Nöth and B. Plannerer. "Schnittstellendefinition für den Worthypothesengraphen. Verbmobil Memo 2". Tech. Rep., Lehrstuhl für Mustererkennung, Friedrich-Alexander-Universität Erlangen-Nürnberg, 1993.

[Noth 99]   E. Nöth, A. Batliner, A. Kießling, R. Kompe, and H. Niemann. "Suprasegmental Modelling". In: K. Ponting, Ed., *Computational Models of Speech Pattern Processing*, pp. 182–199, Springer–Verlag, 1999.

[Ohts 01]   T. Ohtsuka and H. Kasuya. "Aperiodicity control in ARX-based speech analysis-synthesis method". In: *Interspeech 2001 – Eurospeech, 7th European Conference on Speech Communication and Technology, September 3-47, 2001, Aalborg, Denmark, Proceedings*, pp. 2267–2270, 2001.

[Orto 88]  A. Ortony, G. L. Clore, and A. Collins. *The Cognitive Structure of Emotions*. Cambridge University Press, Cambridge, New York, 1988.

[Pank 82]  J. Panksepp. "Towards a general psychobiological theory of emotions". *Behavioral and Brain Sciences*, Vol. 5, No. 3, pp. 407–467, 1982.

[Pank 89]  J. Panksepp. "The neurobiology of emotions: Of animal brains and human feelings". In: H. L. Wagner and A. S. R.Manstead, Eds., *Handbook of Social Psychophysiology*, pp. 5–26, John Wiley and Sons Ltd., London, 1989.

[Plut 62]  R. Plutchik. *The Emotions: Facts, Theories, and a New Model*. Random House, New York, 1962.

[Plut 80]  R. Plutchik. *Emotion: A Psychoevolutionary Synthesis*. Harper & Row, New York, 1980.

[Plut 84]  R. Plutchik. "Emotions: A general psychoevolutionary theory". In: K. R. Scherer and P. Ekman, Eds., *Approaches to Emotion*, pp. 197–219, Erlbaum, Hillsdale, NJ, 1984.

[Plut 94]  R. Plutchik. *The Psychology and Biology of Emotion*. Harpercollins College Div, New York, 1994.

[Poli 81]  J. Polivy. "On the induction of emotion in the laboratory: Discrete moods or multiple affect states?". *Journal of Personality and Social Psychology*, Vol. 41, pp. 803–817, 1981.

[Polz 00]  T. S. Polzin and A. Waibel. "Emotion-sensitive Human-Computer Interfaces". In: *ISCA Tutorial and Research Workshop on Speech and Emotion, September 5-7, 2000, Newcastle, Northern Ireland, Proceedings*, pp. 201–206, 2000.

[Riec 95]  S. Rieck. *Parametrisierung und Klassifikation gesprochener Sprache.* Vol. 353 of *VDI Fortschrittberichte Reihe 10: Informatik/Kommunikationstechnik*, VDI Verlag, Düsseldorf, 1995.

[Rose 84]  I. J. Roseman. "Cognitive determinants of emotion: a structural theory". *Review of Personality and Social Psychology*, Vol. 5, pp. 11–36, 1984.

[Rose 91]  I. J. Roseman. "Appraisal determinants of discrete emotions". *Cognition and Emotion*, Vol. 5, pp. 161–200, 1991.

[Rose 96]  I. J. Roseman, A. A. Antoniou, and P. E. Jose. "Appraisal determinants of emotions: contructing a more accurate and comprehensive theory". *Cognition and Emotion*, Vol. 5, pp. 241–277, 1996.

[Russ 80]  J. A. Russel. "A circumplex model of affect". *Journal of Personality and Social Psychology*, Vol. 39, pp. 1161–1178, 1980.

[Russ 83]  J. A. Russel. "Pancultural aspects of the human conceptual organization of emotions". *Journal of Personality and Social Psychology*, Vol. 45, pp. 1281–1288, 1983.

[Russ 97]  J. A. Russel. "How shall an emotion be called?". In: *Circumplex Models of Personality and Emotions*, Chap. 9, pp. 205–220, American Psychological Association, Washington D.C., 1997.

[Salt 88]    G. Salton and C. Buckley. "Term-weighting Approaches in Automatic
             Text Retrieval". *Information Processing and Management*, Vol. 24, No. 5,
             pp. 513–523, 1988.

[Samm 69]    J. W. Sammon. "A Nonlinear Mapping for Data Structure Analysis".
             *IEEE Transactions on Computers*, Vol. C-18, No. 5, pp. 401–408, 1969.

[Scha 70]    B. Scharf. "Critical Bands". In: J. V. Tobias, Ed., *Foundations of Modern
             Auditory Theory, Vol. 1*, pp. 157–202, Academic Press, New York, 1970.

[Sche 00]    K. R. Scherer. "Psychological models of emotion". In: J. C. Borod, Ed.,
             *The neuropsychology of emotion*, pp. 137–166, Oxford University Press,
             Oxford, New York, 2000.

[Sche 01a]   K. R. Scherer. "Emotion". In: M. Hewstone and W. Stroebe, Eds., *Intro-
             duction to Social Psychology: A European Perspective*, Chap. 6, pp. 151–
             191, Blackwell, Oxford, 2001.

[Sche 01b]   K. R. Scherer, R. Banse, and H. G. Wallbott. "Emotion Inferences from
             Vocal Expression Correlate across Languages and Cultures". *Journal of
             Cross-Cultural Psychology*, Vol. 32, No. 1, pp. 76–92, 2001.

[Sche 03a]   K. R. Scherer. "Vocal communication of emotion: A review of research
             paradigms". *Speech Communication*, Vol. 40, pp. 227–256, 2003.

[Sche 03b]   K. R. Scherer, T. Johnstone, and G. Klasmeyer. "Vocal Expression of
             Emotion". In: R. J. Davidson, K. R. Scherer, and H. H. Goldsmith, Eds.,
             *Handbook of Affective Siences*, Chap. 23, pp. 433–456, Oxford University
             Press, Oxford, New York, 2003.

[Sche 05]    K. R. Scherer. "What are emotions? And how can they be measured?".
             *Social Science Information*, Vol. 44, No. 4, pp. 695–729, 2005.

[Sche 78]    K. R. Scherer. "Personality inference from voice quality: the loud voice of
             extroversion". *European Journal of Social Psychology*, Vol. 8, pp. 467–487,
             1978.

[Sche 84a]   K. R. Scherer. "Emotion as a multicomponent process: a model and some
             cross-cultural data". *Review of Personality and Social Psychology*, Vol. 5,
             pp. 37–63, 1984.

[Sche 84b]   K. R. Scherer. "On the nature and function of emotion: a component
             process approach". In: K. R. Scherer and P. Ekman, Eds., *Approaches to
             Emotion*, pp. 293–318, Erlbaum, Hillsdale, NJ, 1984.

[Sche 86]    K. R. Scherer. "Vocal affect expression: a review and a model for future
             research". *Psychological Bulletin*, Vol. 99, pp. 143–165, 1986.

[Sche 88]    K. R. Scherer. "Criteria for emotion-antecedent appraisal: a review". In:
             V. Hamilton, G. H. Bower, and N. H. Frijda, Eds., *Cognitive Perspectives
             on Emotion and Motivation*, pp. 89–126, Nijhoff, Dordrecht, 1988.

[Sche 89]    K. R. Scherer. "Vocal Correlates of Emotional Arousal and Affective Dis-
             turbance". In: H. L. Wagner and A. S. R.Manstead, Eds., *Handbook of
             Social Psychophysiology*, Chap. 7, pp. 165–197, John Wiley and Sons Ltd.,
             London, 1989.

[Sche 91]  K. R. Scherer, R. Banse, H. G. Wakkbott, and T. Goldbeck. "Vocal Cues in Emotion Encoding and Decoding". *Motivation and Emotion*, Vol. 15, pp. 123–148, 1991.

[Sche 94]  K. R. Scherer. "Towards a concept of modal emotions". In: P. Ekman and R. Davidson, Eds., *The Nature of Emotion: Fundamental Questions*, pp. 25–31, Oxford University Press, Oxford, 1994.

[Sche 97]  K. R. Scherer and G. Ceschi. "Lost Luggage: A Field Study of Emotion-Antecedent Appraisal". *Motivation and Emotion*, Vol. 21, No. 3, pp. 211–235, 1997.

[Sche 99]  K. Scherer. "Appraisal Theory". In: T. Dalgleish and M. Power, Eds., *Handbook of Cognition and Emotion*, pp. 637–663, John Wiley, New York, 1999.

[Schl 54]  H. Schlosberg. "Three dimensions of emotion". *Psychology Review*, Vol. 61, pp. 81–88, 1954.

[Schn 59]  T. C. Schneirla. "An evolutionary and developmental theory of biphasic processes underlying approach and withdrawal". In: M. R. Jones, Ed., *Nebraska Symposium on Motivation*, pp. 1–42, University of Nebraska Press, Lincoln, 1959.

[Schu 03]  B. Schuller, G. Rigoll, and M. Lang. "Hidden Markov Model-Based Speech Emotion Recognition". In: *ICASSP 2003, International Conference on Acoustics, Speech, and Signal Processing, April 6-10, 2003, Hong Kong, China, Proceedings*, pp. II:1–4, 2003.

[Schu 04]  B. Schuller, G. Rigoll, and M. Lang. "Speech Emotion Recognition Combining Acoustic Features and Linguistic Information in a Hybrid Support Vector Machine-Belief Network Architecture". In: *ICASSP 2004, International Conference on Acoustics, Speech, and Signal Processing, May 17-21, 2004, Montreal, Canada, Proceedings*, pp. I:577–580, 2004.

[Schu 05]  B. Schuller, R. Jiménez Villar, G. Rigoll, and M. Lang. "Meta-Classifiers in Acoustic and Linguistic Feature Fusion-based Affect Recognition". In: *ICASSP 2005, International Conference on Acoustics, Speech, and Signal Processing, March 19-23, 2005, Philadelphia, U. S. A., Proceedings*, pp. I:325–328, 2005.

[Schu 06]  B. Schuller, D. Arsić, F. Wallhoff, and G. Rigoll. "Emotion Recognition in the Noise Applying Large Acoustic Feature Sets". In: *Speech Prodody 2006, May 2-5, 2006, Dresden, Germany, Proceedings*, 2006. No pagination.

[Schu 07a]  B. Schuller. *Mensch, Maschine, Emotion – Erkennung aus sprachlicher und manueller Interaktion*. VDM Verlag Dr. Müller, Saarbrücken, 2007.

[Schu 07b]  B. Schuller, A. Batliner, D. Seppi, S. Steidl, T. Vogt, J. Wagner, L. Devillers, L. Vidrascu, N. Amir, L. Kessous, and V. Aharonson. "The relevance of feature type for the automatic classification of emotional user states: low level descriptors and functionals". In: *Interspeech 2007 – Eurospeech, 10th European Conference on Speech Communication and Technology, August 27-31, 2007, Antwerp, Belgium, Proceedings*, pp. 2253–2256, 2007.

[Schu 07c]  B. Schuller, D. Seppi, A. Batliner, A. Maier, and S. Steidl. "Towards more Reality in the Recognition of Emotional Speech". In: *ICASSP 2007, International Conference on Acoustics, Speech, and Signal Processing, April 15-20, 2007, Honolulu, U. S. A., Proceedings*, pp. 941–944, 2007.

[Schu 08]   B. Schuller, A. Batliner, S. Steidl, and D. Seppi. "Does Affect Affect Automatic Recognition of Children's Speech". In: *WOCCI 2008, 1st Workshop on Child, Computer and Interaction, October 23, 2008, Chania, Crete, Greece, Proceedings*, 2008. No pagination.

[Schu 95]   E. G. Schukat-Talamazzini. *Automatische Spracherkennung – Grundlagen, statistische Modelle und effiziente Algorithmen*. Vieweg Verlag, Braunschweig, Wiesbaden, 1995. freely available at http://www.minet.uni-jena.de/fakultaet/schukat/asebuch.html, last visited 01/12/2009.

[Sepp 08a]  D. Seppi, A. Batliner, B. Schuller, S. Steidl, T. Vogt, J. Wagner, L. Devillers, L. Vidrascu, N. Amir, and V. Aharonson. "Patterns, Prototypes, Performance: Classifying Emotional User States". In: *Interspeech 2008 – ICSLP, 10th International Conference on Spoken Language Processing, September 22-26, 2008, Brisbane, Australia, Proceedings*, pp. 601–604, 2008.

[Sepp 08b]  D. Seppi, B. Schuller, A. Batliner, and S. Steidl. "Detecting Problems in Spoken Child-Computer Interaction". In: *WOCCI 2008, 1st Workshop on Child, Computer and Interaction, October 23, 2008, Chania, Crete, Greece, Proceedings*, 2008. No pagination.

[Seth 07]   V. Sethu, E. Ambikairajah, and J. Epps. "Group Delay Features for Emotion Detection". In: *Interspeech 2007 – Eurospeech, 10th European Conference on Speech Communication and Technology, August 27-31, 2007, Antwerp, Belgium, Proceedings*, pp. 2273–2276, 2007.

[Shaf 05]   I. Shafran and M. Mohri. "A Comparison of Classifiers for Detecting Emotion from Speech". In: *ICASSP 2005, International Conference on Acoustics, Speech, and Signal Processing, March 19-23, 2005, Philadelphia, U. S. A., Proceedings*, pp. 341–344, 2005.

[Shan 48]   C. E. Shannon. "A Mathematical Theory of Communication". *Bell System Technical Journal*, Vol. 27, pp. 379–423 and 623–656, 1948. reprint available at http://cm.bell-labs.com/cm/ms/what/shannonday/paper.html, last visited 01/12/2009.

[Shav 87]   P. Shaver, J. Schwartz, D. Kirson, and C. O'Connor. "Emotion knowledge: Further exploration of a prototype approach". *Journal of Personality and Social Psychology*, Vol. 52, pp. 1061–1086, 1987.

[Smit 85]   C. A. Smith and P. C. Ellsworth. "Patterns of cognitive appraisal in emotion". *Journal of Personality and Social Psychology*, Vol. 48, pp. 813–838, 1985.

[Sony 06]   "Sony AIBO Europe – Official Website". 2006. http://support.sony-europe.com/aibo/index.asp, last visited 01/12/2009.

[Stei 03]   S. Steidl, G. Stemmer, C. Hacker, E. Nöth, and H. Niemann. "Improving Children's Speech Recognition by HMM Interpolation with an Adults' Speech Recognizer". In: B. Michaelis and G. Krel, Eds., *Pattern Recognition, 25th DAGM Symposium, September 10-12, 2003, Magdeburg, Germany, Proceedings*, pp. 600–607, Springer, Berlin, Heidelberg, 2003.

[Stei 05]  S. Steidl, M. Levit, A. Batliner, E. Nöth, and H. Niemann. "'Of All Things the Measure is Man' – Automatic Classification of Emotions and Inter-Labeler Consistency". In: *ICASSP 2005, International Conference on Acoustics, Speech, and Signal Processing, March 19-23, 2005, Philadelphia, U. S. A., Proceedings*, pp. 317–320, 2005.

[Stei 08]  S. Steidl, A. Batliner, E. Nöth, and J. Hornegger. "Quantification of Segmentation and F0 Errors and Their Effect on Emotion Recognition". In: P. Sojka, I. Kopecek, and K. Pala, Eds., *Text, Speech and Dialogue, 11th International Conference, September 08-12, 2008, Brno, Czech Republic, Proceedings*, pp. 525–534, Springer, Berlin, Heidelberg, 2008.

[Stei 92]  N. Stein and K. Oatley. "Basic emotions: Theory and measurement". *Cognition and Emotion*, Vol. 6, pp. 161–168, 1992.

[Stem 01]  G. Stemmler, M. Heldmann, C. A. Pauls, and T. Scherer. "Constraints for emotion specifity in fear and anger: the context counts". *Psychophysiology*, Vol. 69, pp. 275–291, 2001.

[Stem 05]  G. Stemmer. *Modeling Variability in Speech Recognition*. Logos Verlag, Berlin, 2005.

[Step 93]  S. Stepper and F. Strack. "Proprioceptive determinants of emotional and nonemotional feelings". *Journal of Personality and Social Psychology*, Vol. 64, pp. 211–220, 1993.

[Stev 37]  S. S. Stevens, J. Volkmann, and E. B. Newman. "A Scale for the Measurement of the Psychological Magnitude Pitch". *Journal of the Acoustical Society of America*, Vol. 8, No. 3, pp. 185–190, 1937.

[Stor 87]  C. Storm and T. Storm. "A taxonomic study of the vocabulary of emotion". *Journal of Personality and Social Psychology*, Vol. 53, pp. 805–816, 1987.

[Stra 88]  F. Strack, S. Stepper, and L. L. Martin. "Inhibiting and facilitating conditions of the human smile: A nonobstrusive test of the facial feedback hypothesis". *Journal of Personality and Social Psychology*, Vol. 54, pp. 768–777, 1988.

[Taga 98]  H. D. Tagare. "A Gentle Introduction to the EM Algorithm. Part I: Theory". Tech. Rep., Yale School of Medicine, New Haven, CT, U. S. A., 1998.

[Take 93]  A. Takeuchi and K. Nagao. "Communicative Facial Displays as a New Conversational Modality". In: *ACM/IFIP INTERCHI 1993, Amsterdam, Proceedings*, pp. 187–193, 1993.

[Talk 95]  D. Talkin. "A Robust Algorithm for Pitch Tracking (RAPT)". In: W. B. Kleijn and K. K. Paliwal, Eds., *Speech Coding and Synthesis*, Elsevier, New York, 1995.

[Teag 80]  H. M. Teager. "Some Observations on Oral Air Flow During Phonation". *IEEE Transactions on Acoustics, Speech, and Signal Processing*, Vol. 28, No. 5, pp. 599–601, 1980.

[Teag 83]  H. M. Teager and S. M. Teager. "A Phenomenological Model for Vowel Production in the Vocal Tract". In: R. G. Daniloff, Ed., *Speech Sciences: Recent Advances*, pp. 73–109, College Hill Press, San Diego, 1983.

[Teag 90]  H. M. Teager and S. M. Teager. "Evidence for Nonlinear Sound Production Mechanisms in the Vocal Tract". *NATO Advanced Study Institute on Speech Production and Speech Modelling*, Vol. 55, pp. 241–261, 1990.

[Titz 92]  I. R. Titze. "Acoustic Interpretation of the Voice Range Profile". *Speech Hearing Research*, Vol. 35, No. 1, pp. 21–34, 1992.

[Tomk 62]  S. S. Tomkins. *Affect, Imagery, Consciousness*. Vol. 1 and 2, Springer, New York, 1962.

[Tomk 84]  S. S. Tomkins. "Affect theory". In: K. R. Scherer and P. Ekman, Eds., *Approaches to Emotion*, pp. 163–196, Erlbaum, Hillsdale, NJ, 1984.

[Tran 04]  V. Tran. *The influence of emotions on decision-making processes in management teams*. PhD thesis, University of Geneva, Switzerland, 2004.

[Truo 07]  K. P. Truong and D. A. van Leeuwen. "Visualizing acoustic similarities between emotions in speech: an acoustic map of emotions". In: *Interspeech 2007 – Eurospeech, 10th European Conference on Speech Communication and Technology, August 27-31, 2007, Antwerp, Belgium, Proceedings*, pp. 2265–2268, 2007.

[Verv 03]  D. Ververidis and C. Kotropoulos. "A Review of Emotional Speech Databases". In: *PCI 2003, 9th Panhellenic Conference on Informatics, November 1-23, 2003, Thessaloniki, Greece*, pp. 560–574, 2003.

[Vidr 05]  L. Vidrascu and L. Devillers. "Annotation and Detection of Blended Emotions in Real Human-Human Dialogs Recorded in a Call-Center". In: *ICME 2005, 6th IEEE International Conference on Multimedia and Expo, July 6-8, 2005, Amsterdam, Netherlands, Proceedings*, p. , 2005.

[Vidr 07]  L. Vidrascu and L. Devillers. "Five emotion classes in real-world call center data: the use of various types of paralinguistic features". In: M. Schröder, A. Batliner, and C. d'Alessandro, Eds., *ParaLing 2007, International Workshop on Paralinguistic Speech - between Models and Data, August 3, 2007, Saarbrücken*, pp. 11–16, 2007.

[Vlas 07]  B. Vlasenko, B. Schuller, A. Wendemuth, and G. Rigoll. "Combining Frame and Turn-Level Information for Robust Recognition of Emotions within Speech". In: *Interspeech 2007 – Eurospeech, 10th European Conference on Speech Communication and Technology, August 27-31, 2007, Antwerp, Belgium, Proceedings*, pp. 2249–2252, 2007.

[Vogt 05]  T. Vogt and E. André. "Comparing Feature Sets for Acted and Spontaneous Speech in View of Automatic Emotion Recognition". In: *ICME 2005, 6th IEEE International Conference on Multimedia and Expo, July 6-8, 2005, Amsterdam, Netherlands, Proceedings*, pp. 474–477, 2005.

[Wahl 06]  W. Wahlster, Ed. *SmartKom: Foundations of Multimodal Dialogue Systems*. Springer, Berlin, Heidelberg, 2006.

[Walk 01]  M. Walker, J. Aberdeen, J. Boland, E. Bratt, J. Garafolo, L. Hirschman, A. Le, S. Lee, S. Narayanan, K. Papineni, B. Pellom, J. Polifroni, A. Potamianos, P. Prabhu, A. Rudnicky, G. Sanders, S. Seneff, D. Stallard, and S. Whittaker. "DARPA Communicater dialog travel planning systems: The June 2000 data collection". In: *Interspeech 2001 – Eurospeech, 7th European Conference on Speech Communication and Technology, September 3-47, 2001, Aalborg, Denmark, Proceedings*, pp. 1371–1374, 2001.

[Warn 03]  V. Warnke. *Integrierte Segmentierung und Klassifikation von Äußerungen und Dialogakten mit heterogenen Wissensquellen.* Logos Verlag, Berlin, 2003.

[Whis 89]  C. Whissell. "The dictionary of affect in language". In: R. Plutchik and H. Kellerman, Eds., *Emotion: Theory, Research and Experience. Vol. 4, The Measurement of Emotions,* pp. 113–131, Academic Press, New York, 1989.

[Wigh 92]  C. Wightman. *Automatic Detection of Prosodic Constituents.* PhD thesis, Boston University Graduate School, 1992.

[Wund 10]  W. Wundt. *Grundzüge der Physiologischen Psychologie.* Vol. 2, Alfred Kröner Verlag, Leipzig, 6th Ed., 1910.

[Yaco 03]  S. Yacoub, S. Simske, X. Lin, and J. Burns. "Recognition of Emotions in Interactive Voice Response Systems". In: *Interspeech 2003 – Eurospeech, 8th European Conference on Speech Communication and Technology, September 1-4, 2003, Geneva, Switzerland, Proceedings,* pp. 729–732, 2003.

[Yild 04]  S. Yildirim, M. Bulut, C. M. Lee, A. Kazemzadeh, C. Busso, Z. Deng, S. Lee, and S. Narayanan. "An acoustic study of emotions expressed in speech". In: *Interspeech 2004 – ICSLP, 8th International Conference on Spoken Language Processing, October 4-8, 2004, Jeju Island, Korea, Proceedings,* 2004. No pagination.

[Ying 07]  T. Yingthawornsuk, H. Kaymaz Keskinpala, D. M. Wilkes, R. G. Shiavi, and R. M. Salomon. "Direct Acoustic Feature Using Iterative EM Algorithm and Spectral Energy for Classifying Suicidal Speech". In: *Interspeech 2007 – Eurospeech, 10th European Conference on Speech Communication and Technology, August 27-31, 2007, Antwerp, Belgium, Proceedings,* pp. 766–769, 2007.

[Zamm 98]  V. L. Zammuner. "Concepts of emotion: "emotionness" and dimensional ratings of Italian words". *Cognition and Emotion,* Vol. 12, pp. 243–272, 1998.

[Zeis 06]  V. Zeißler, J. Adelhardt, A. Batliner, C. Frank, E. Nöth, R. P. Shi, and H. Niemann. "The Prosody Module". In: W. Wahlster, Ed., *SmartKom: Foundations of Multimodal Dialogue Systems,* pp. 139–152, Springer, Berlin, Heidelberg, 2006.

[Zeis 09]  V. Zeißler. *Robuste Erkennung der prosodischen Phänomene und der emotionalen Benutzerzustände in einem multimodalen Dialogsystem.* PhD thesis, Lehrstuhl für Informatik 5 (Mustererkennung), Universität Erlangen-Nürnberg, 2009. To appear.

[Zhou 01]  G. Zhou, J. H. L. Hansen, and J. F. Kaiser. "Nonlinear Feature Based Classification of Speech Under Stress". *IEEE Transactions on Speech and Audio Processing,* Vol. 9, No. 3, pp. 201–216, 2001.